Ayu
Watanabe

L♥DK

エルディーケー

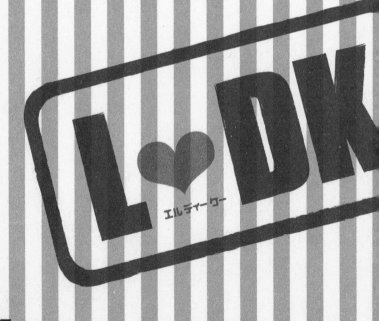

4

L♥DK

Ayu Watanabe

4

c o n t e n t s

#13 Unforgivable

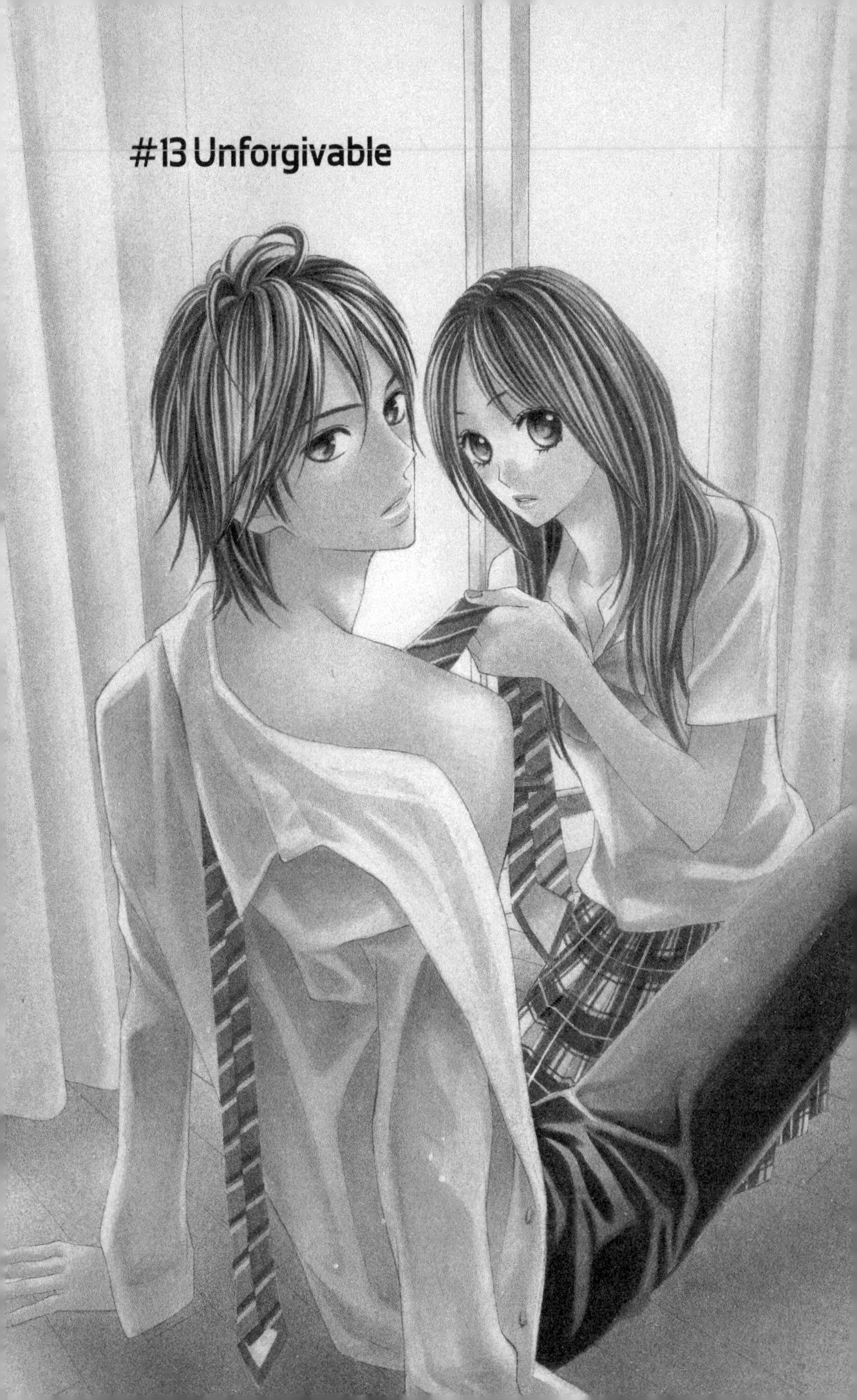

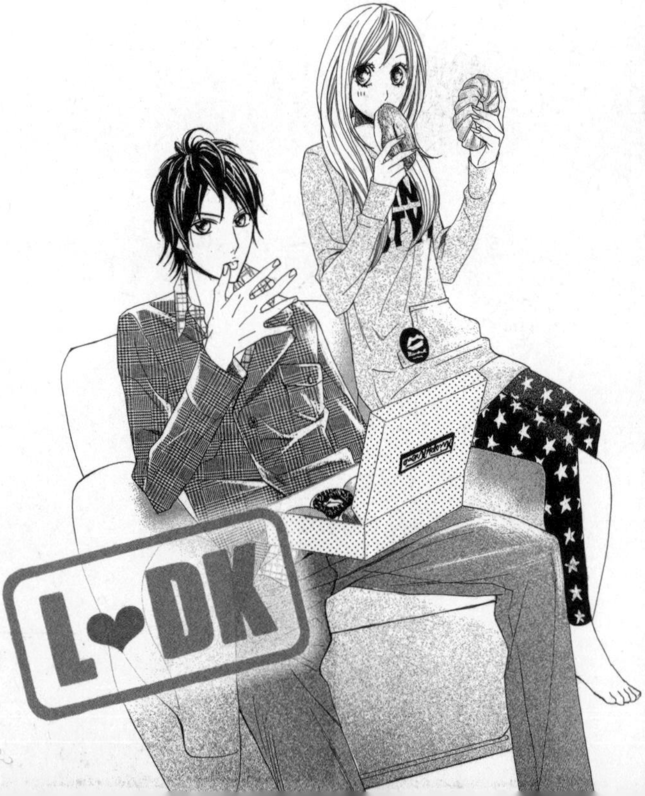
L♥DK

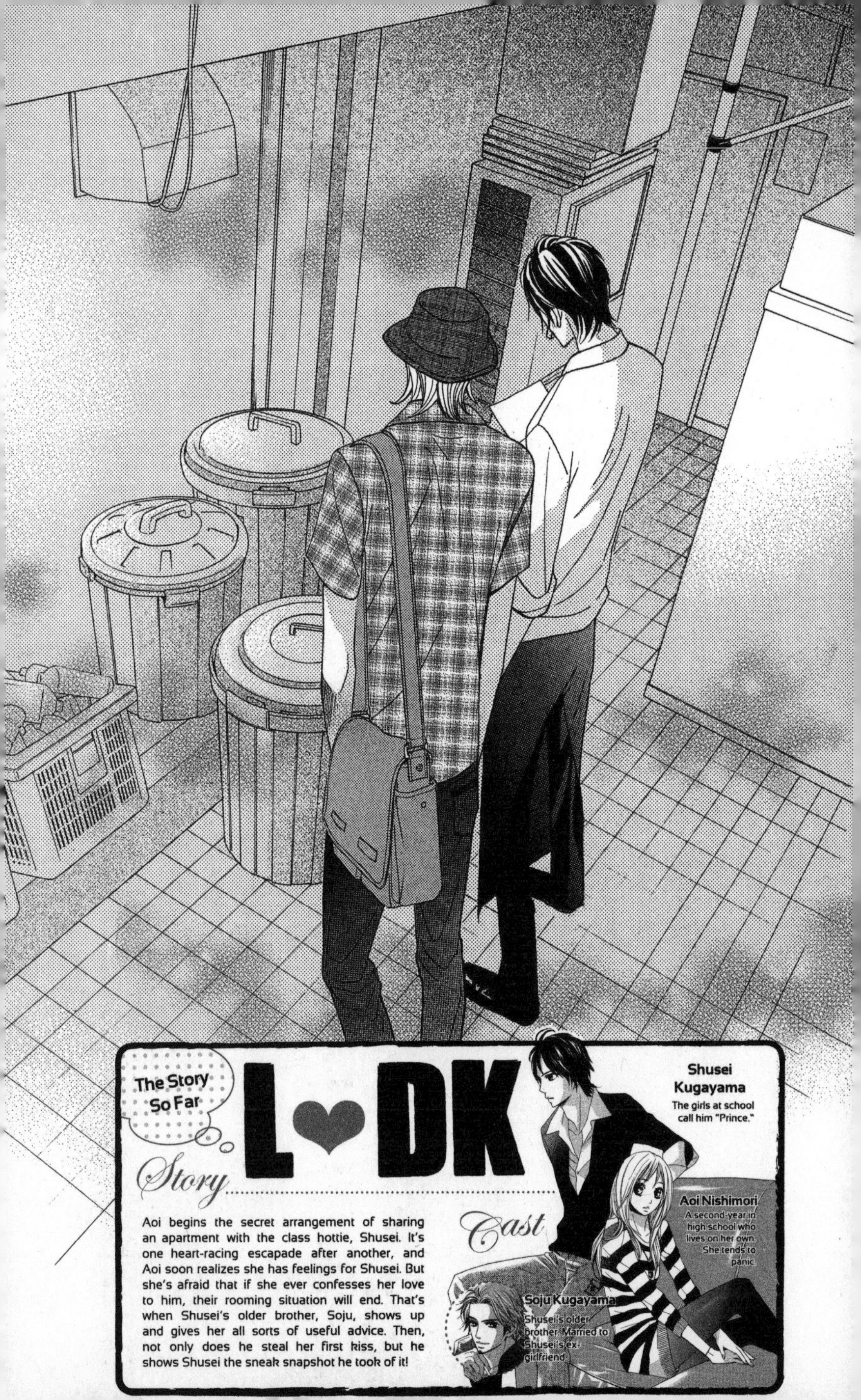

The Story So Far

L♥DK

Story

Aoi begins the secret arrangement of sharing an apartment with the class hottie, Shusei. It's one heart-racing escapade after another, and Aoi soon realizes she has feelings for Shusei. But she's afraid that if she ever confesses her love to him, their rooming situation will end. That's when Shusei's older brother, Soju, shows up and gives her all sorts of useful advice. Then, not only does he steal her first kiss, but he shows Shusei the sneak snapshot he took of it!

Cast

Shusei Kugayama
The girls at school call him "Prince."

Aoi Nishimori
A second-year in high school who lives on her own. She tends to panic.

Soju Kugayama
Shusei's older brother. Married to Shusei's ex-girlfriend.

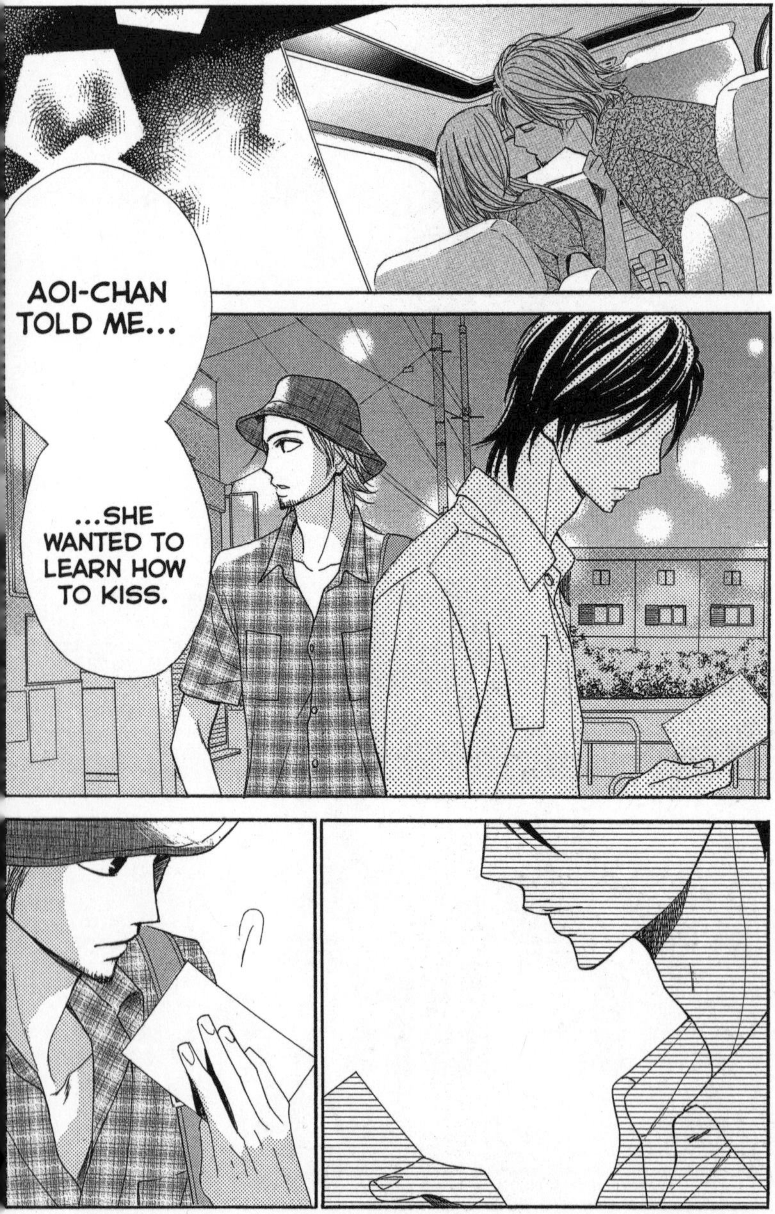
AOI-CHAN TOLD ME...
...SHE WANTED TO LEARN HOW TO KISS.

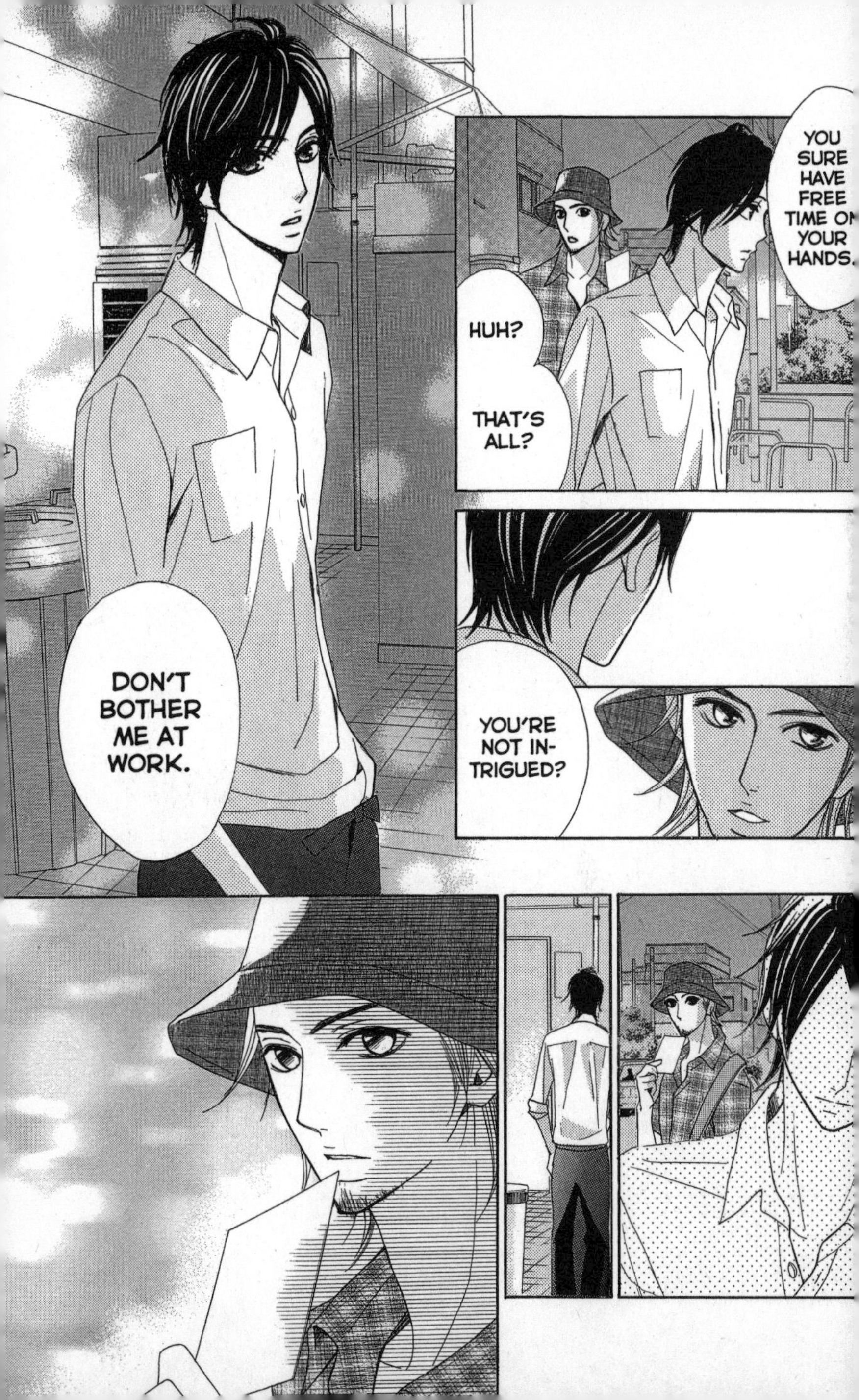
YOU SURE HAVE FREE TIME ON YOUR HANDS.
HUH? THAT'S ALL?
YOU'RE NOT IN-TRIGUED?
DON'T BOTHER ME AT WORK.

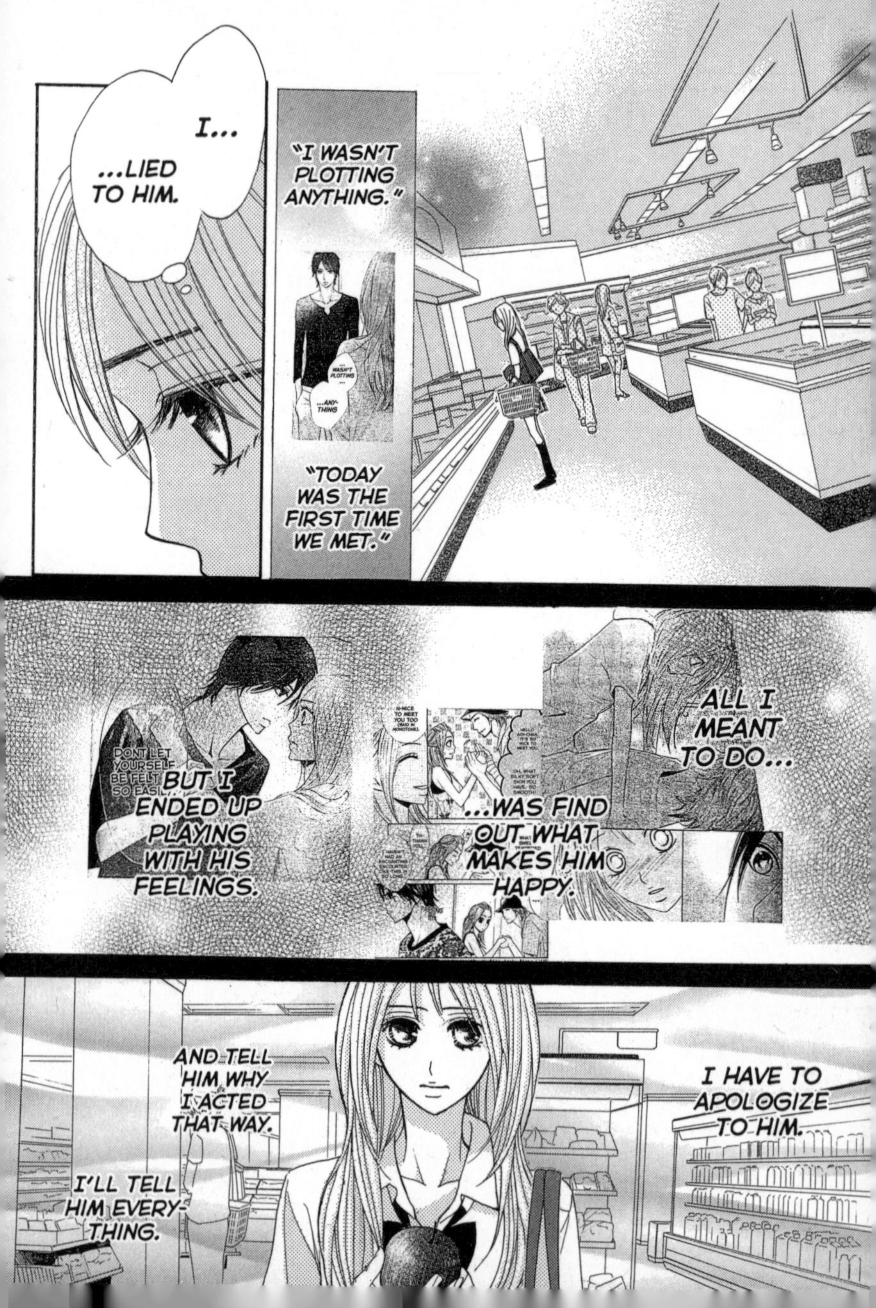
"I WASN'T PLOTTING ANYTHING."
...WASN'T PLOTTING...
...ANY-THING
"TODAY WAS THE FIRST TIME WE MET."
I...
...LIED TO HIM.
ALL I MEANT TO DO...
HELLO AOI-CHAN, IT'S SO NICE TO MEET YOU.
OH, WHAT SILKY-SOFT SKIN YOU HAVE. SO SMOOTH!
N-NICE TO MEET YOU TOO (SAID IN MONOTONE).
TH-THANK YOU.
I HAVEN'T HAD AN ENCHANTING ENCOUNTER LIKE THIS IN SO LONG.
...WAS FIND OUT WHAT MAKES HIM HAPPY.
DON'T LET YOURSELF BE FELT SO EASIL...
BUT I ENDED UP PLAYING WITH HIS FEELINGS.
I HAVE TO APOLOGIZE TO HIM.
AND TELL HIM WHY I ACTED THAT WAY.
I'LL TELL HIM EVERY-THING.

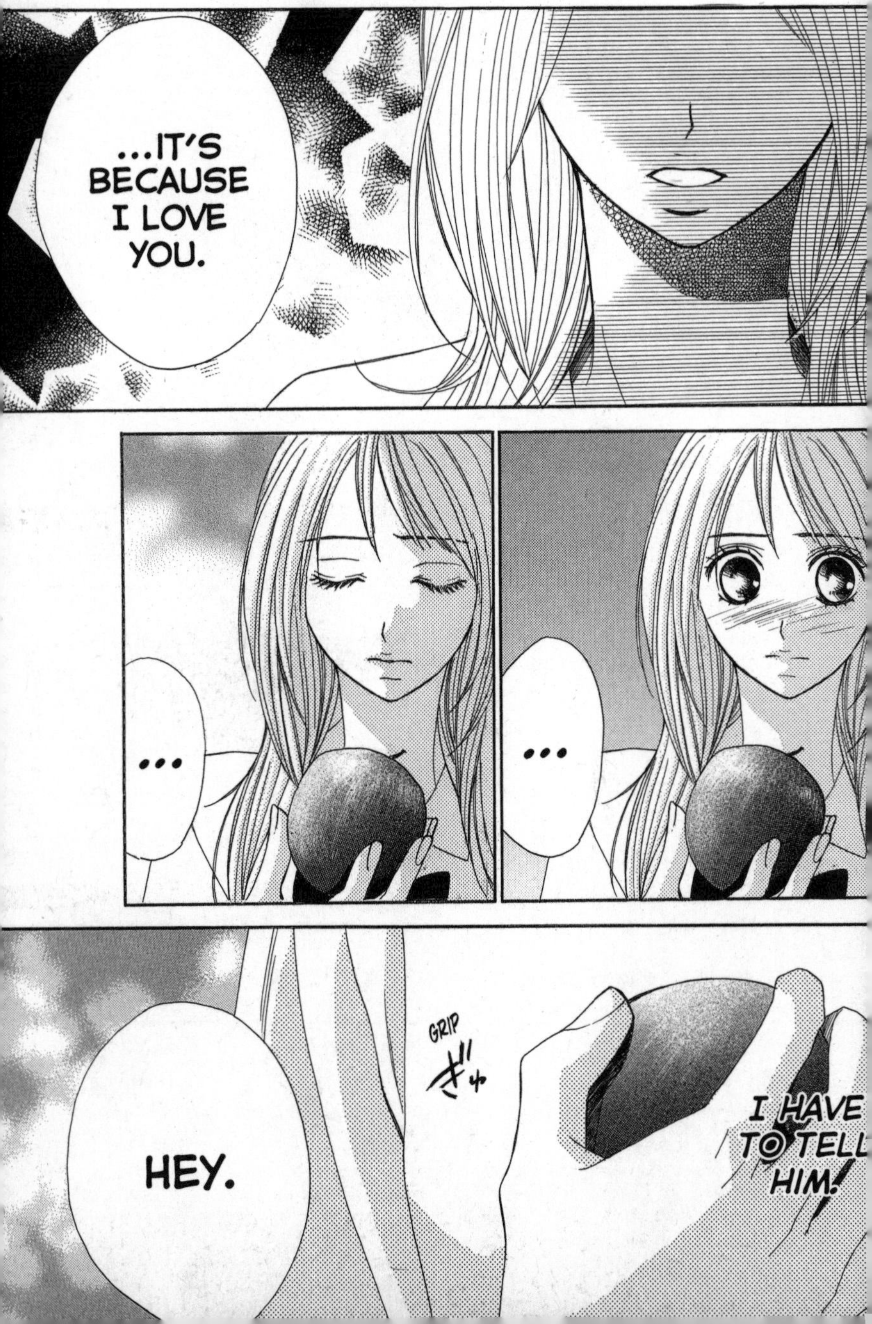
...IT'S BECAUSE I LOVE YOU.
...
...
I HAVE TO TELL HIM!
GRIP
HEY.

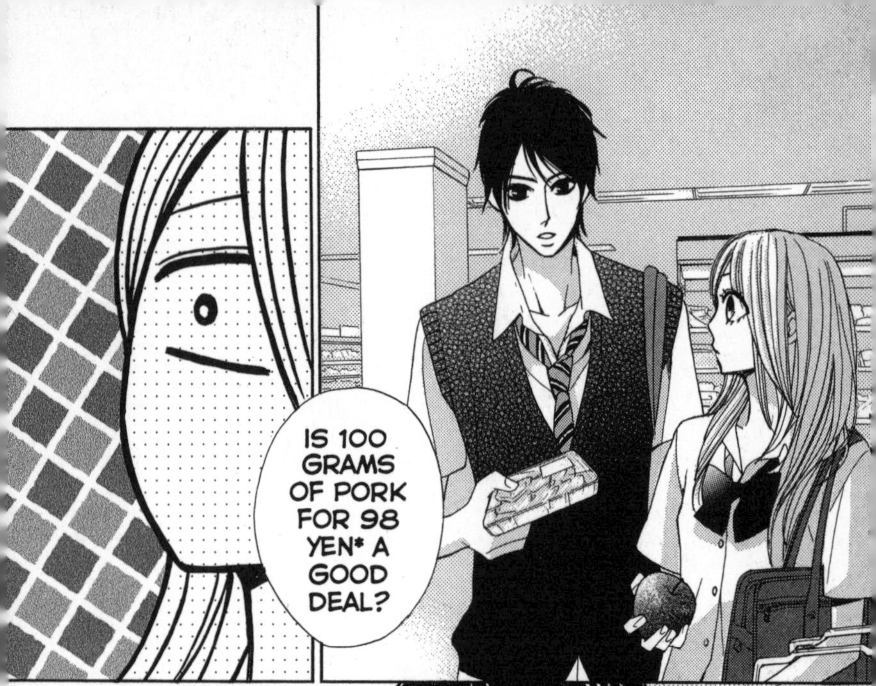
IS 100 GRAMS OF PORK FOR 98 YEN* A GOOD DEAL?

*Approximately 1/4 pound for $1.

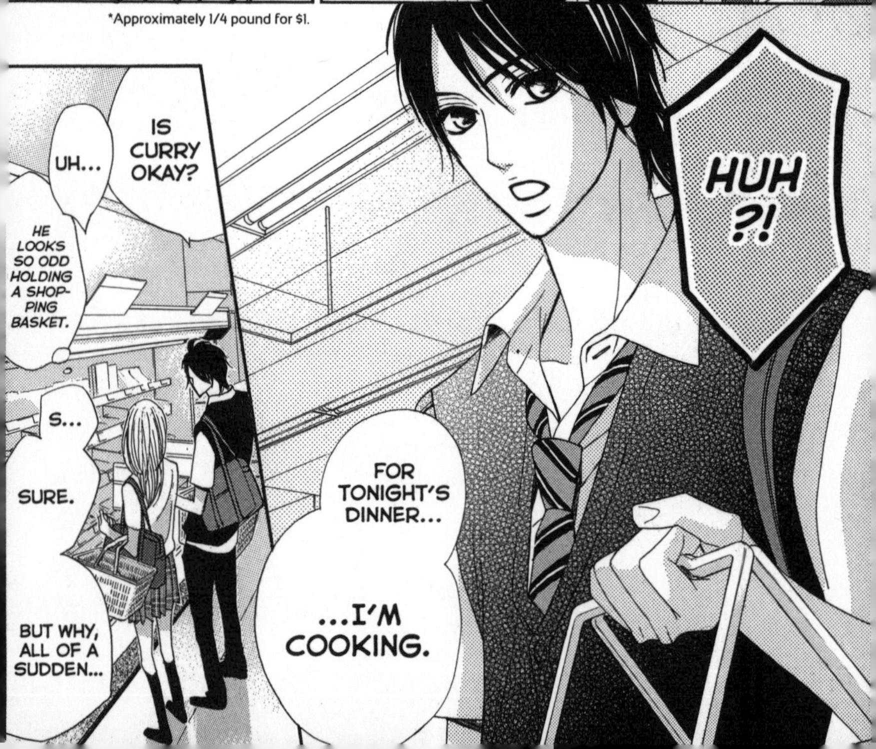
HUH ?!
FOR TONIGHT'S DINNER...
...I'M COOKING.
IS CURRY OKAY?
UH...
HE LOOKS SO ODD HOLDING A SHOP-PING BASKET.
S...
SURE.
BUT WHY, ALL OF A SUDDEN...

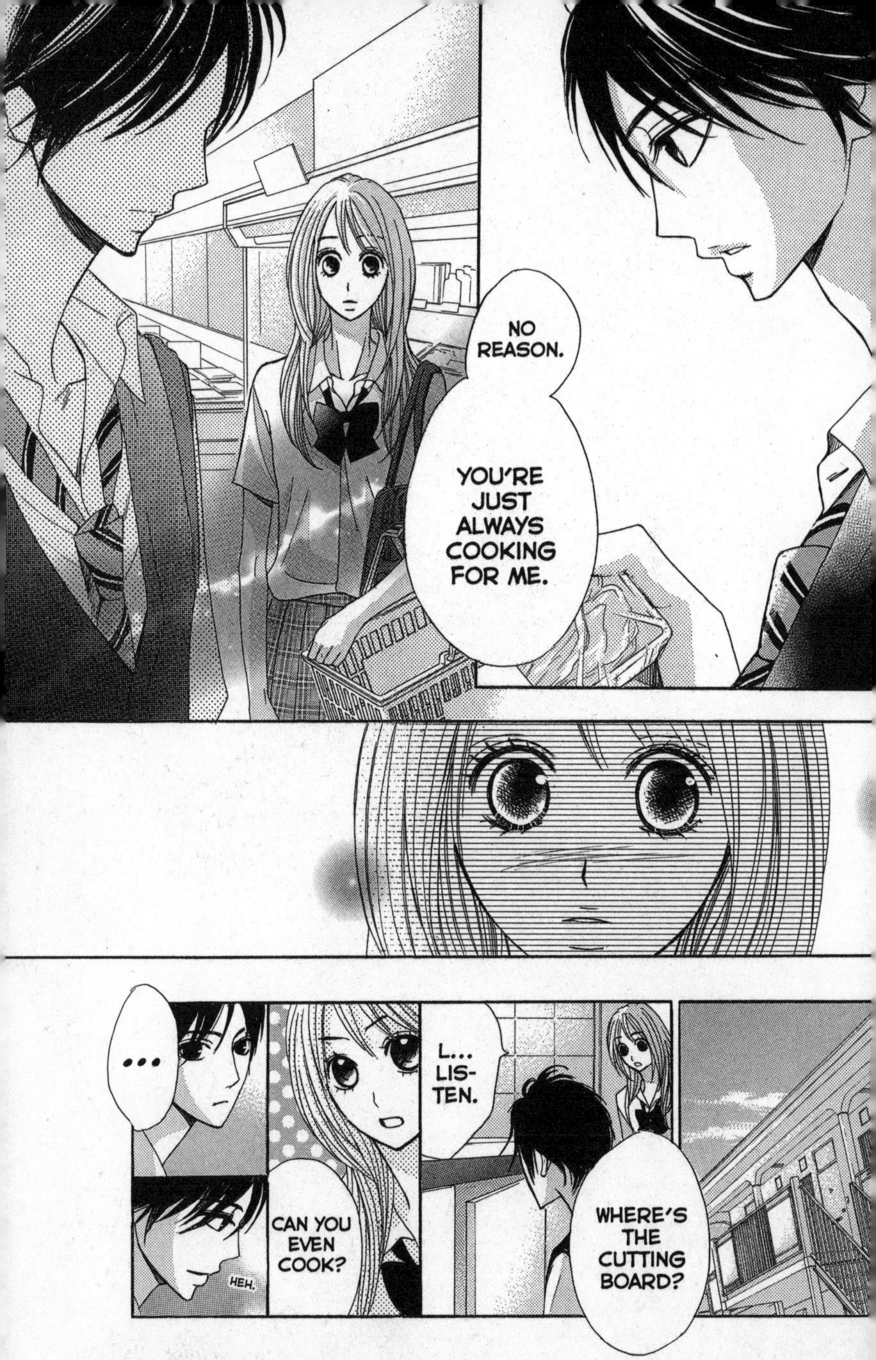
NO REASON.
YOU'RE JUST ALWAYS COOKING FOR ME.
WHERE'S THE CUTTING BOARD?
L... LIS- TEN.
CAN YOU EVEN COOK?
...
HEH.

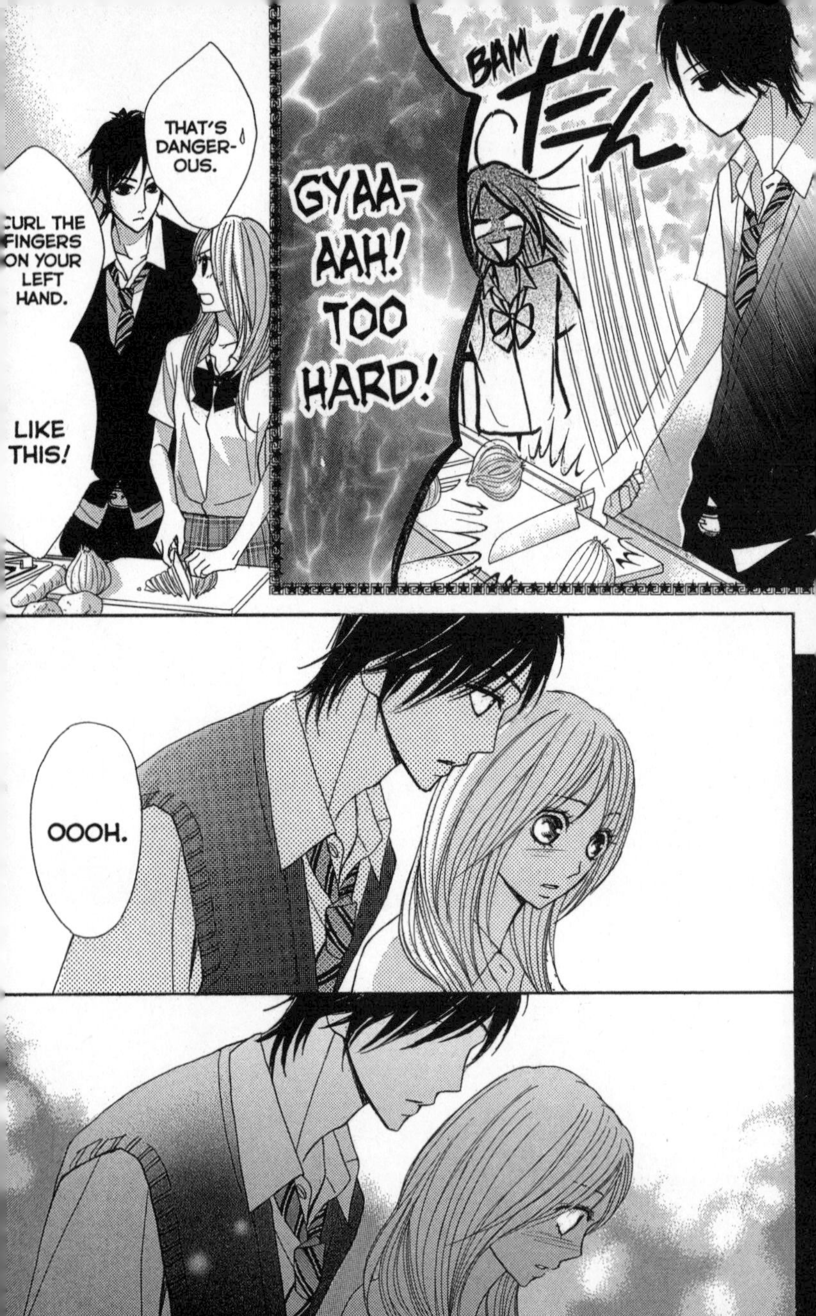
BAM
GYAA-AAH! TOO HARD!
THAT'S DANGER-OUS.
CURL THE FINGERS ON YOUR LEFT HAND.
LIKE THIS!
OOOH.

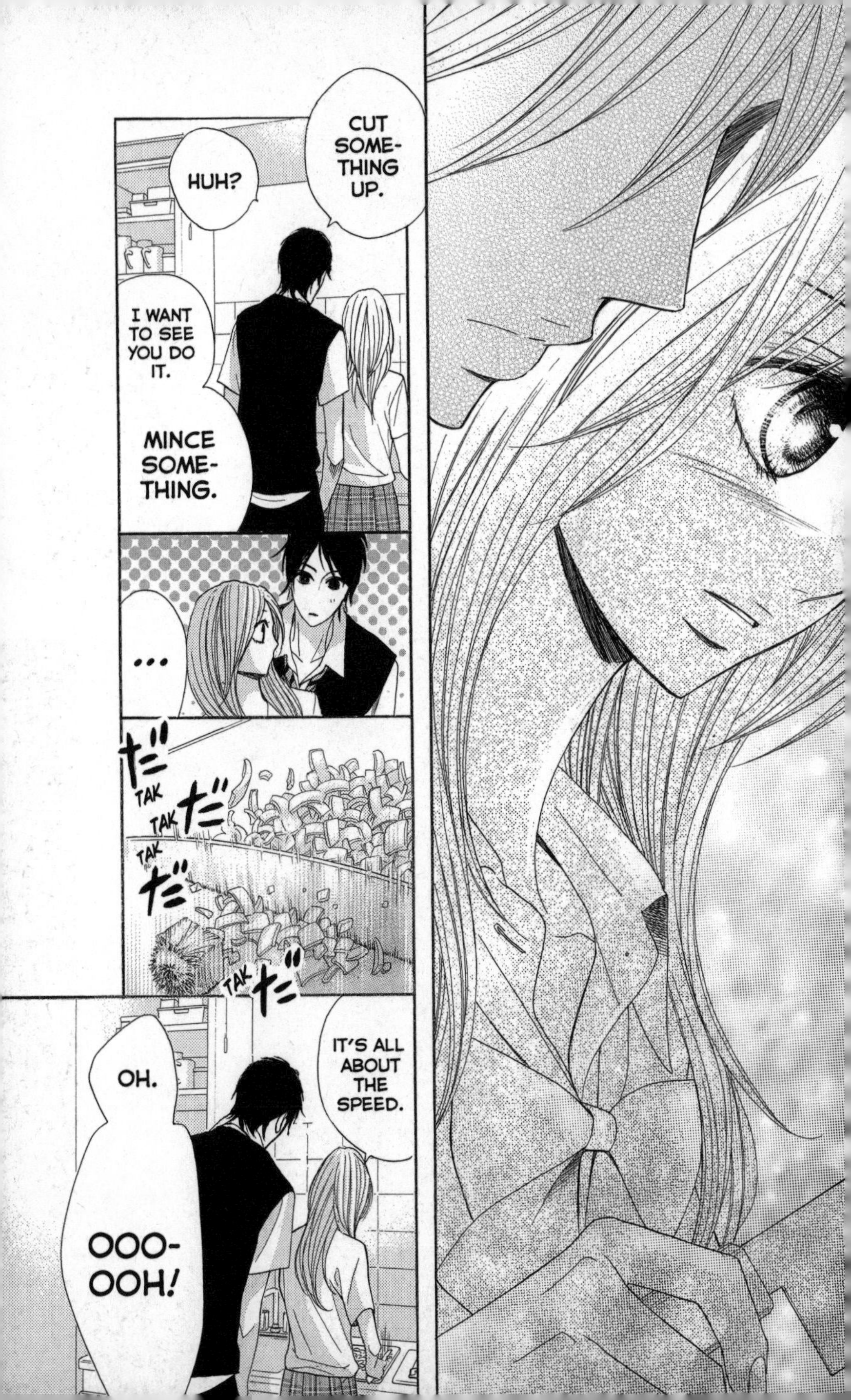
CUT SOME-THING UP.
HUH?
I WANT TO SEE YOU DO IT.
MINCE SOME-THING.
...
だ TAK
だ TAK
だ TAK
だ TAK
IT'S ALL ABOUT THE SPEED.
OH.
OOO-OOH!

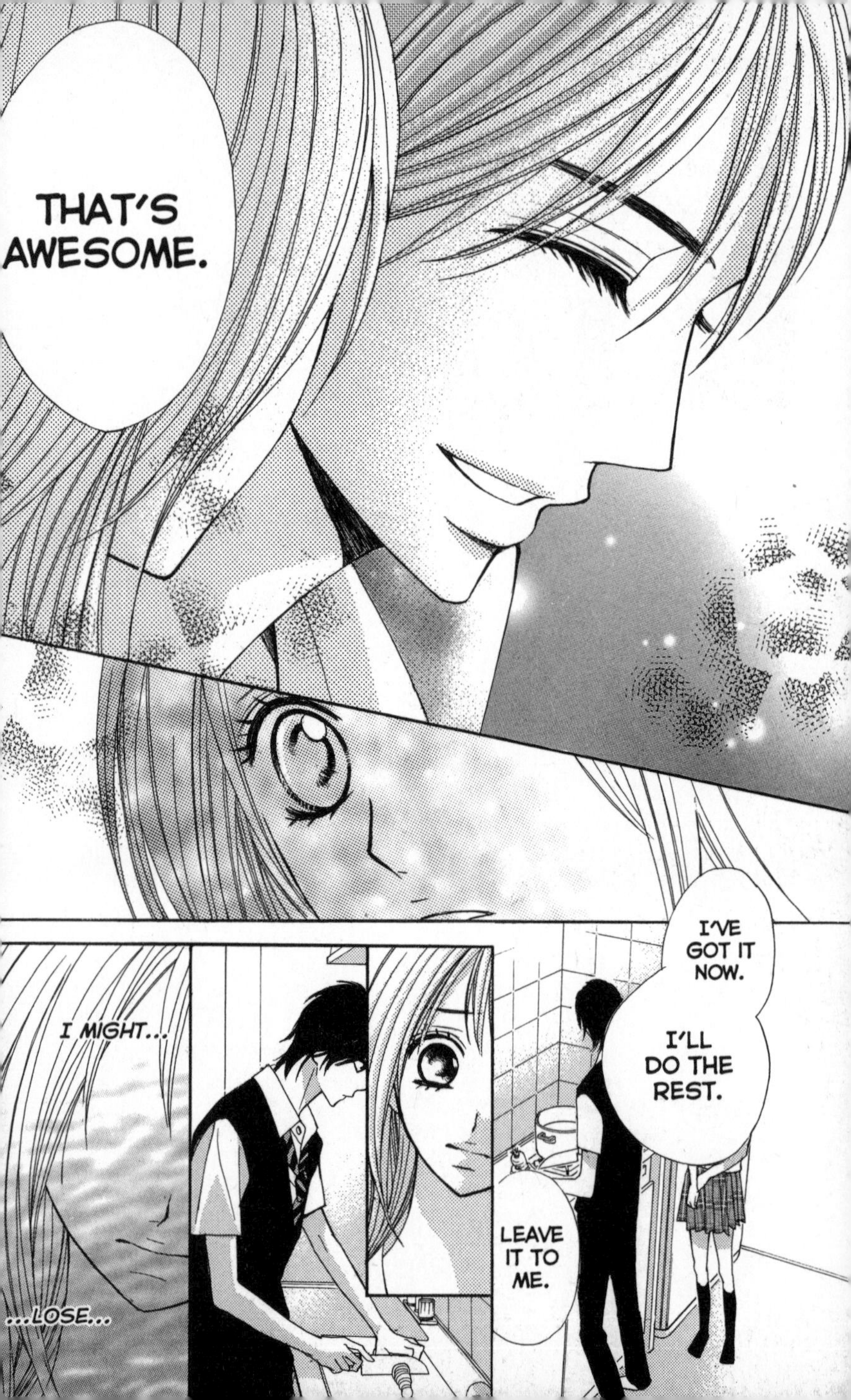
THAT'S AWESOME.
I'VE GOT IT NOW.
I'LL DO THE REST.
LEAVE IT TO ME.
I MIGHT...
...LOSE...

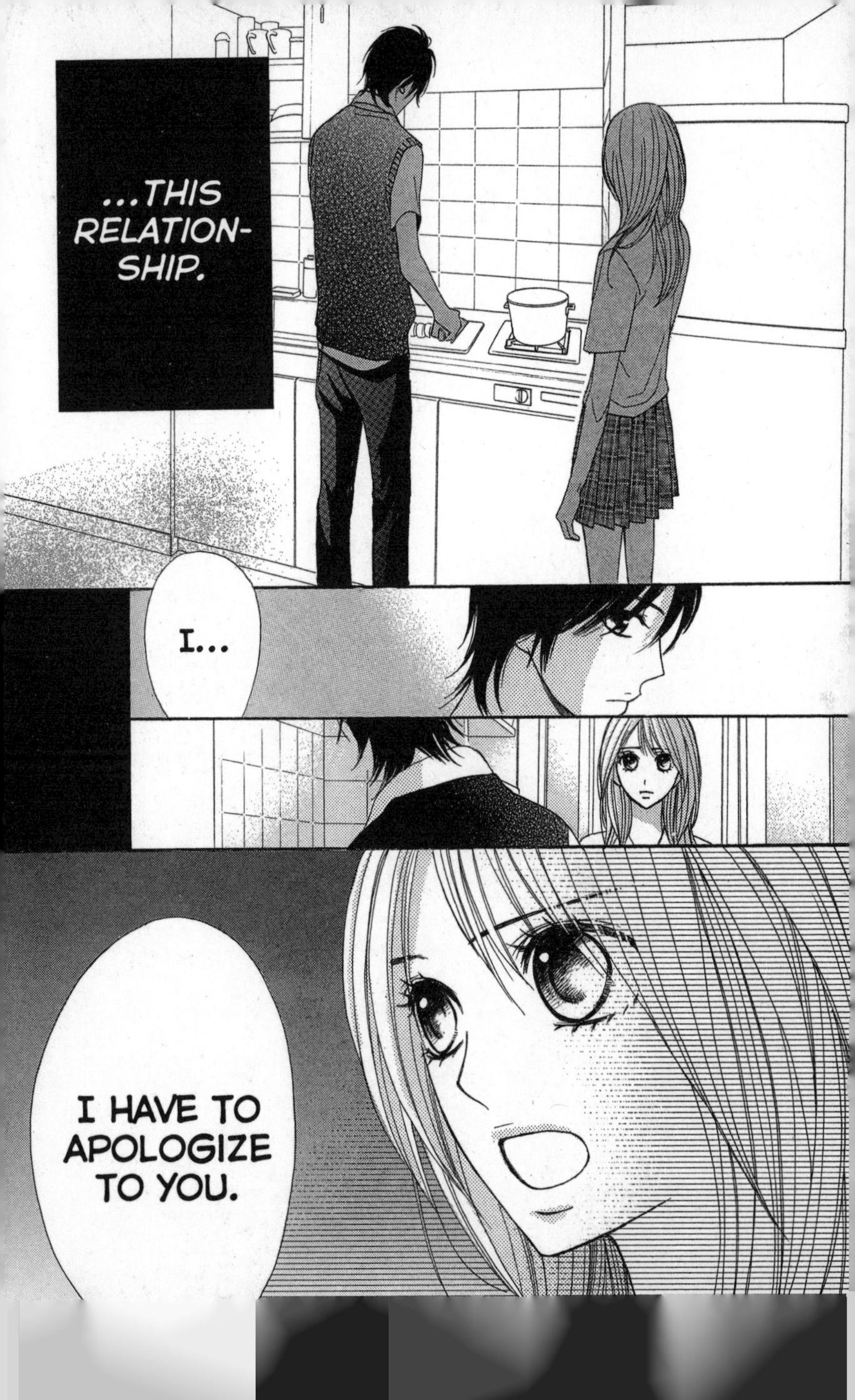
...THIS RELATION-SHIP.
I...
I HAVE TO APOLOGIZE TO YOU.

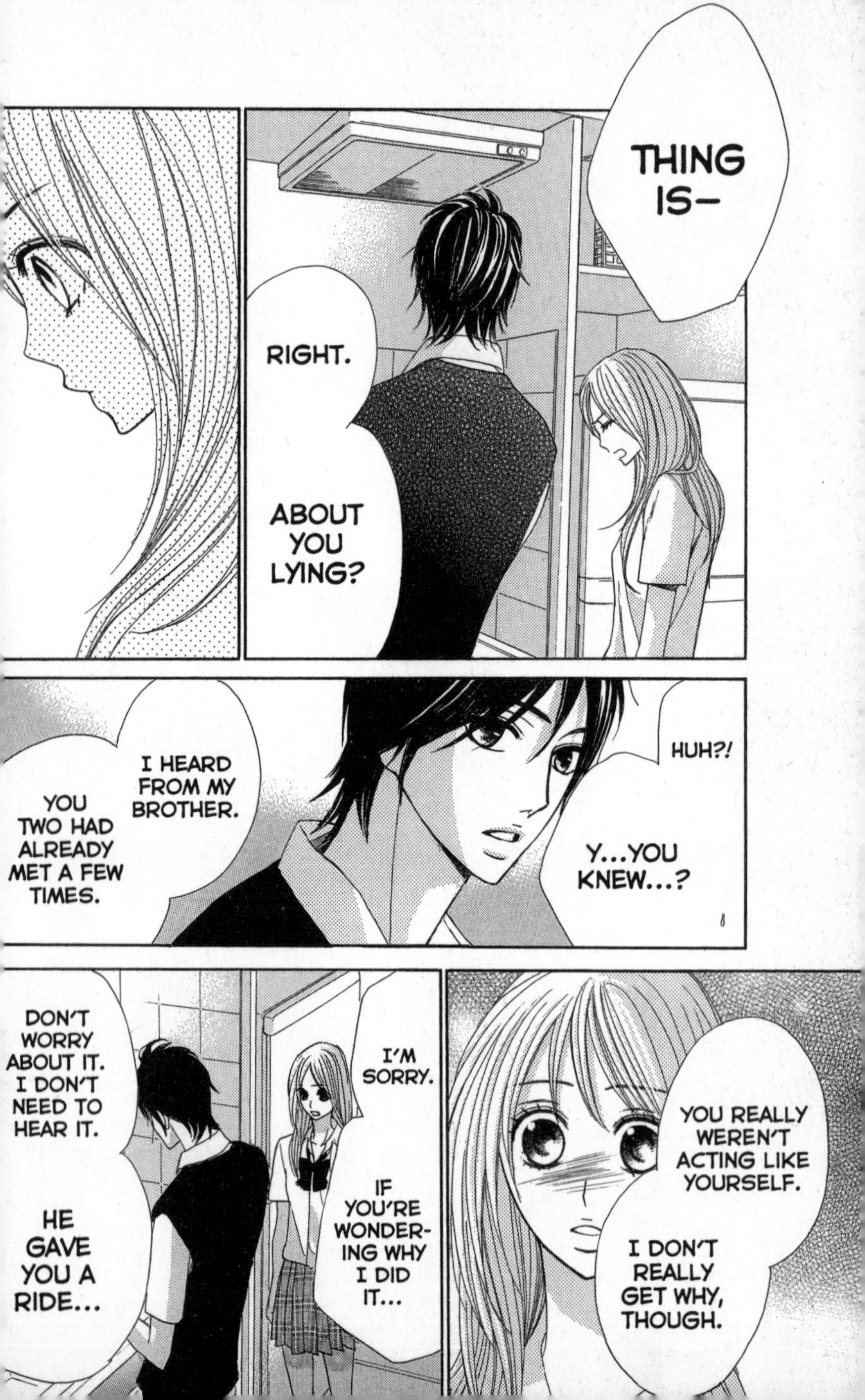
THING IS–
RIGHT.
ABOUT YOU LYING?
HUH?!
Y...YOU KNEW...?
I HEARD FROM MY BROTHER.
YOU TWO HAD ALREADY MET A FEW TIMES.
YOU REALLY WEREN'T ACTING LIKE YOURSELF.
I DON'T REALLY GET WHY, THOUGH.
I'M SORRY.
IF YOU'RE WONDERING WHY I DID IT...
DON'T WORRY ABOUT IT. I DON'T NEED TO HEAR IT.
HE GAVE YOU A RIDE...

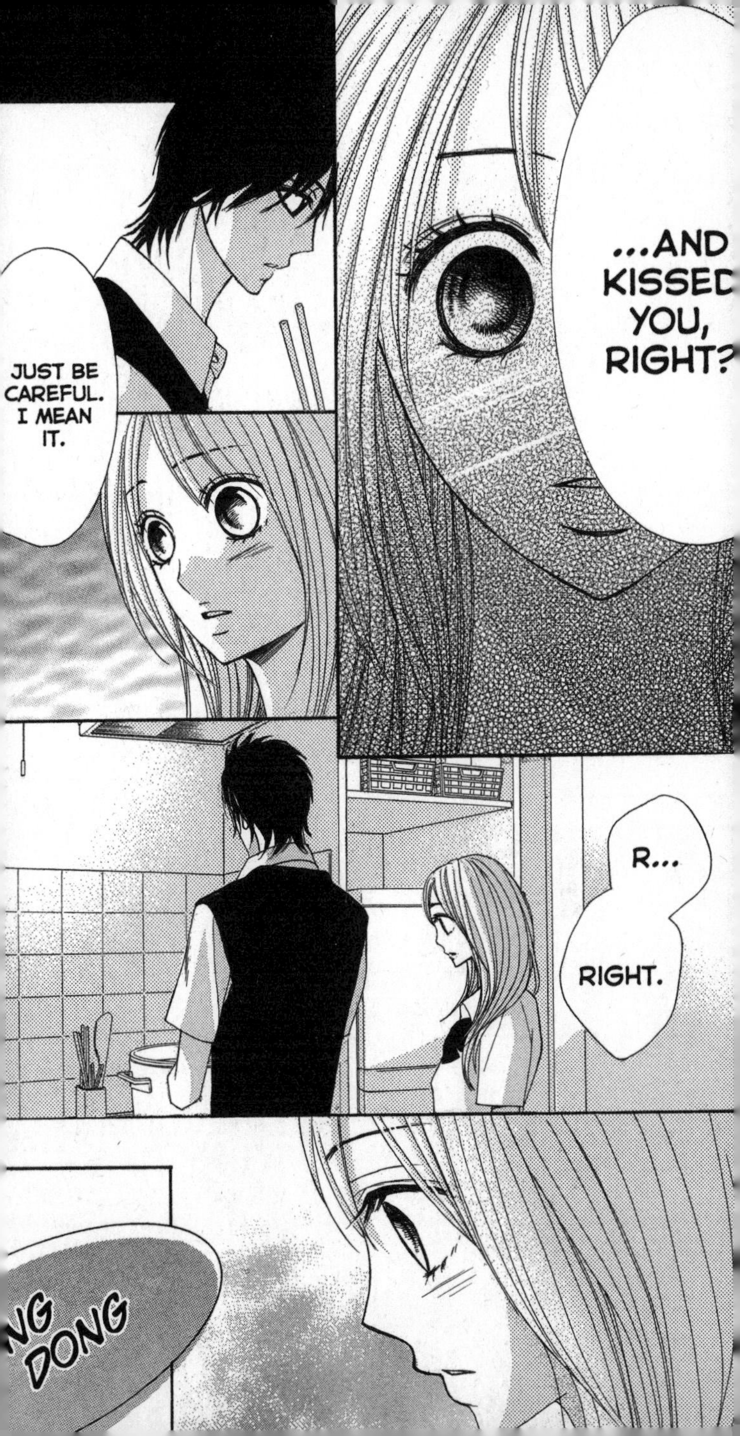
...AND KISSED YOU, RIGHT?
JUST BE CAREFUL. I MEAN IT.
R...
RIGHT.
NG DONG

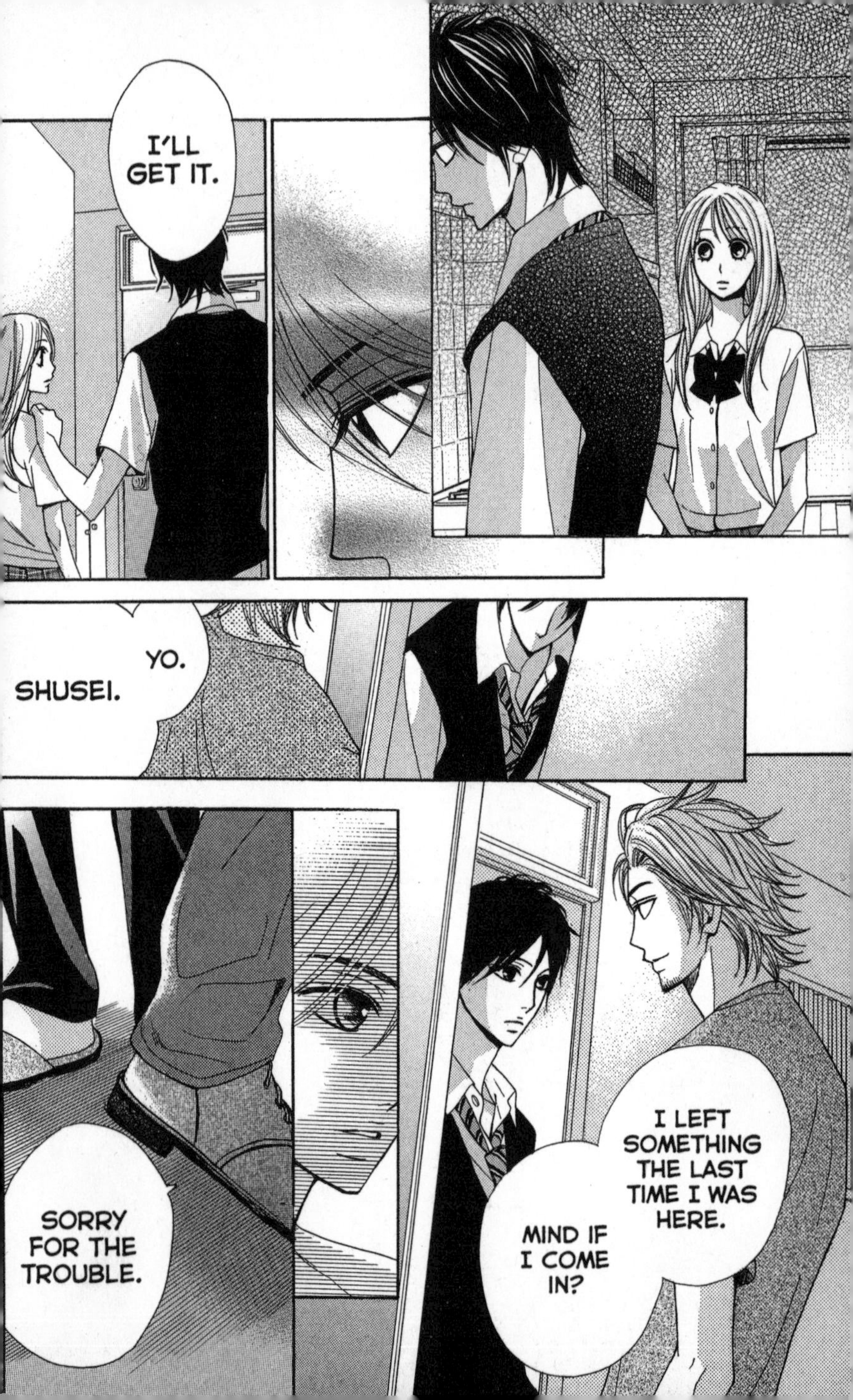
I'LL GET IT.
YO. SHUSEI.
I LEFT SOMETHING THE LAST TIME I WAS HERE.
MIND IF I COME IN?
SORRY FOR THE TROUBLE.

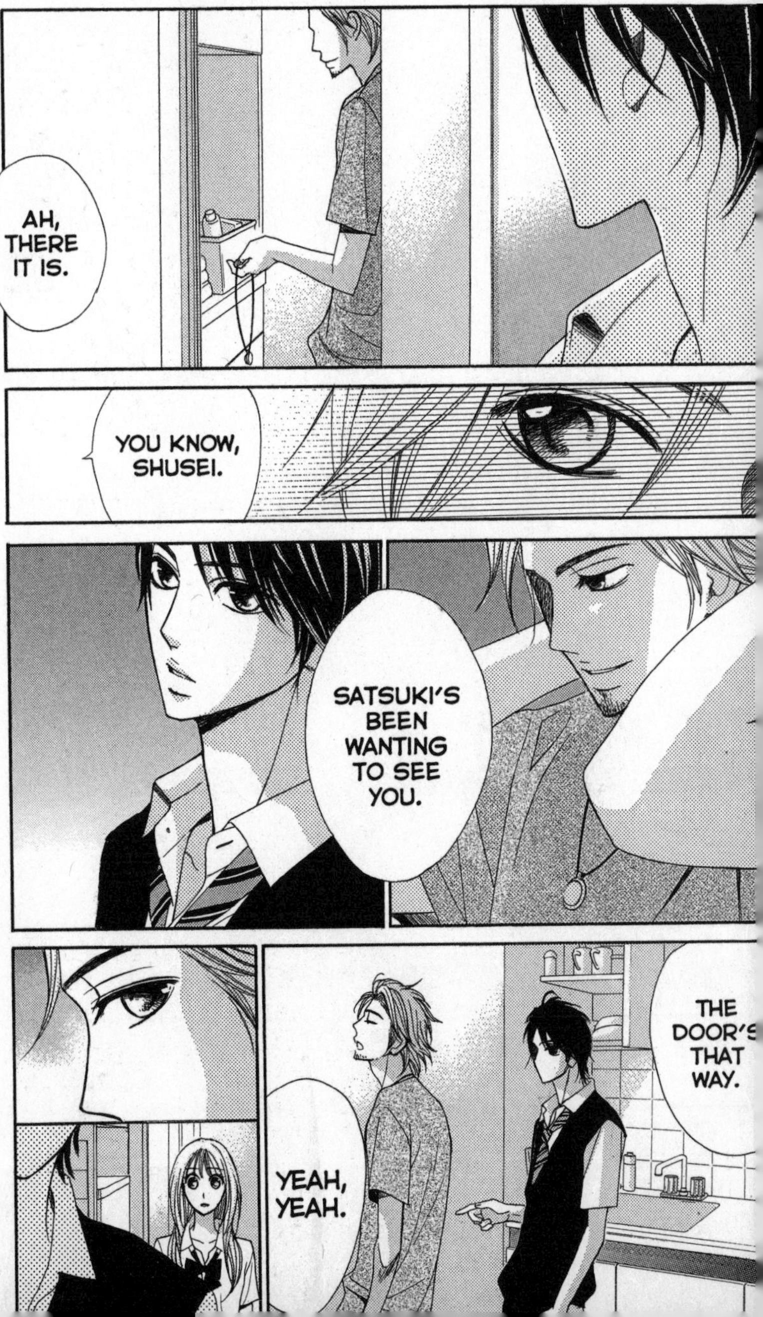
AH, THERE IT IS.
YOU KNOW, SHUSEI.
SATSUKI'S BEEN WANTING TO SEE YOU.
THE DOOR'S THAT WAY.
YEAH, YEAH.

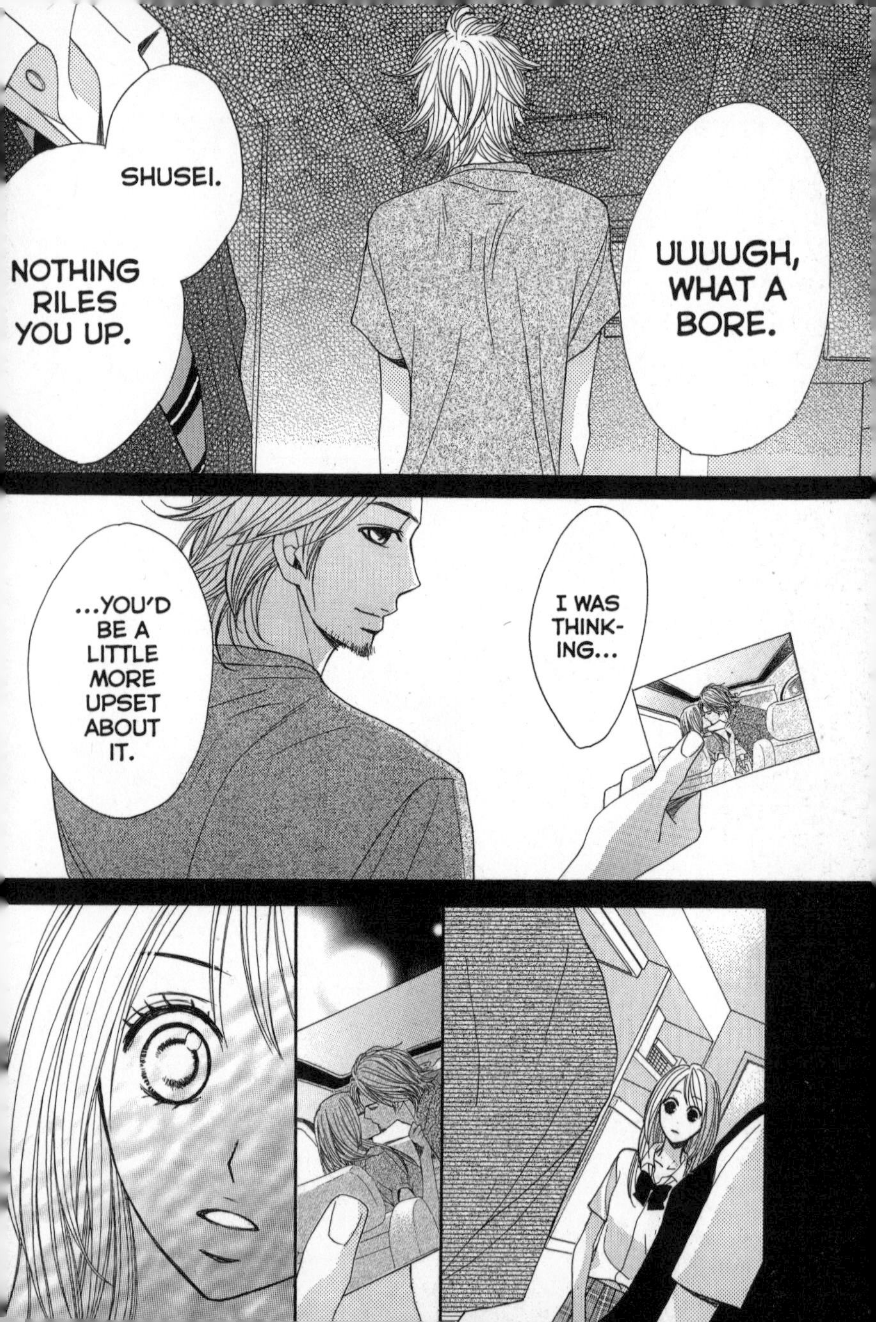
UUUUGH, WHAT A BORE.
SHUSEI.
NOTHING RILES YOU UP.
I WAS THINK-ING...
...YOU'D BE A LITTLE MORE UPSET ABOUT IT.

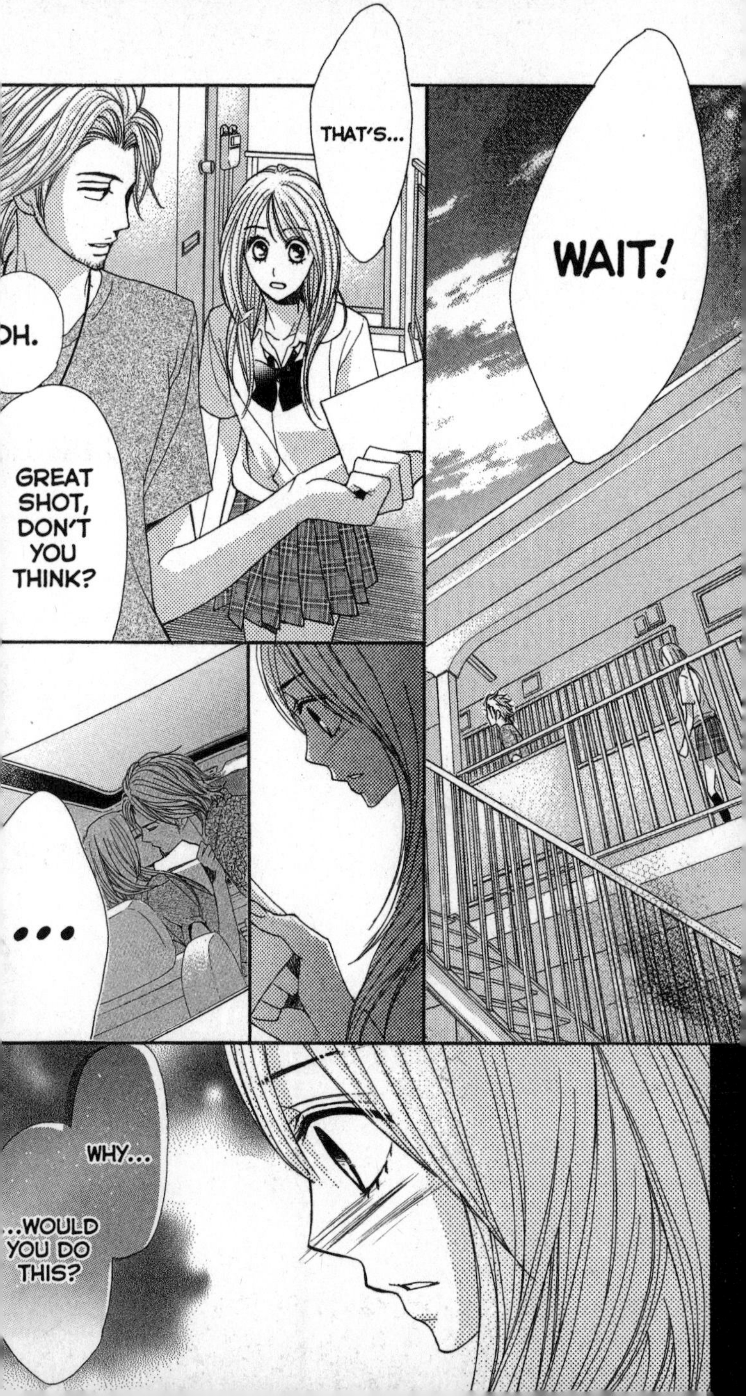
WAIT!
THAT'S...
OH.
GREAT SHOT, DON'T YOU THINK?
...
WHY...
...WOULD YOU DO THIS?

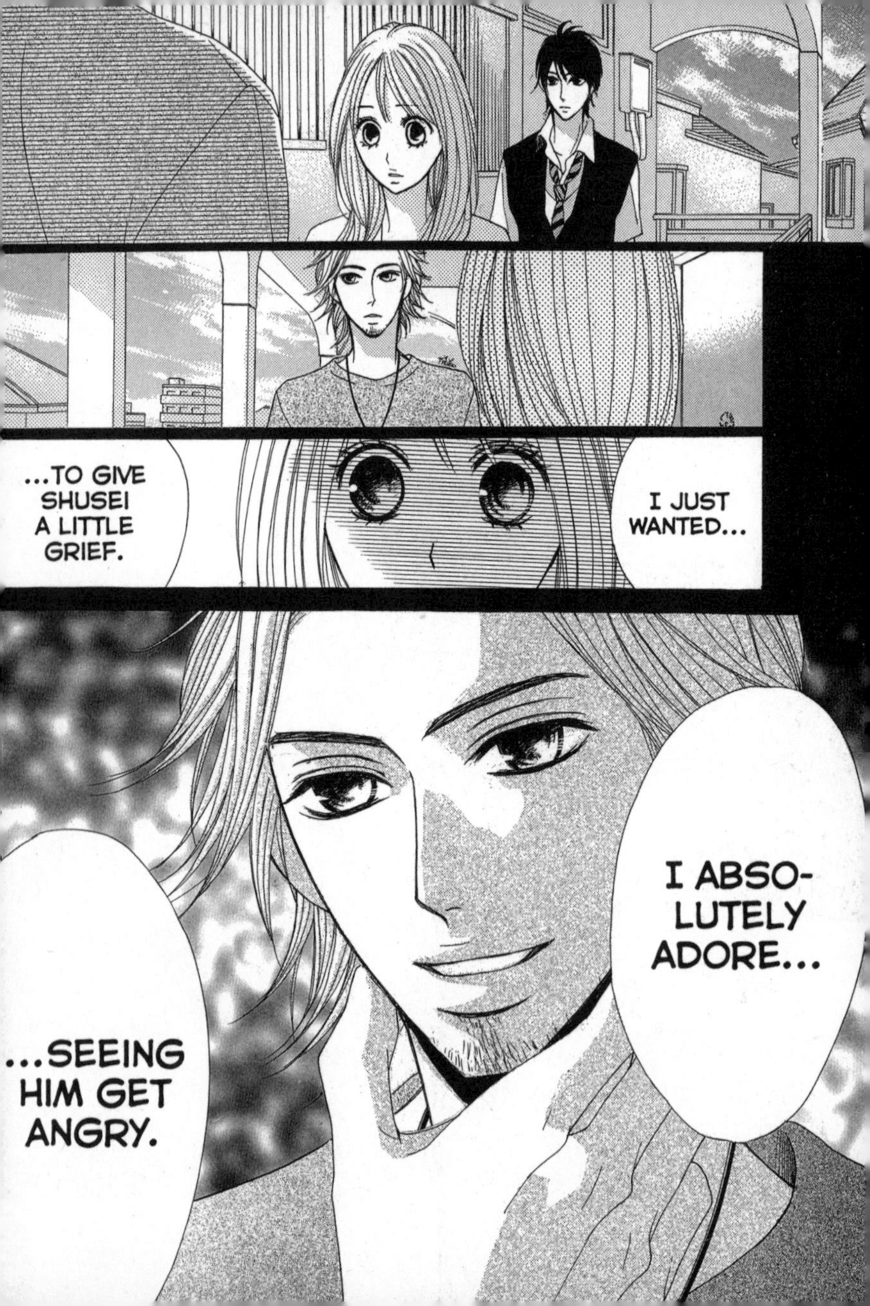
I JUST WANTED...
...TO GIVE SHUSEI A LITTLE GRIEF.
I ABSO-LUTELY ADORE...
...SEEING HIM GET ANGRY.

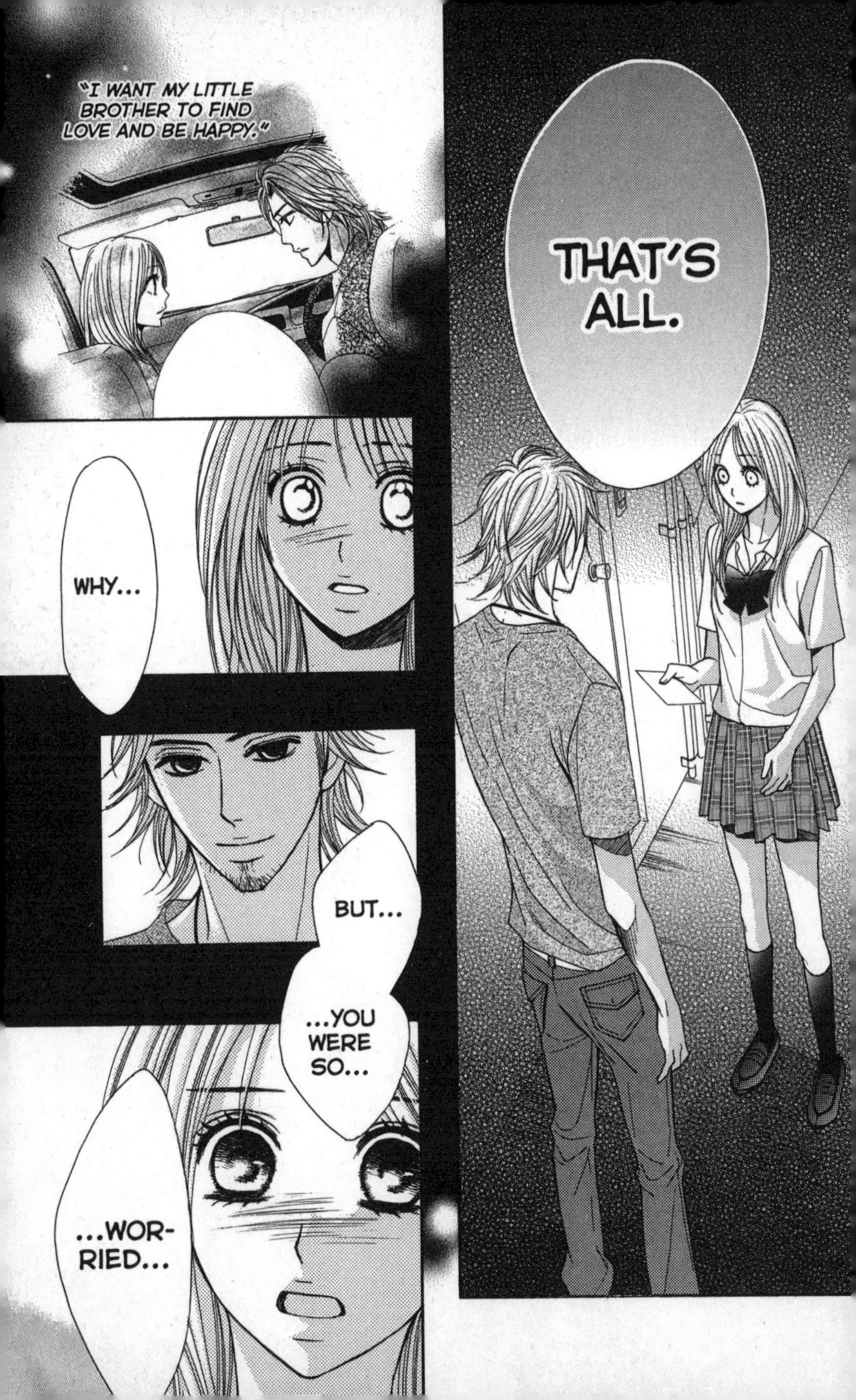
THAT'S ALL.
"I WANT MY LITTLE BROTHER TO FIND LOVE AND BE HAPPY."
WHY...
BUT...
...YOU WERE SO...
...WOR-RIED...

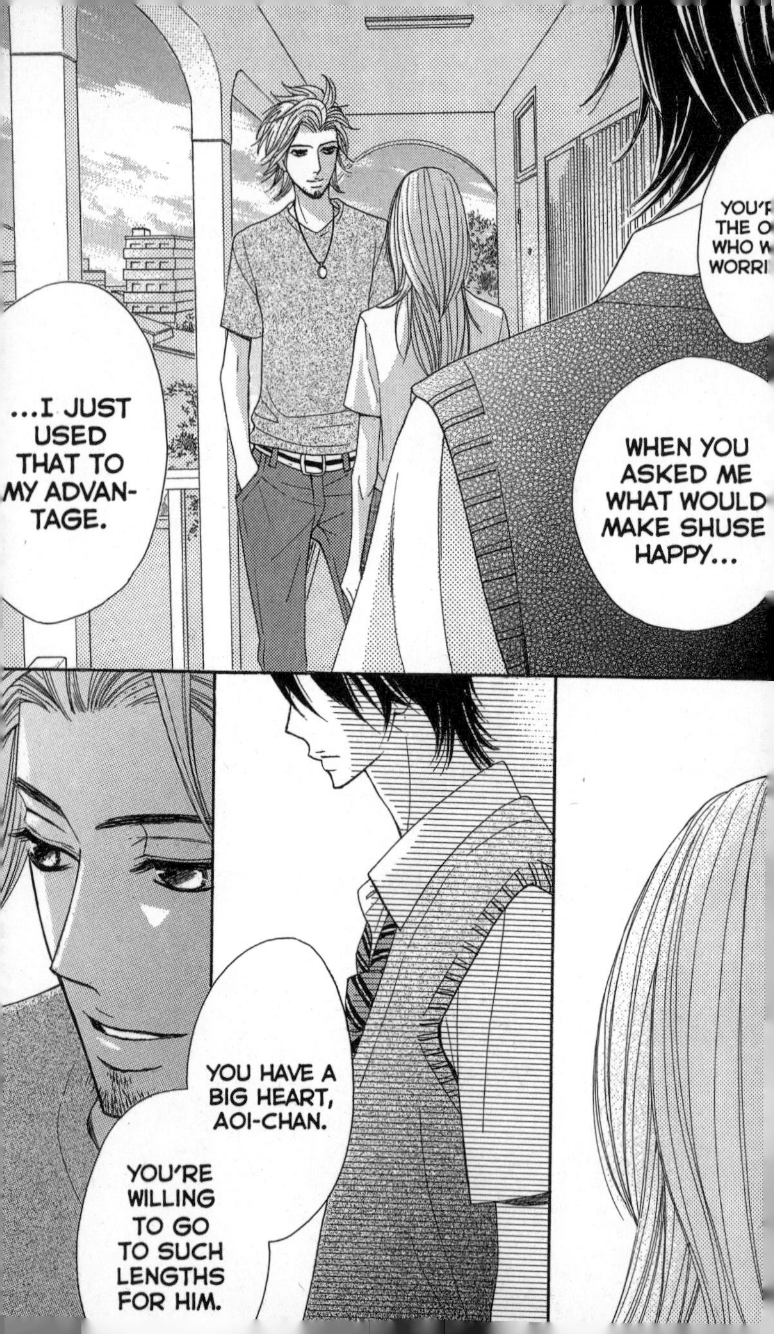
YOU'R THE O WHO W WORRI
WHEN YOU ASKED ME WHAT WOULD MAKE SHUSE HAPPY...
...I JUST USED THAT TO MY ADVANTAGE.
YOU HAVE A BIG HEART, AOI-CHAN.
YOU'RE WILLING TO GO TO SUCH LENGTHS FOR HIM.

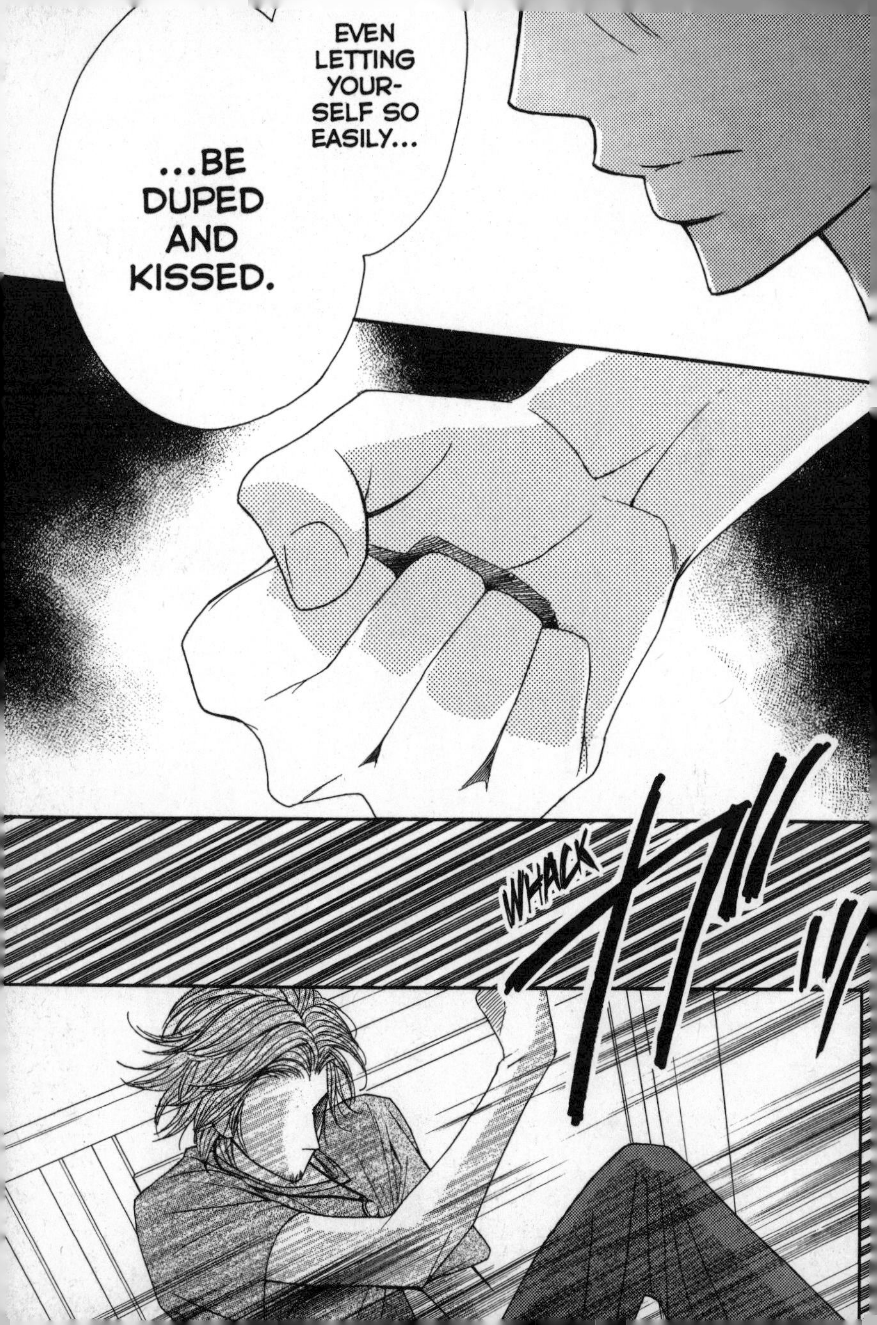
EVEN LETTING YOUR-SELF SO EASILY...
...BE DUPED AND KISSED.
WHACK

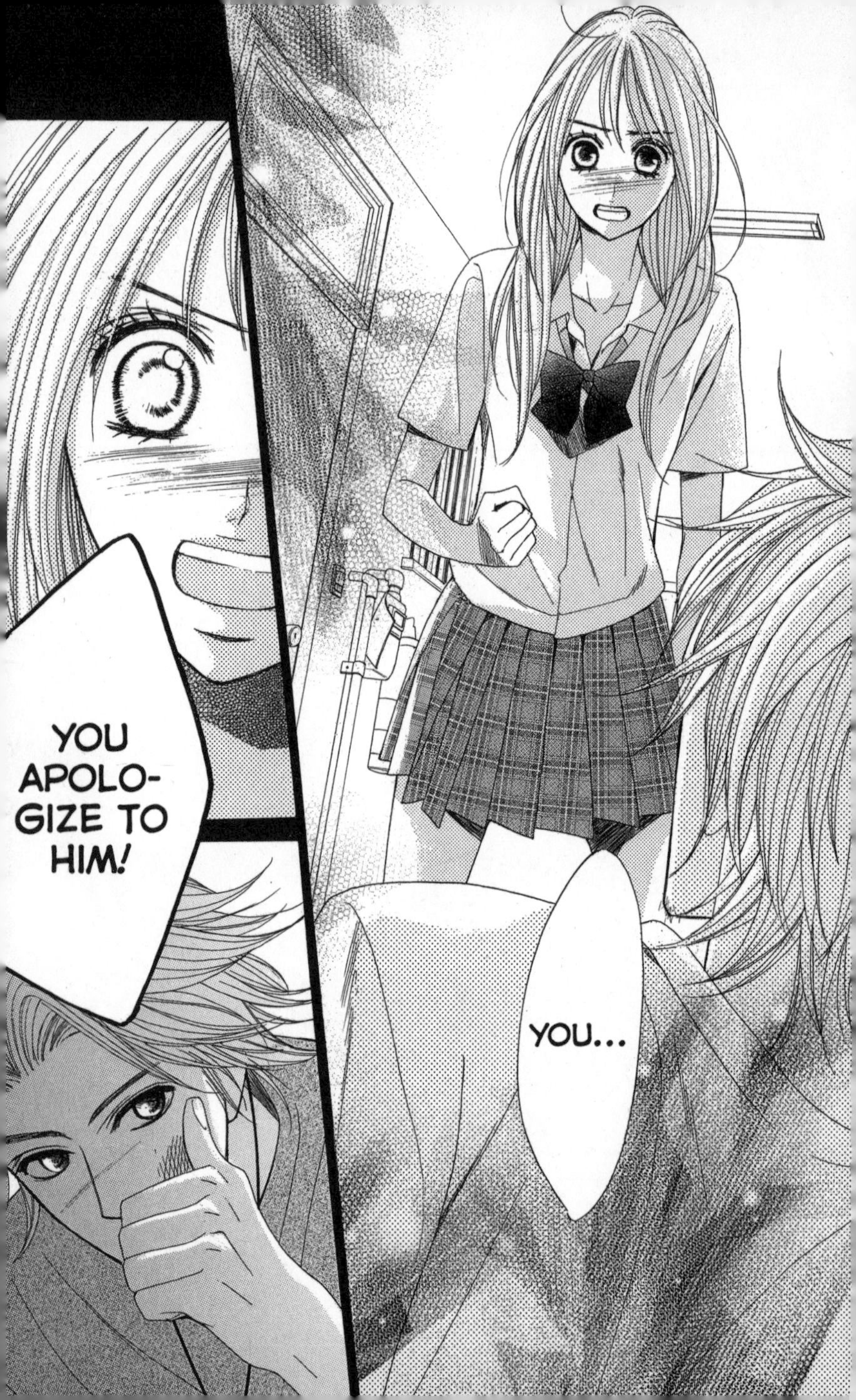
YOU...
YOU APOLOGIZE TO HIM!

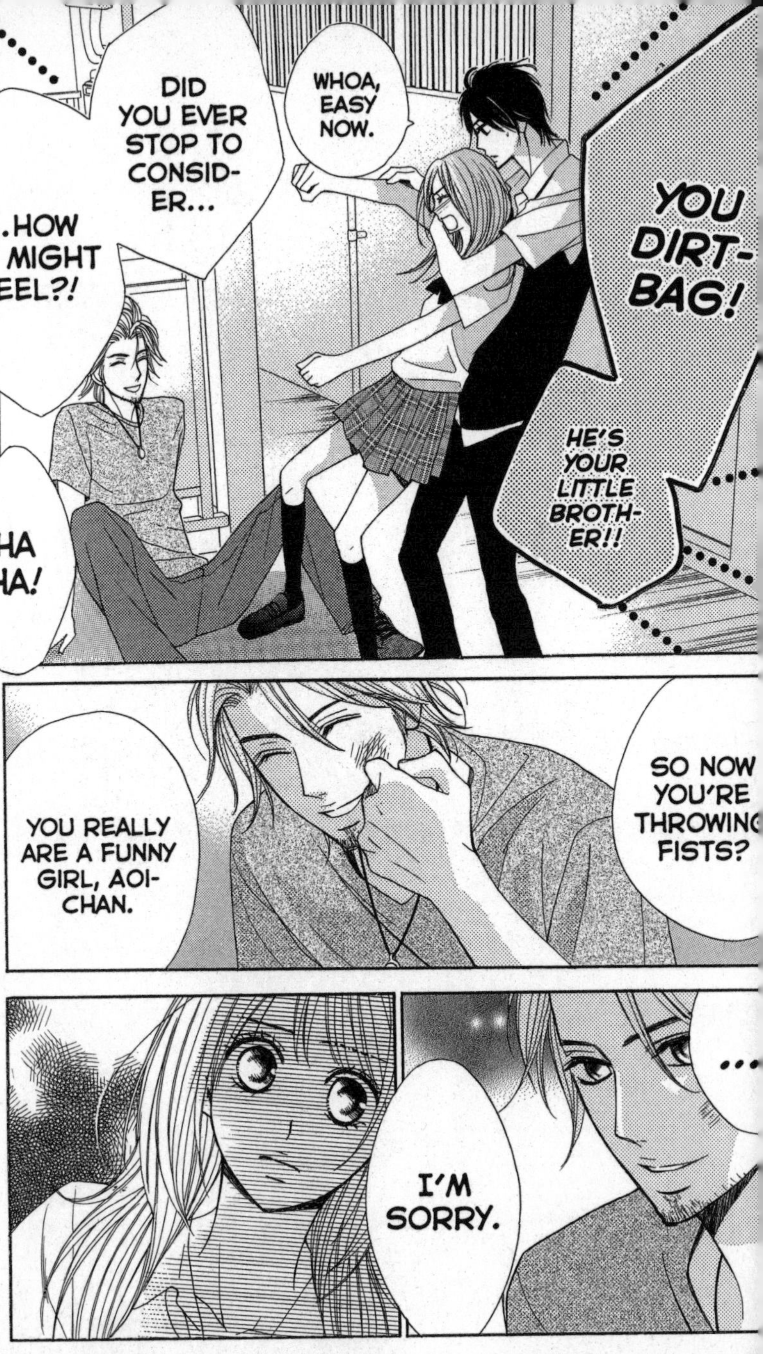
YOU DIRT-BAG!
HE'S YOUR LITTLE BROTHER!!
WHOA, EASY NOW.
DID YOU EVER STOP TO CONSIDER...
...HOW HE MIGHT FEEL?!
HA HA!
SO NOW YOU'RE THROWING FISTS?
YOU REALLY ARE A FUNNY GIRL, AOI-CHAN.
...
I'M SORRY.

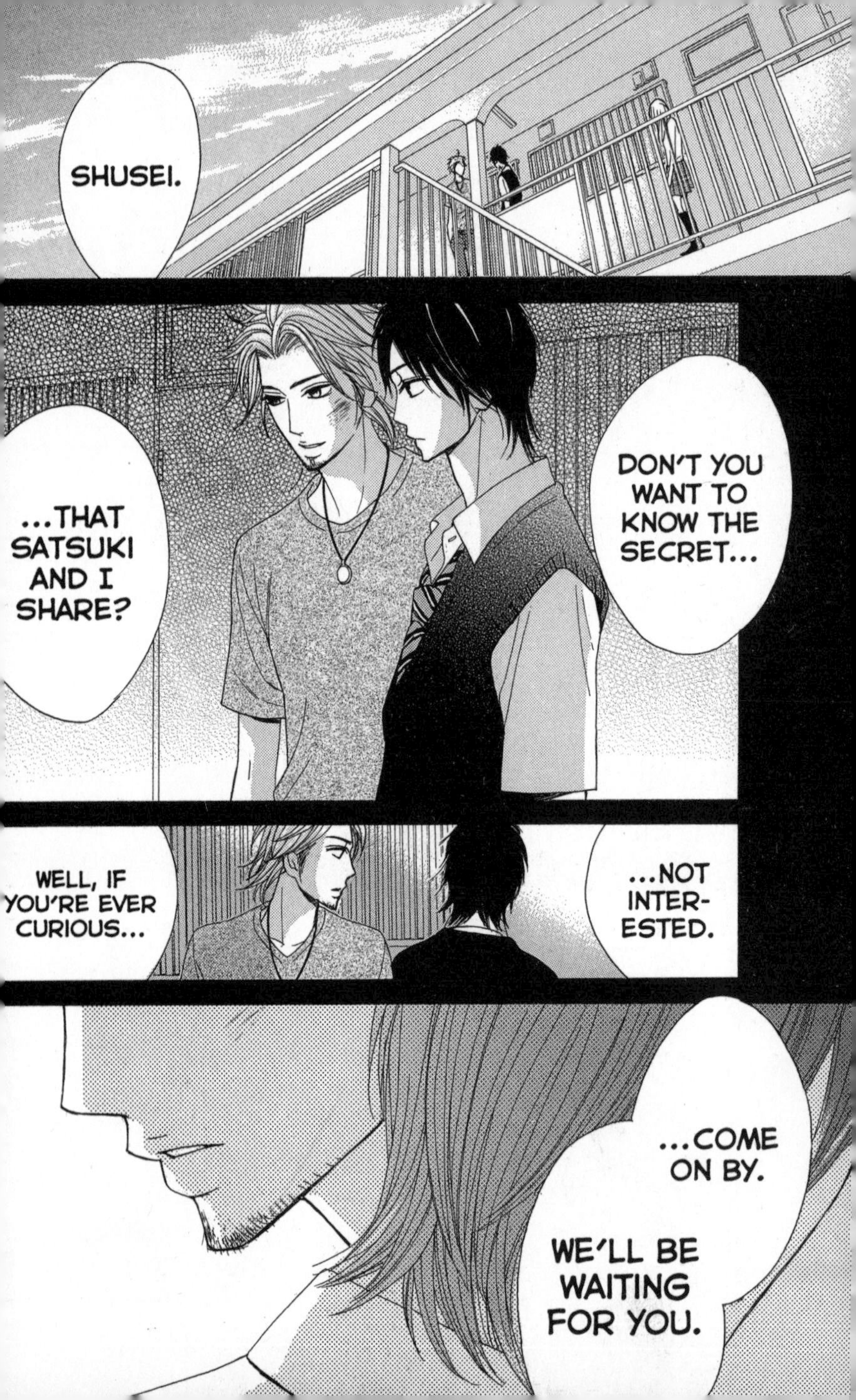
SHUSEI.
DON'T YOU WANT TO KNOW THE SECRET...
...THAT SATSUKI AND I SHARE?
...NOT INTER-ESTED.
WELL, IF YOU'RE EVER CURIOUS...
...COME ON BY.
WE'LL BE WAITING FOR YOU.

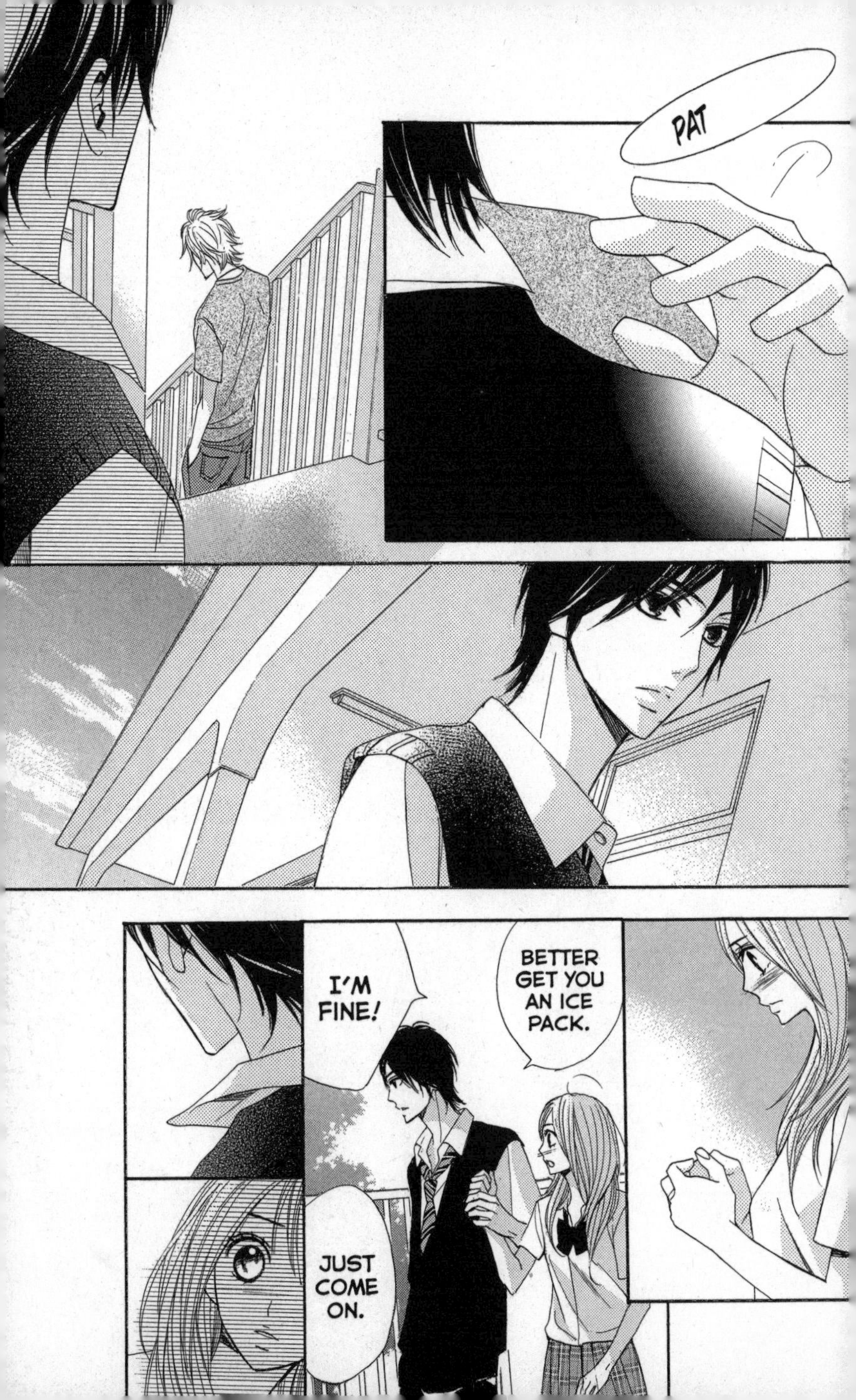
PAT
BETTER GET YOU AN ICE PACK.
I'M FINE!
JUST COME ON.

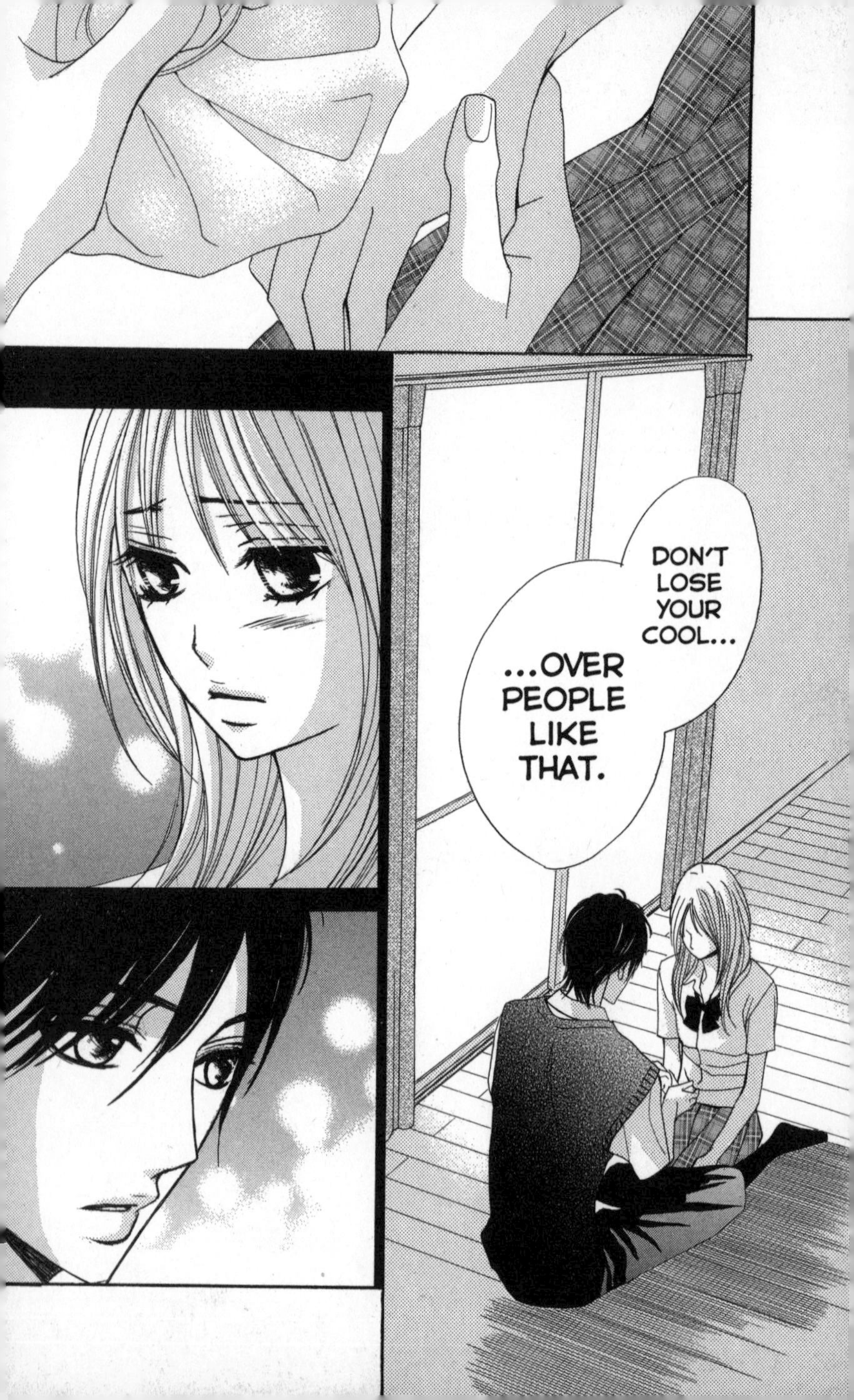
DON'T LOSE YOUR COOL...
...OVER PEOPLE LIKE THAT.

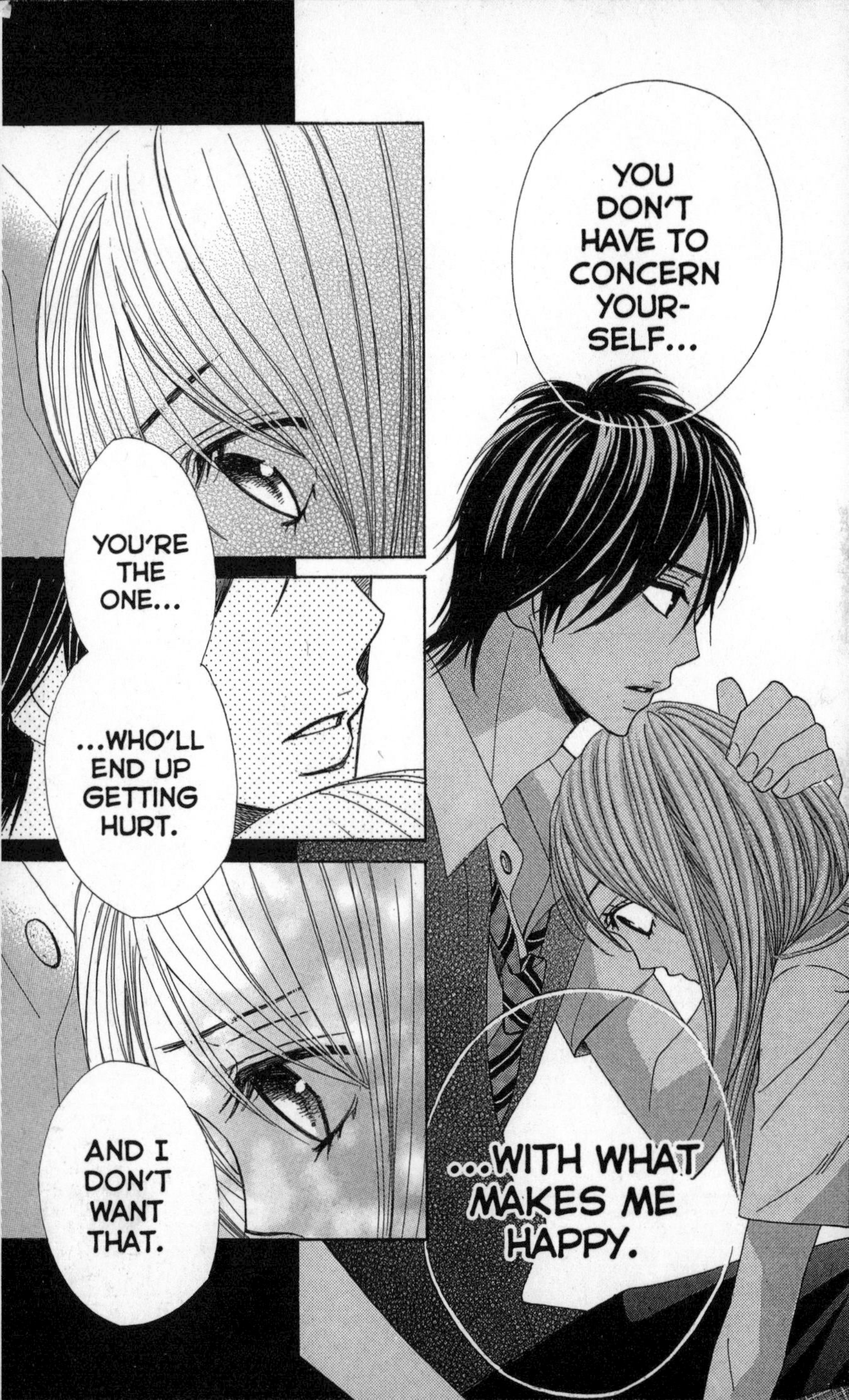
YOU DON'T HAVE TO CONCERN YOUR-SELF...
...WITH WHAT MAKES ME HAPPY.
YOU'RE THE ONE...
...WHO'LL END UP GETTING HURT.
AND I DON'T WANT THAT.

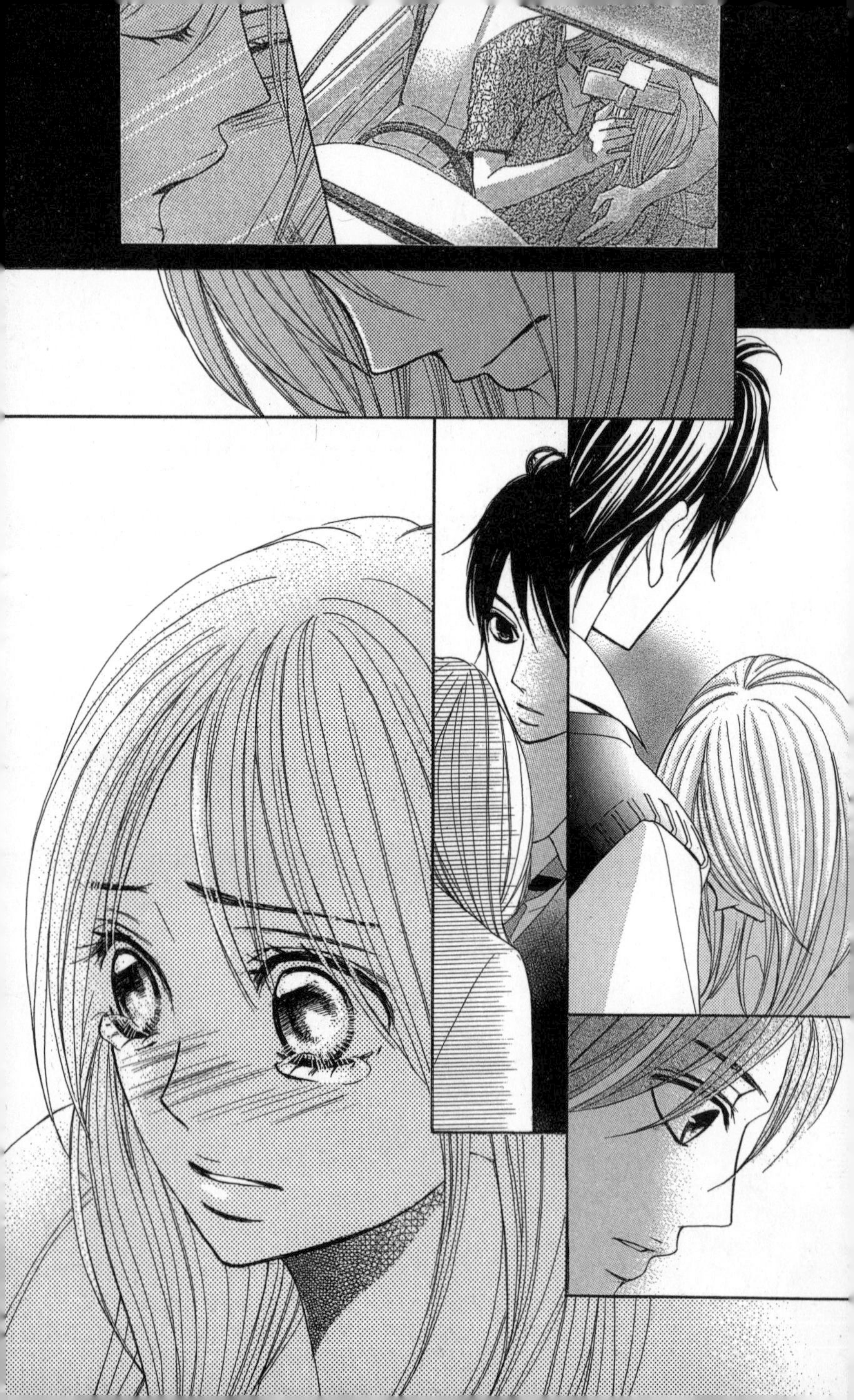

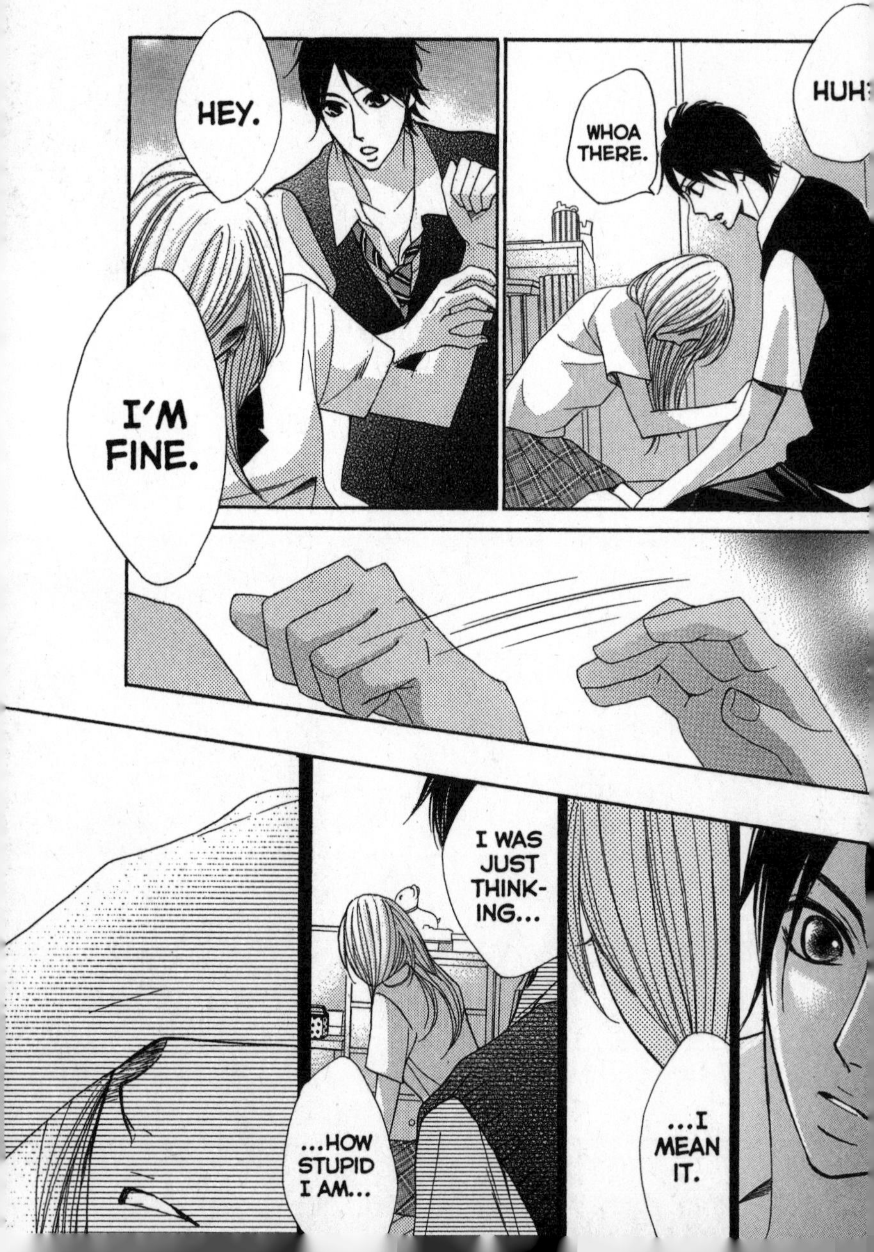
HUH
WHOA THERE.
HEY.
I'M FINE.
...I MEAN IT.
I WAS JUST THINKING...
...HOW STUPID I AM...

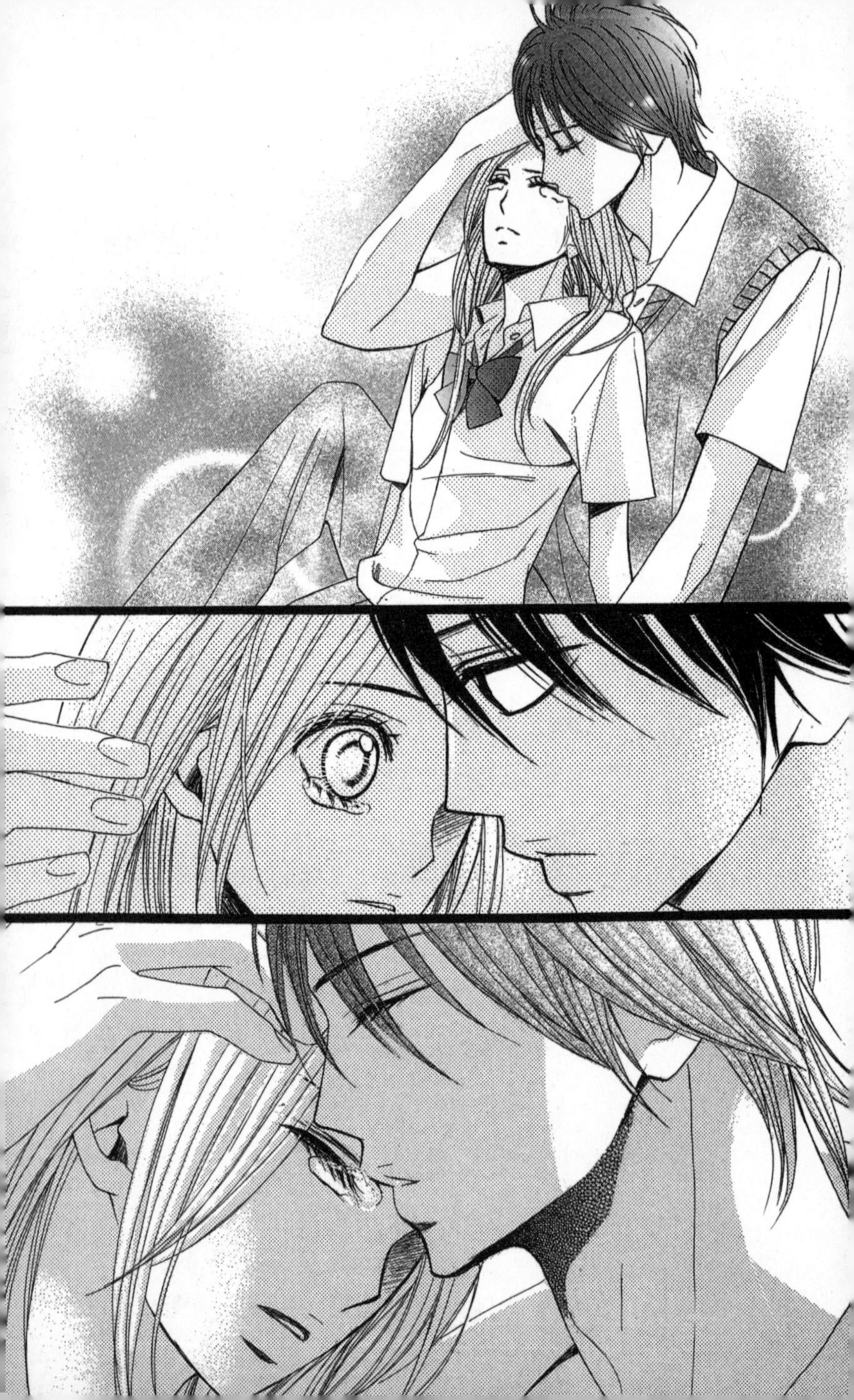

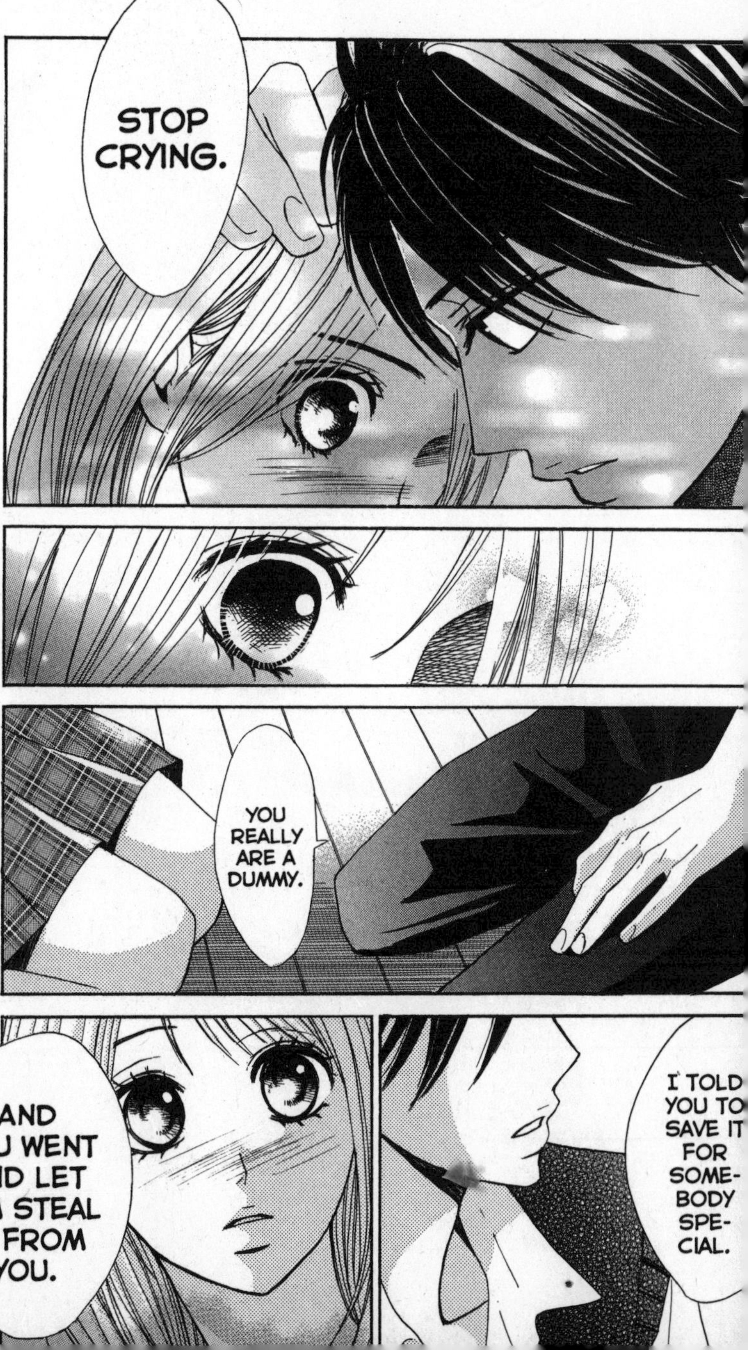
STOP CRYING.
YOU REALLY ARE A DUMMY.
I TOLD YOU TO SAVE IT FOR SOMEBODY SPECIAL.
AND YOU WENT AND LET HIM STEAL IT FROM YOU.

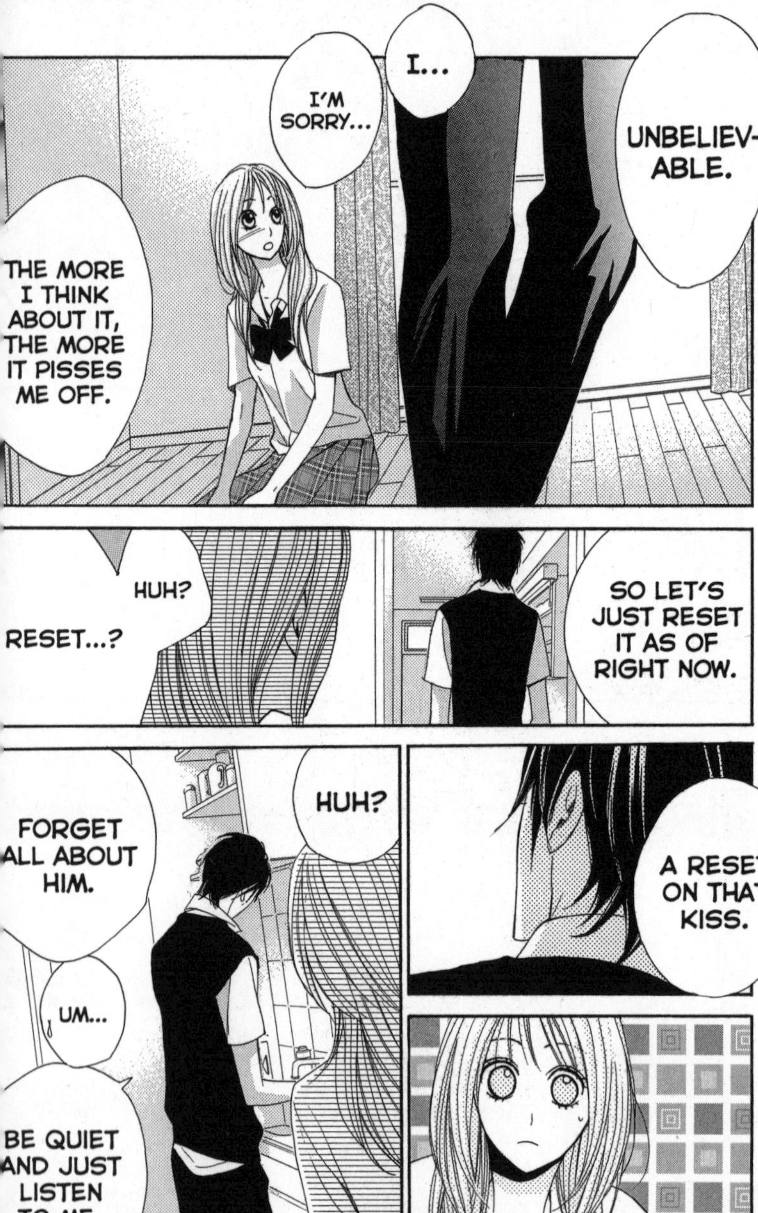
UNBELIEV-ABLE.
I...
I'M SORRY...
THE MORE I THINK ABOUT IT, THE MORE IT PISSES ME OFF.
SO LET'S JUST RESET IT AS OF RIGHT NOW.
HUH?
RESET...?
A RESET ON THAT KISS.
HUH?
FORGET ALL ABOUT HIM.
UM...
BE QUIET AND JUST LISTEN TO ME.

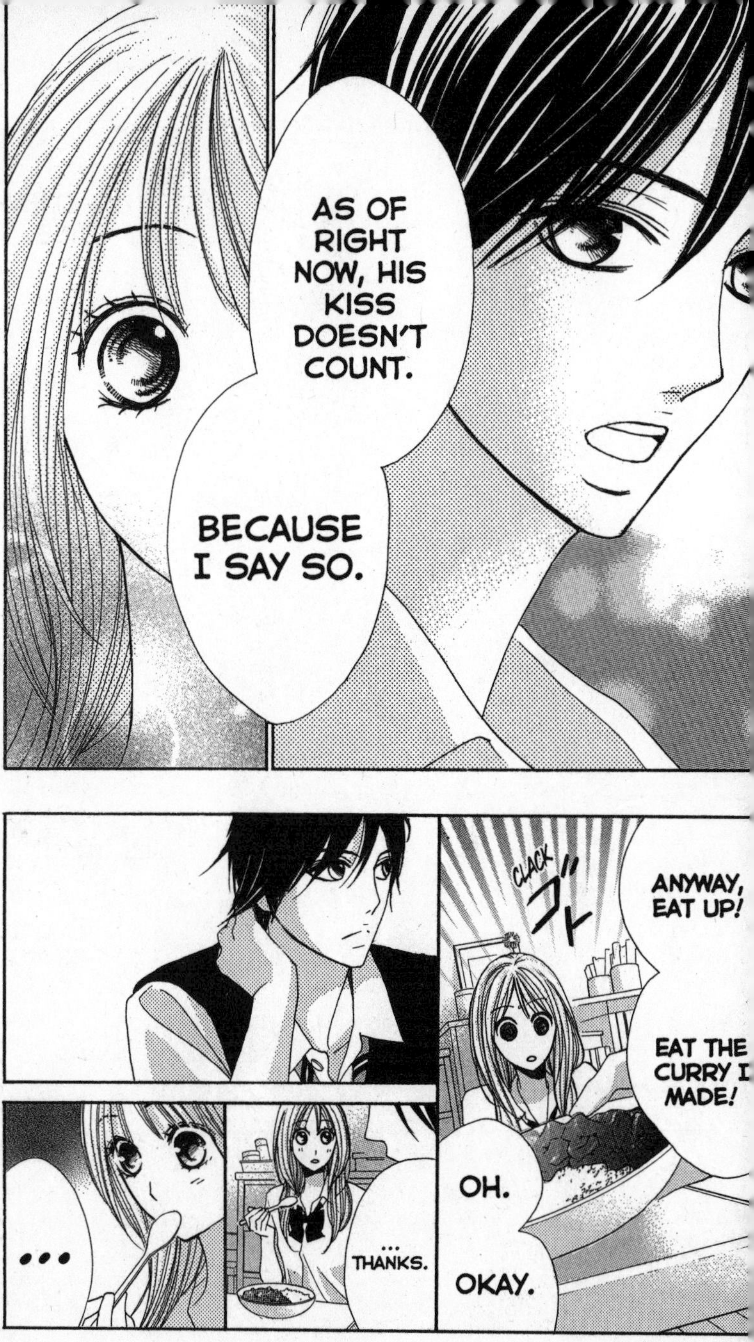
AS OF RIGHT NOW, HIS KISS DOESN'T COUNT.
BECAUSE I SAY SO.
CLACK
ANYWAY, EAT UP!
EAT THE CURRY I MADE!
OH.
OKAY.
...THANKS.
...

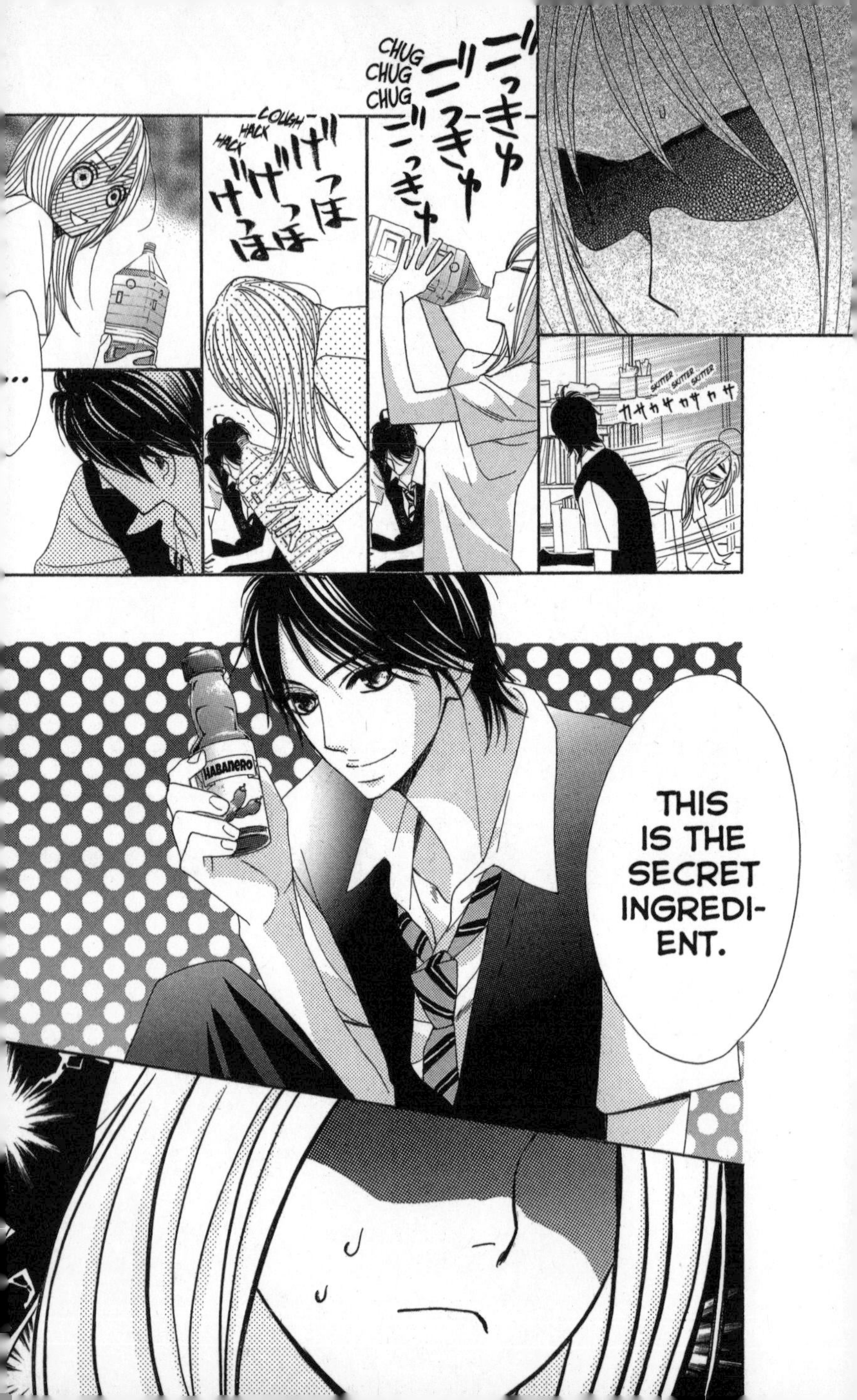
SKITTER SKITTER SKITTER
カサカサカサカサ
CHUG CHUG CHUG
ゴっきゅ ゴっきゅ ゴっきゅ
COUGH HACK HACK
げっほ げっほ げほ
...
HABANERO
THIS IS THE SECRET INGREDIENT.

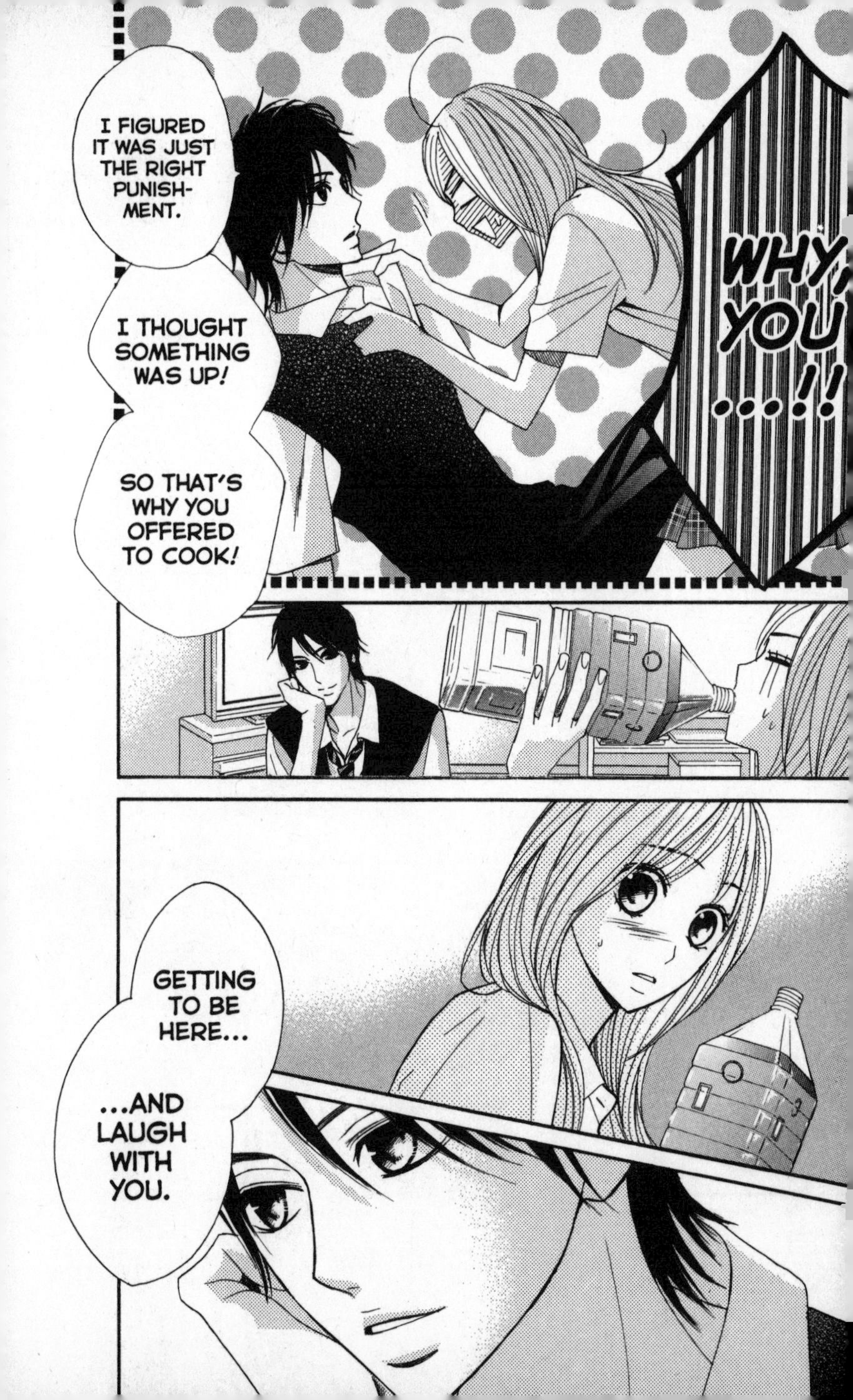
I FIGURED IT WAS JUST THE RIGHT PUNISH-MENT.
WHY, YOU ...!!
I THOUGHT SOMETHING WAS UP!
SO THAT'S WHY YOU OFFERED TO COOK!
GETTING TO BE HERE...
...AND LAUGH WITH YOU.

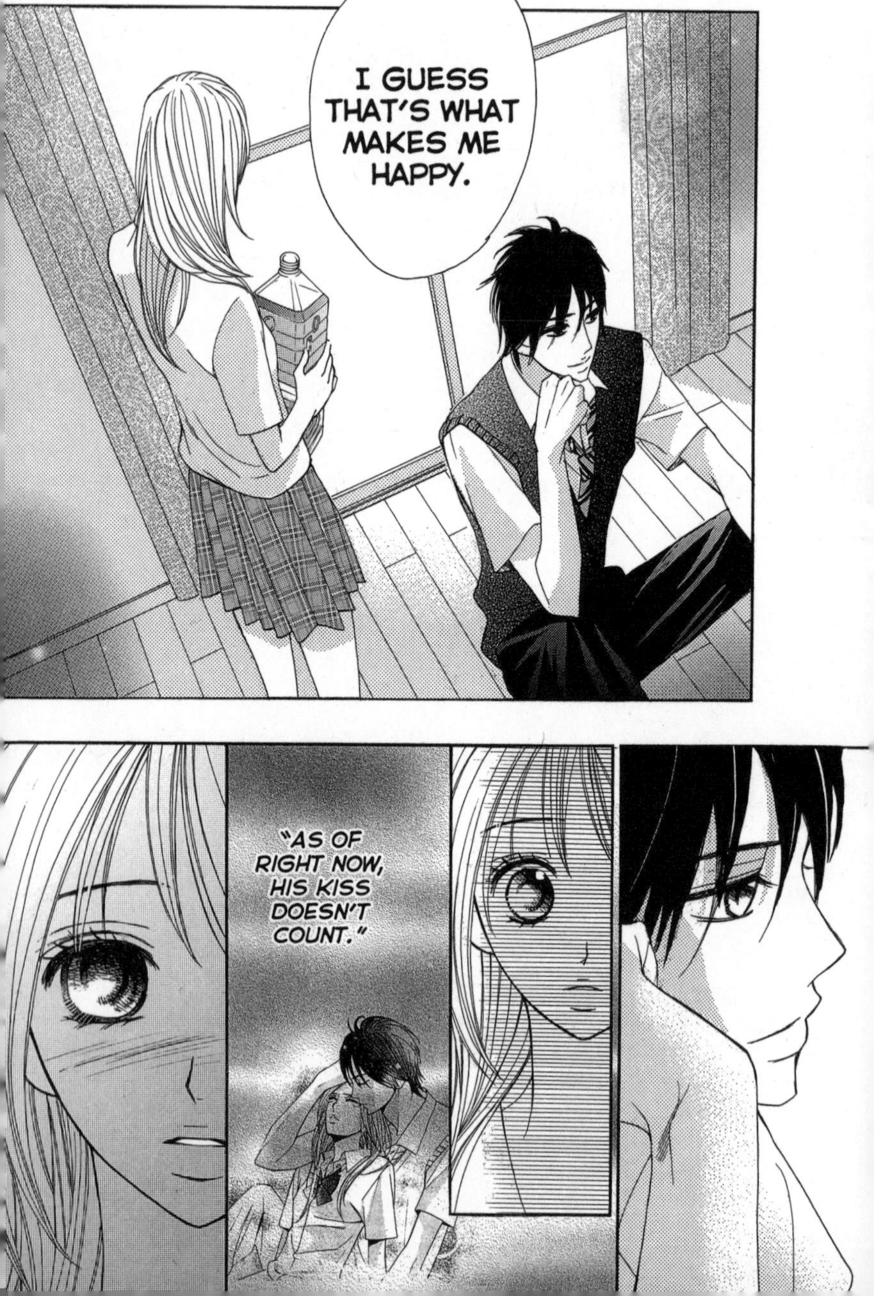
I GUESS THAT'S WHAT MAKES ME HAPPY.
"AS OF RIGHT NOW, HIS KISS DOESN'T COUNT."

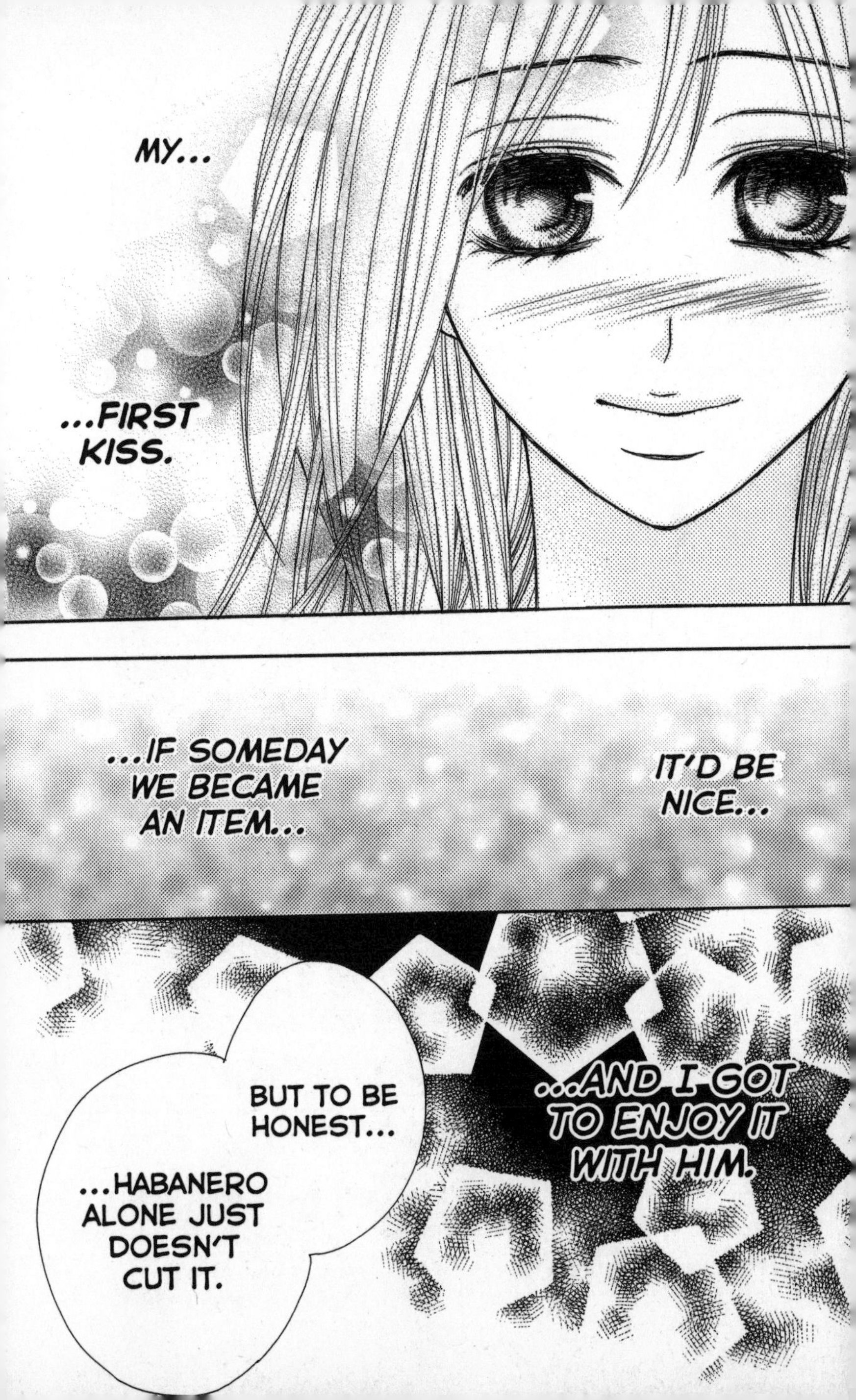
MY...
...FIRST KISS.
IT'D BE NICE...
...IF SOMEDAY WE BECAME AN ITEM...
...AND I GOT TO ENJOY IT WITH HIM.
BUT TO BE HONEST...
...HABANERO ALONE JUST DOESN'T CUT IT.

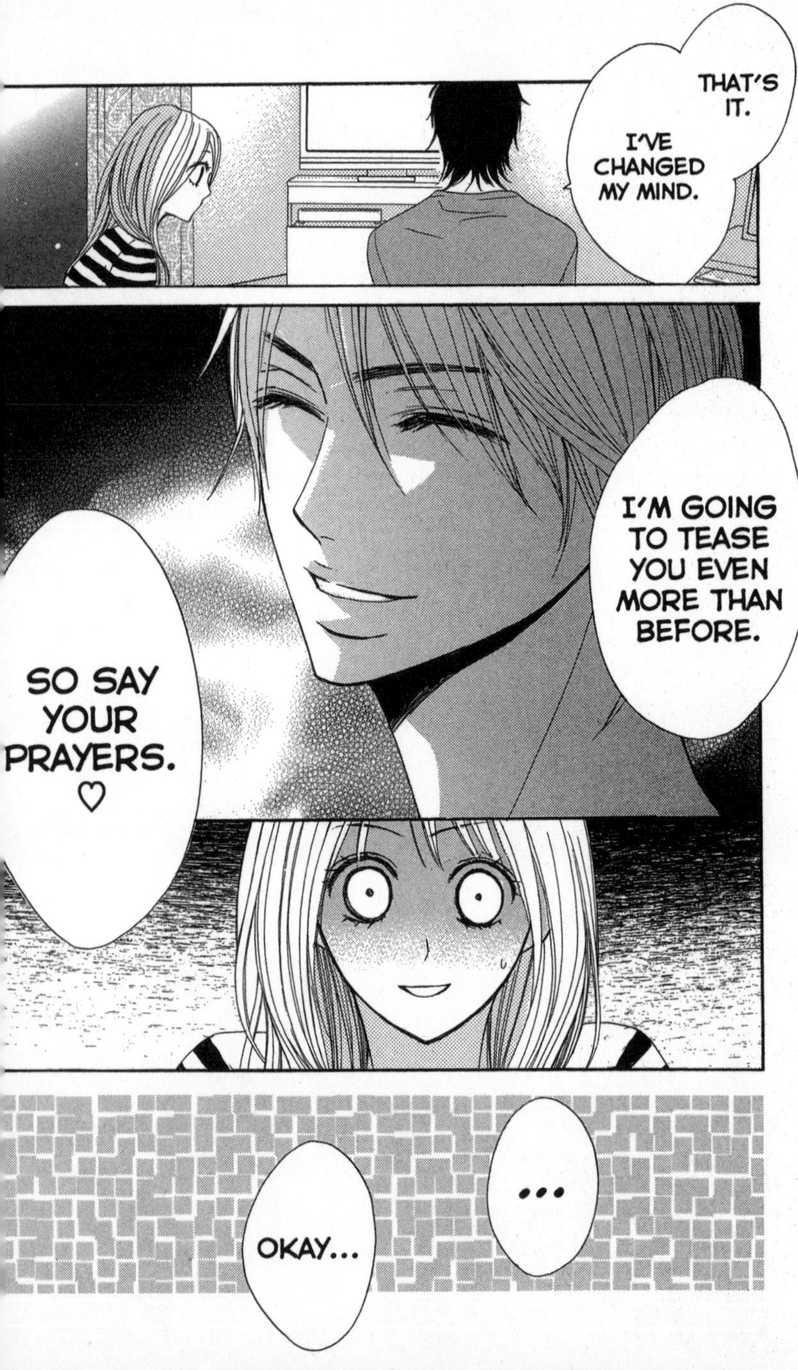
THAT'S IT.
I'VE CHANGED MY MIND.
I'M GOING TO TEASE YOU EVEN MORE THAN BEFORE.
SO SAY YOUR PRAYERS. ♡
...
OKAY...

L♥DK

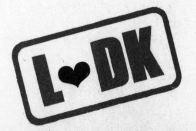

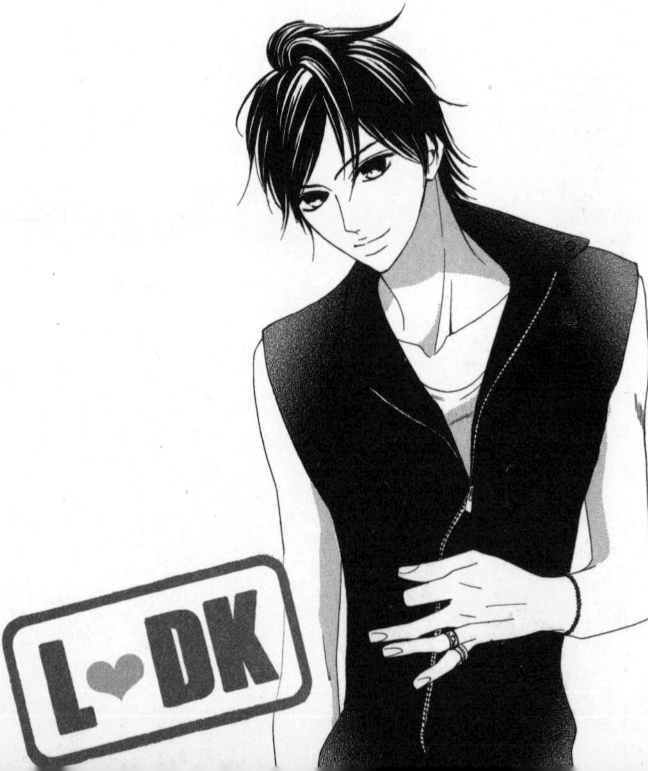
L♥DK

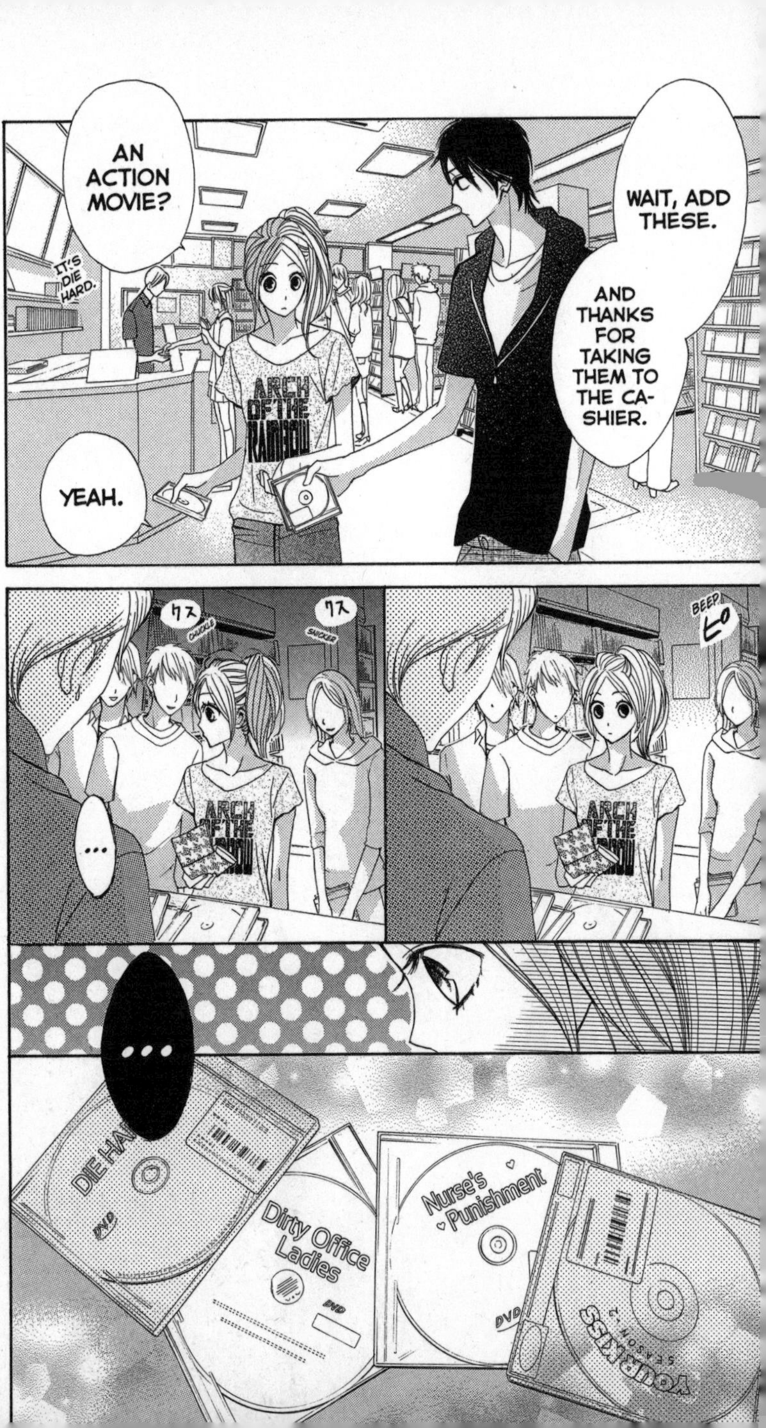

WAIT, ADD THESE.
AND THANKS FOR TAKING THEM TO THE CA-SHIER.
AN ACTION MOVIE?
IT'S DIE HARD.
YEAH.
BEEP ピ
クス CHUCKLE
クス SNICKER
...
...
Nurse's Punishment
Dirty Office Ladies
DVD
SEASON 2

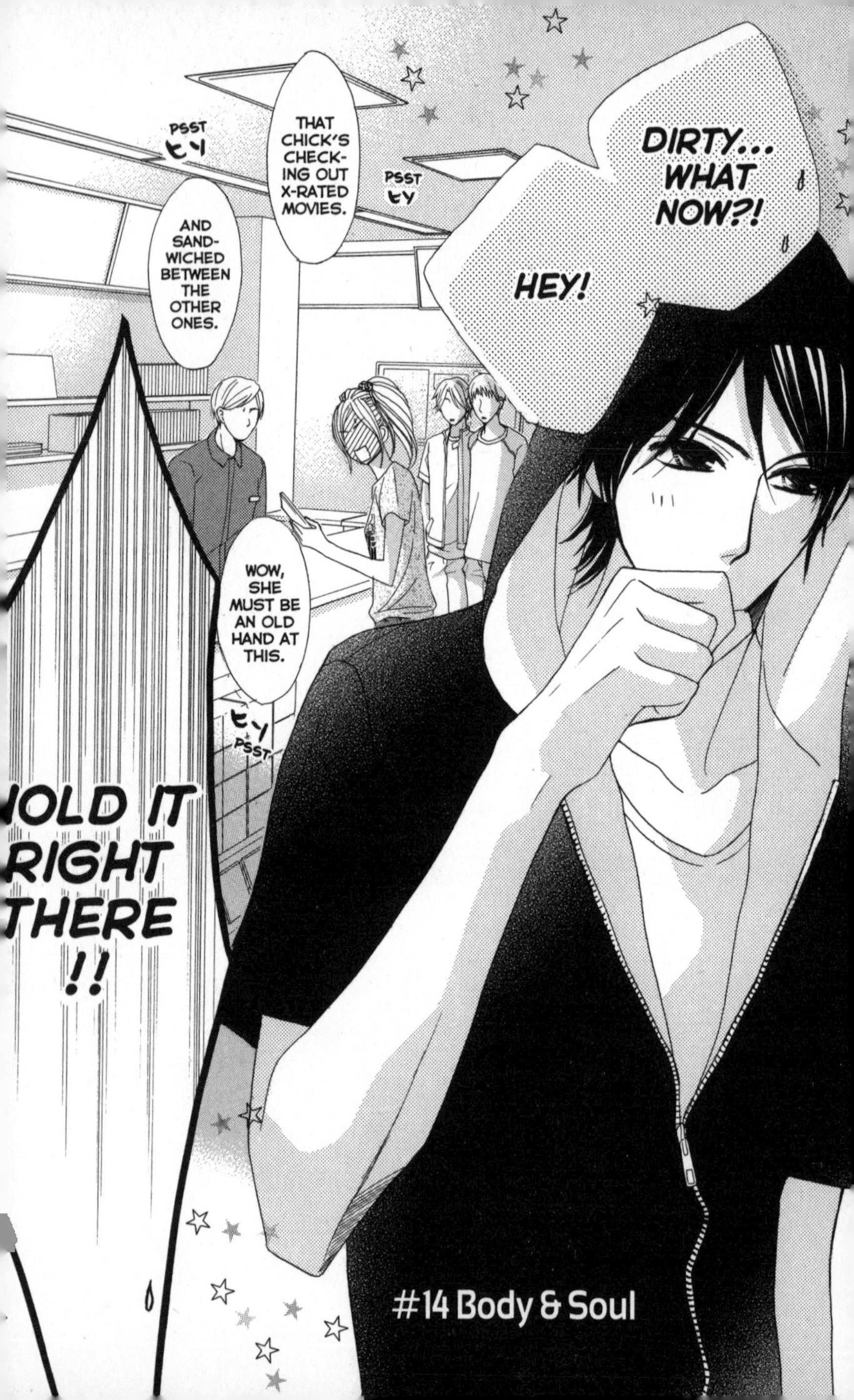
HEY!
DIRTY... WHAT NOW?!
PSST ヒソ
THAT CHICK'S CHECKING OUT X-RATED MOVIES.
PSST ヒソ
AND SANDWICHED BETWEEN THE OTHER ONES.
WOW, SHE MUST BE AN OLD HAND AT THIS.
ヒソ PSST
OLD IT RIGHT THERE !!

#14 Body & Soul

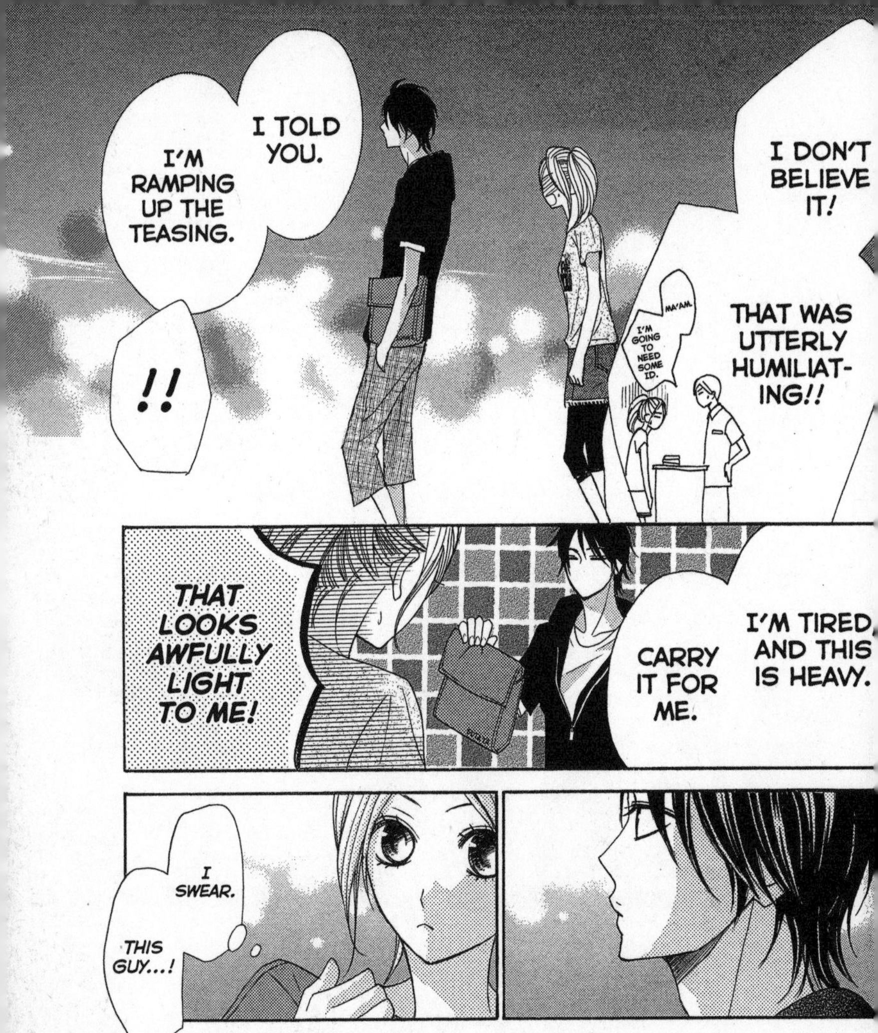
I DON'T BELIEVE IT!
THAT WAS UTTERLY HUMILIAT-ING!!
MA'AM. I'M GOING TO NEED SOME ID.
I TOLD YOU. I'M RAMPING UP THE TEASING.
!!
I'M TIRED, AND THIS IS HEAVY.
CARRY IT FOR ME.
THAT LOOKS AWFULLY LIGHT TO ME!
I SWEAR.
THIS GUY...!

L♥DK

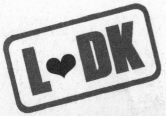

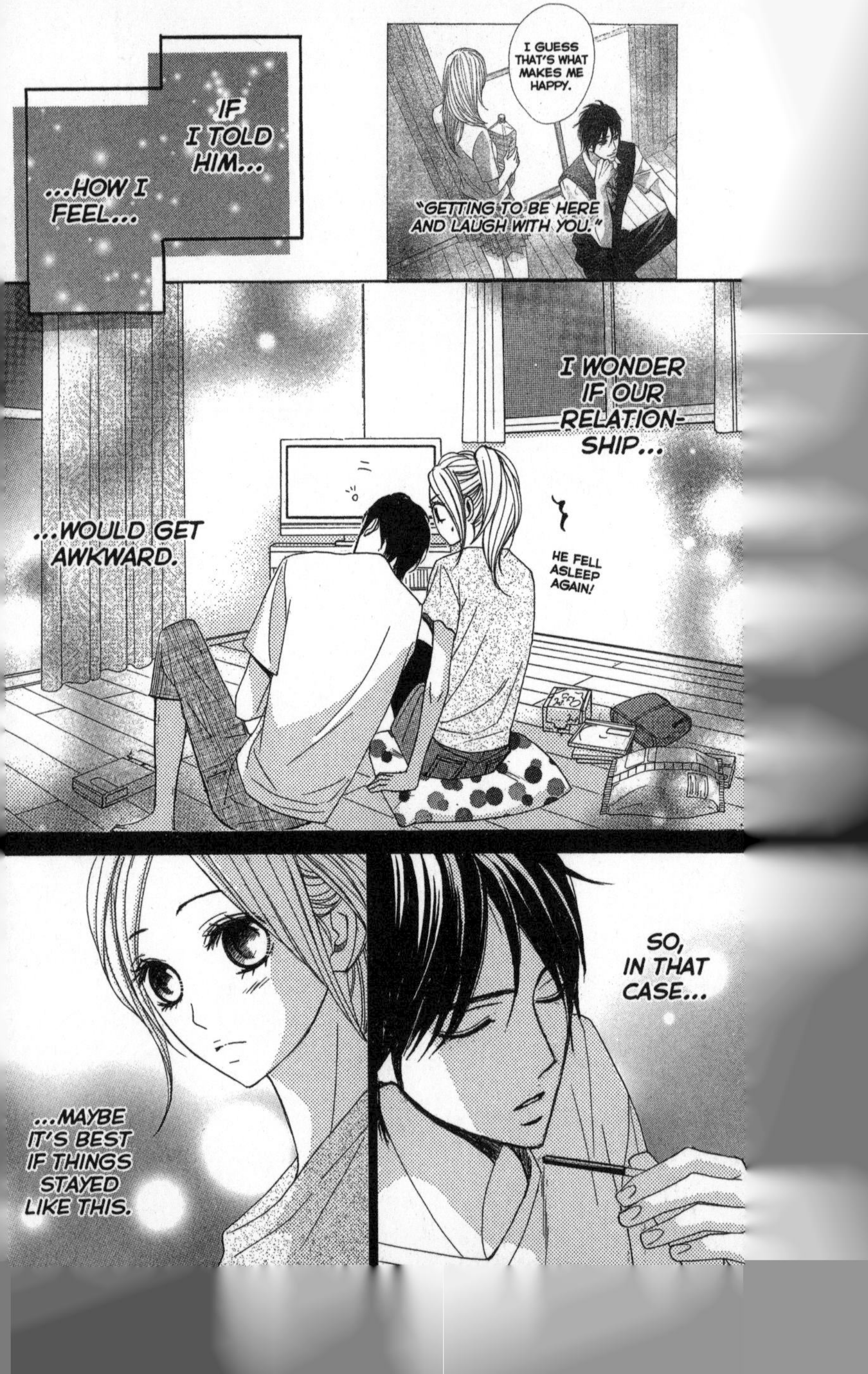
I GUESS THAT'S WHAT MAKES ME HAPPY.
"GETTING TO BE HERE AND LAUGH WITH YOU."
IF I TOLD HIM...
...HOW I FEEL...
I WONDER IF OUR RELATION-SHIP...
HE FELL ASLEEP AGAIN!
...WOULD GET AWKWARD.
SO, IN THAT CASE...
...MAYBE IT'S BEST IF THINGS STAYED LIKE THIS.

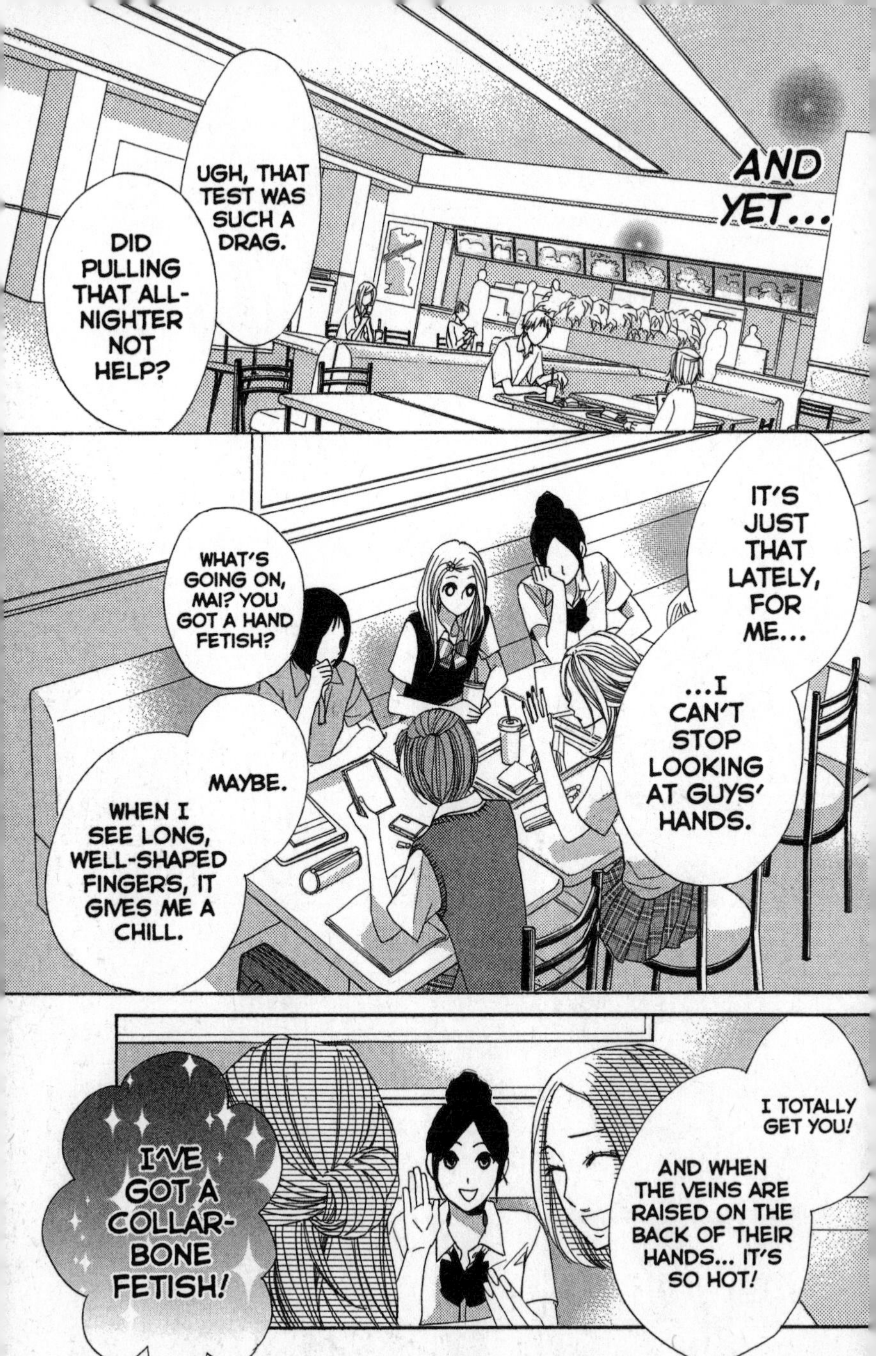
AND YET...
UGH, THAT TEST WAS SUCH A DRAG.
DID PULLING THAT ALL-NIGHTER NOT HELP?
IT'S JUST THAT LATELY, FOR ME...
...I CAN'T STOP LOOKING AT GUYS' HANDS.
WHAT'S GOING ON, MAI? YOU GOT A HAND FETISH?
MAYBE.
WHEN I SEE LONG, WELL-SHAPED FINGERS, IT GIVES ME A CHILL.
I TOTALLY GET YOU!
AND WHEN THE VEINS ARE RAISED ON THE BACK OF THEIR HANDS... IT'S SO HOT!
I'VE GOT A COLLAR-BONE FETISH!

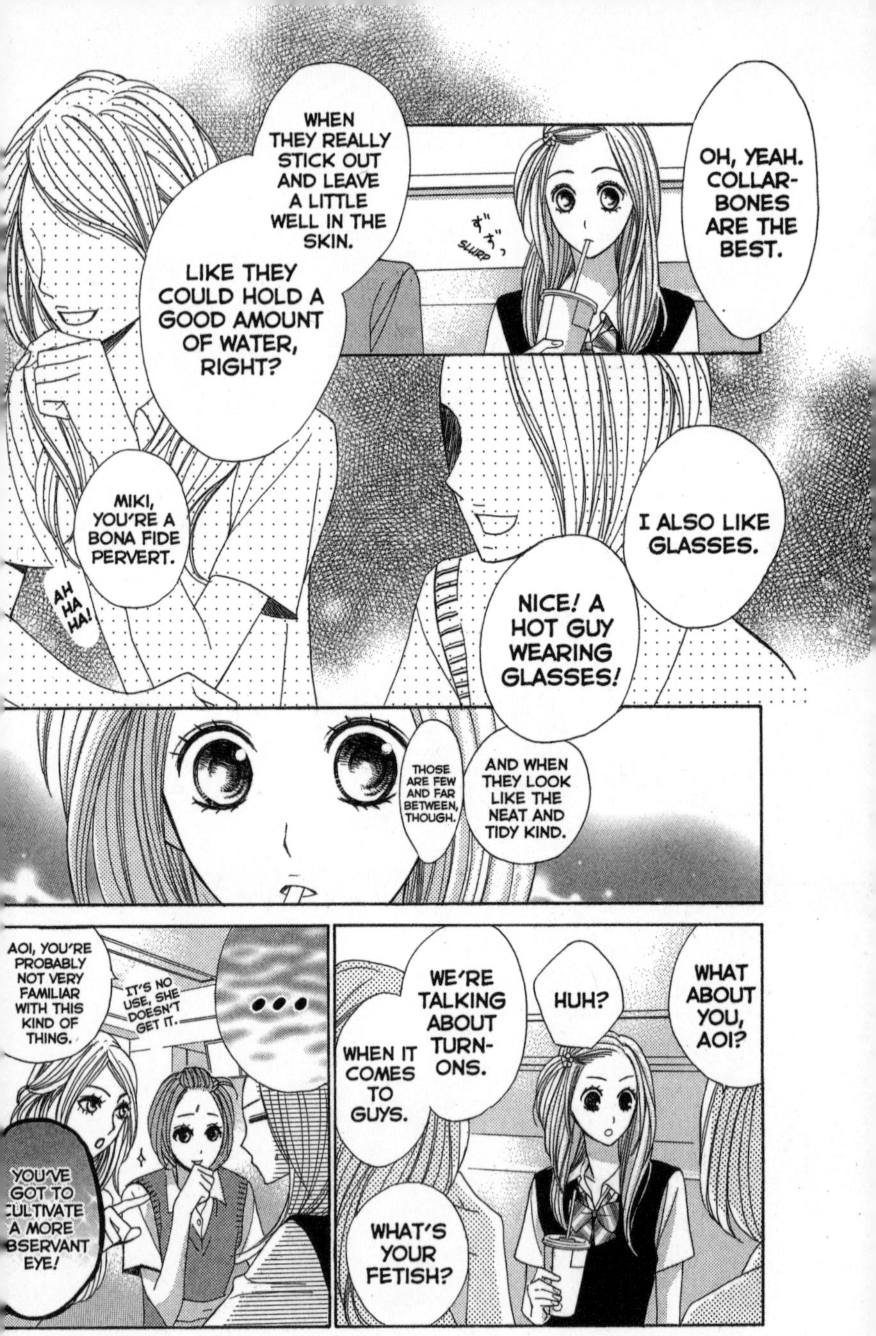
OH, YEAH. COLLAR-BONES ARE THE BEST.
ずずっ
SLURP
WHEN THEY REALLY STICK OUT AND LEAVE A LITTLE WELL IN THE SKIN.
LIKE THEY COULD HOLD A GOOD AMOUNT OF WATER, RIGHT?
I ALSO LIKE GLASSES.
NICE! A HOT GUY WEARING GLASSES!
MIKI, YOU'RE A BONA FIDE PERVERT.
AH HA HA!
AND WHEN THEY LOOK LIKE THE NEAT AND TIDY KIND.
THOSE ARE FEW AND FAR BETWEEN, THOUGH.
WHAT ABOUT YOU, AOI?
HUH?
WE'RE TALKING ABOUT TURN-ONS.
WHEN IT COMES TO GUYS.
WHAT'S YOUR FETISH?
...
AOI, YOU'RE PROBABLY NOT VERY FAMILIAR WITH THIS KIND OF THING.
IT'S NO USE, SHE DOESN'T GET IT.
YOU'VE GOT TO CULTIVATE A MORE BSERVANT EYE!

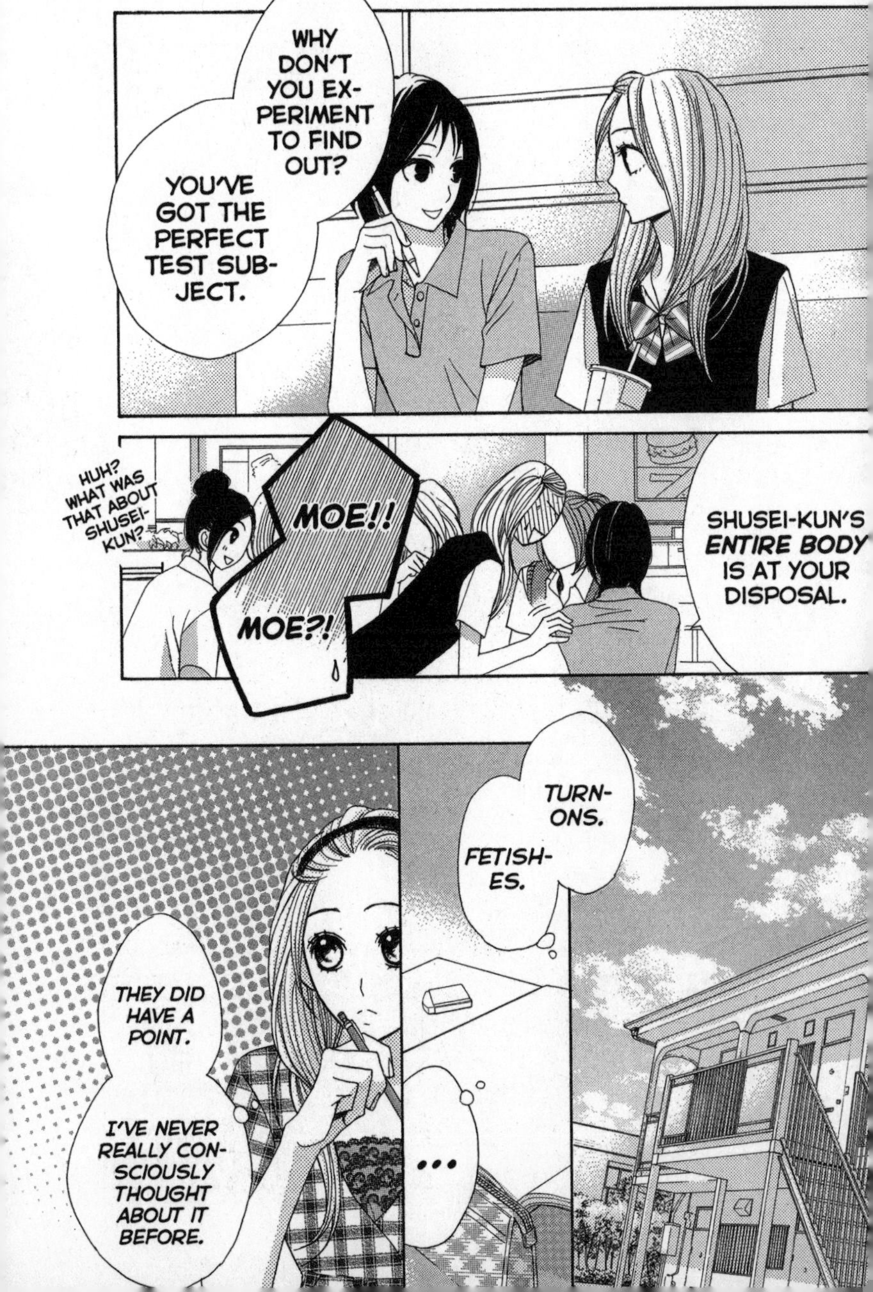
WHY DON'T YOU EXPERIMENT TO FIND OUT?
YOU'VE GOT THE PERFECT TEST SUBJECT.
SHUSEI-KUN'S *ENTIRE BODY* IS AT YOUR DISPOSAL.
MOE!!
MOE?!
HUH? WHAT WAS THAT ABOUT SHUSEI-KUN?
TURN-ONS.
FETISHES.
...
THEY DID HAVE A POINT.
I'VE NEVER REALLY CONSCIOUSLY THOUGHT ABOUT IT BEFORE.

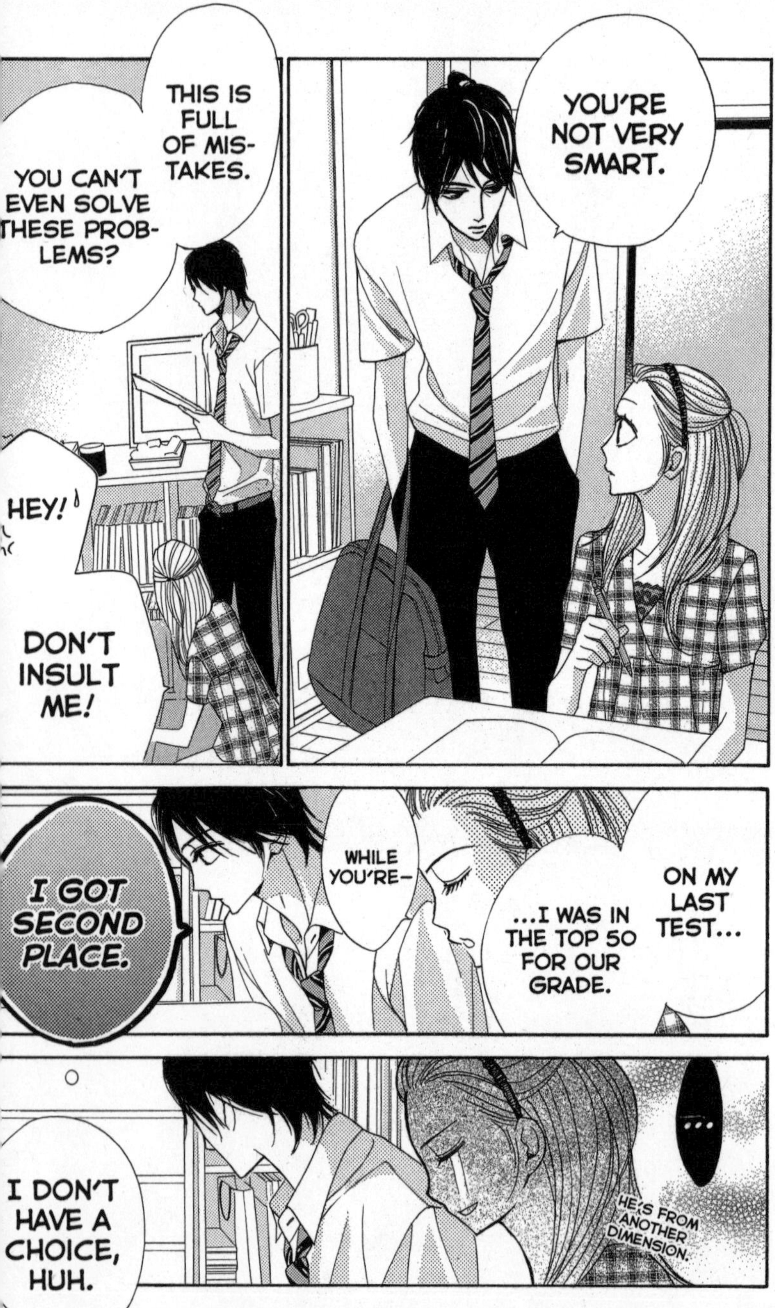
YOU'RE NOT VERY SMART.
THIS IS FULL OF MIS-TAKES.
YOU CAN'T EVEN SOLVE THESE PROB-LEMS?
HEY!
DON'T INSULT ME!
ON MY LAST TEST...
...I WAS IN THE TOP 50 FOR OUR GRADE.
WHILE YOU'RE—
I GOT SECOND PLACE.
...
HE'S FROM ANOTHER DIMENSION.
I DON'T HAVE A CHOICE, HUH.

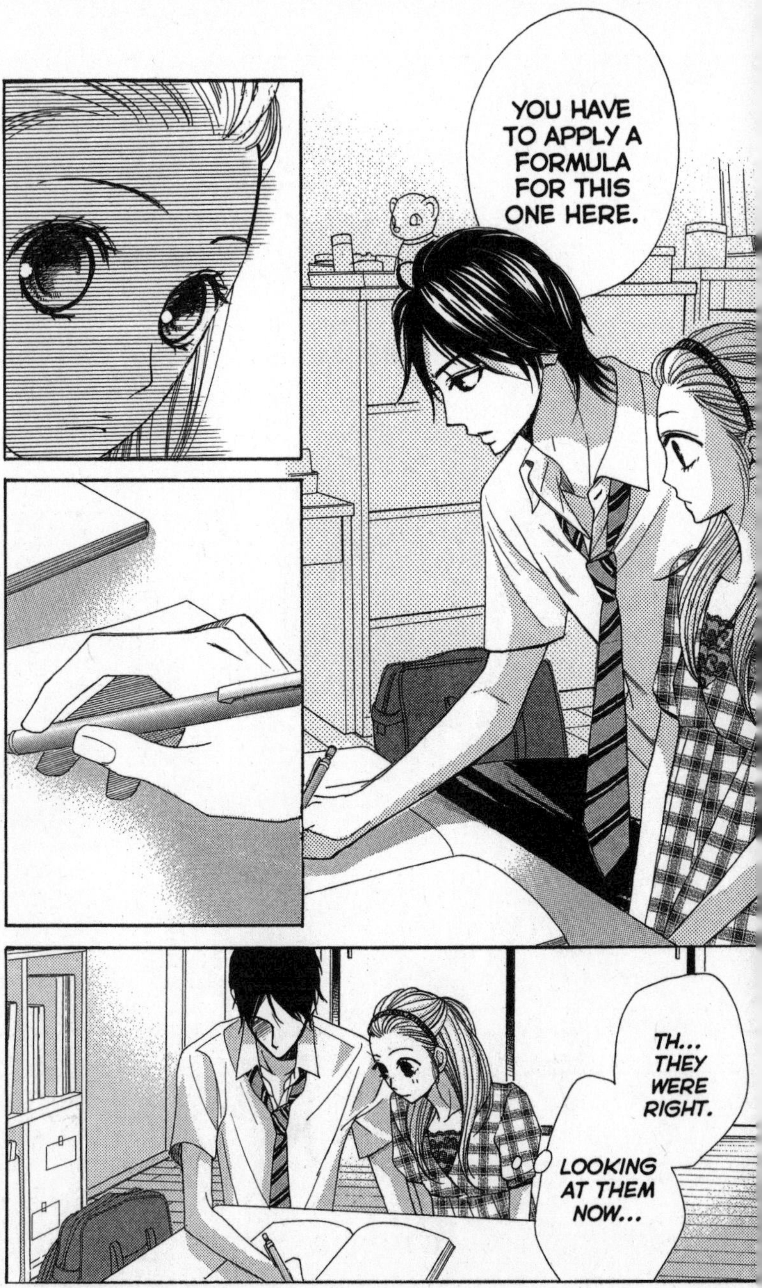
YOU HAVE TO APPLY A FORMULA FOR THIS ONE HERE.
TH... THEY WERE RIGHT.
LOOKING AT THEM NOW...

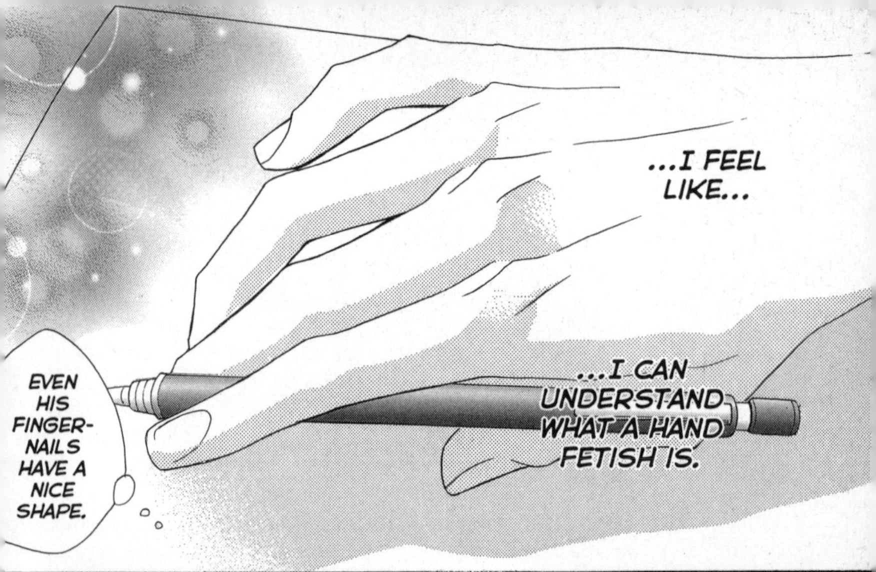
...I FEEL LIKE...
...I CAN UNDERSTAND WHAT A HAND FETISH IS.
EVEN HIS FINGER-NAILS HAVE A NICE SHAPE.

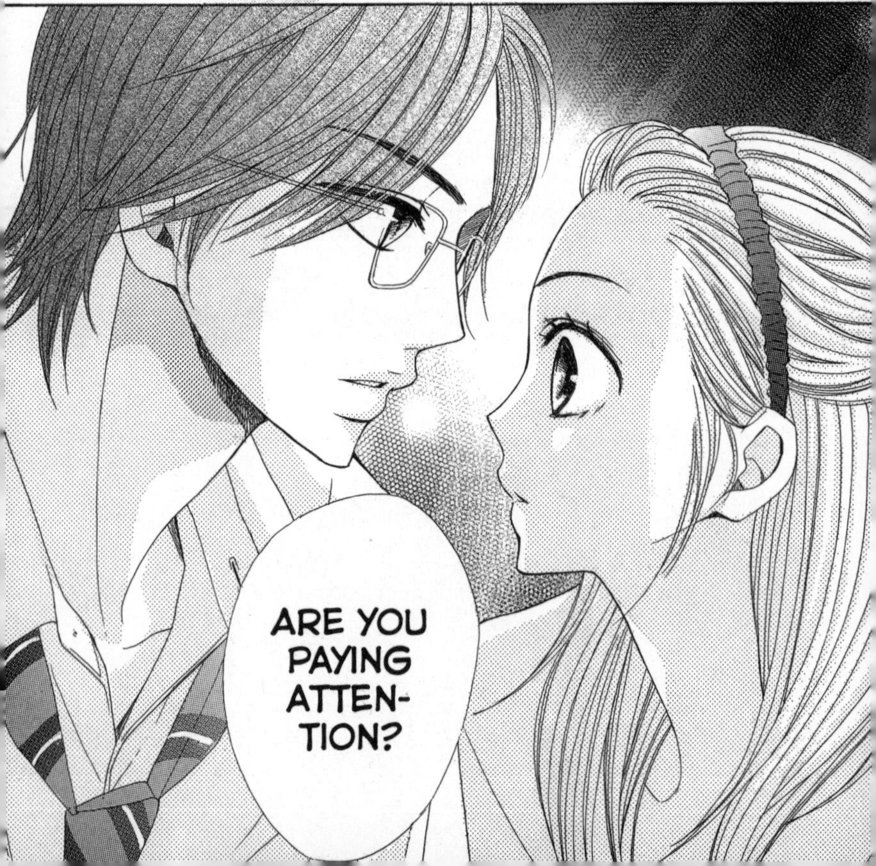
ARE YOU PAYING ATTEN-TION?

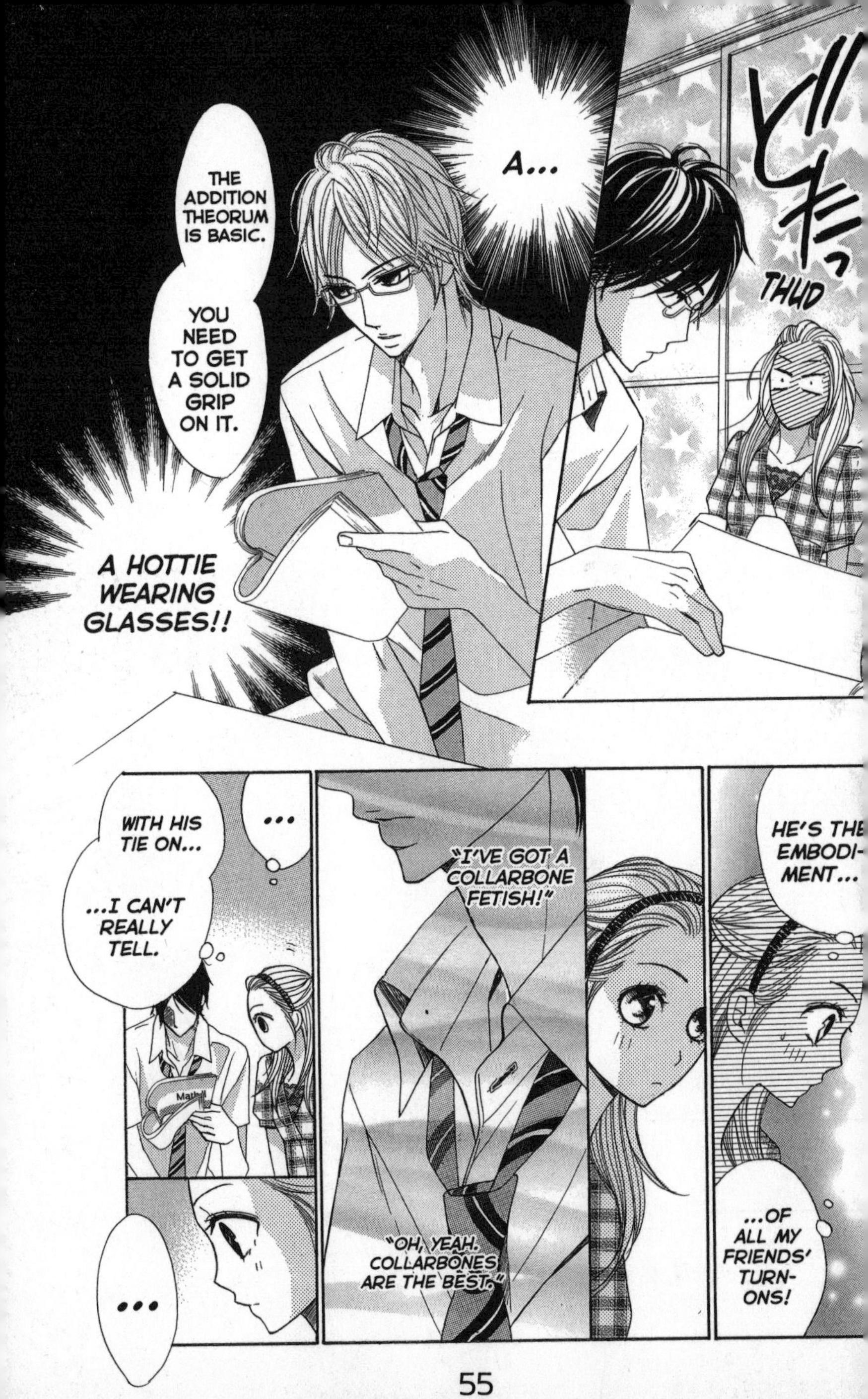
THUD
A...
THE ADDITION THEORUM IS BASIC.
YOU NEED TO GET A SOLID GRIP ON IT.
A HOTTIE WEARING GLASSES!!
HE'S THE EMBODIMENT...
...OF ALL MY FRIENDS' TURN-ONS!
"I'VE GOT A COLLARBONE FETISH!"
"OH, YEAH. COLLARBONES ARE THE BEST."
...
WITH HIS TIE ON...
...I CAN'T REALLY TELL.
...

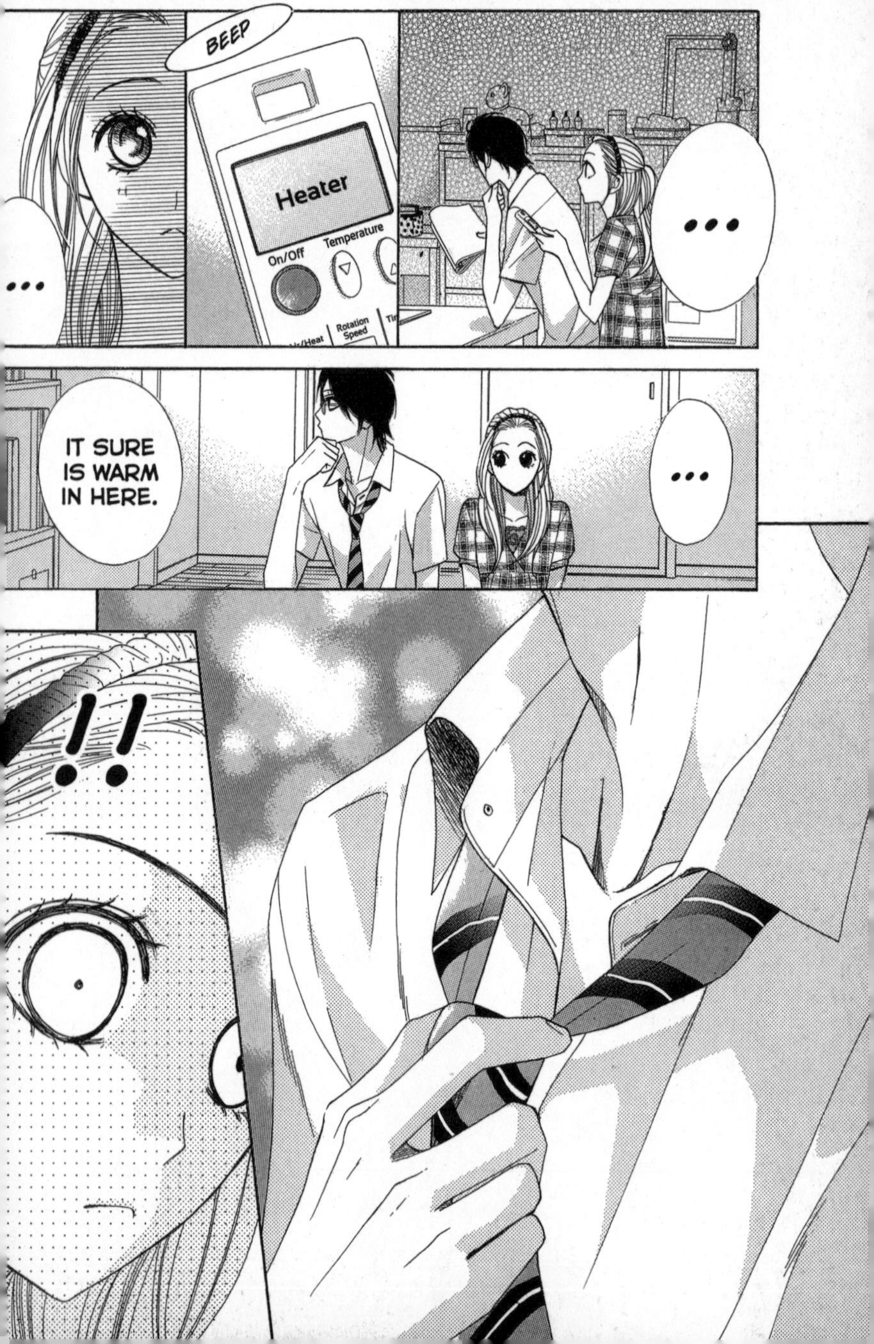
...
BEEP
Heater
Temperature
On/Off
Rotation Speed
...
...
IT SURE IS WARM IN HERE.
!!

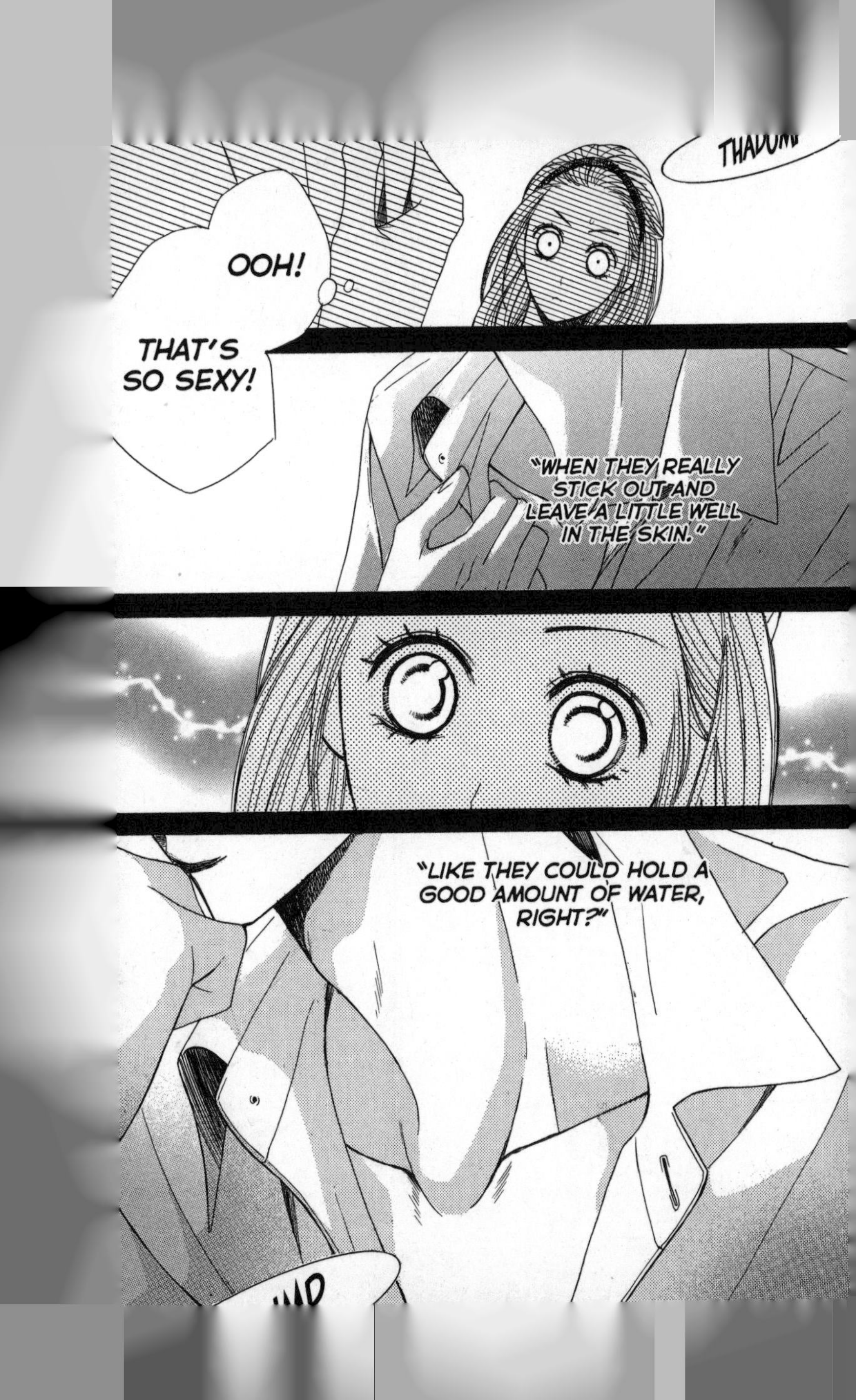
THADUN
OOH!
THAT'S SO SEXY!
"WHEN THEY REALLY STICK OUT AND LEAVE A LITTLE WELL IN THE SKIN."
"LIKE THEY COULD HOLD A GOOD AMOUNT OF WATER, RIGHT?"

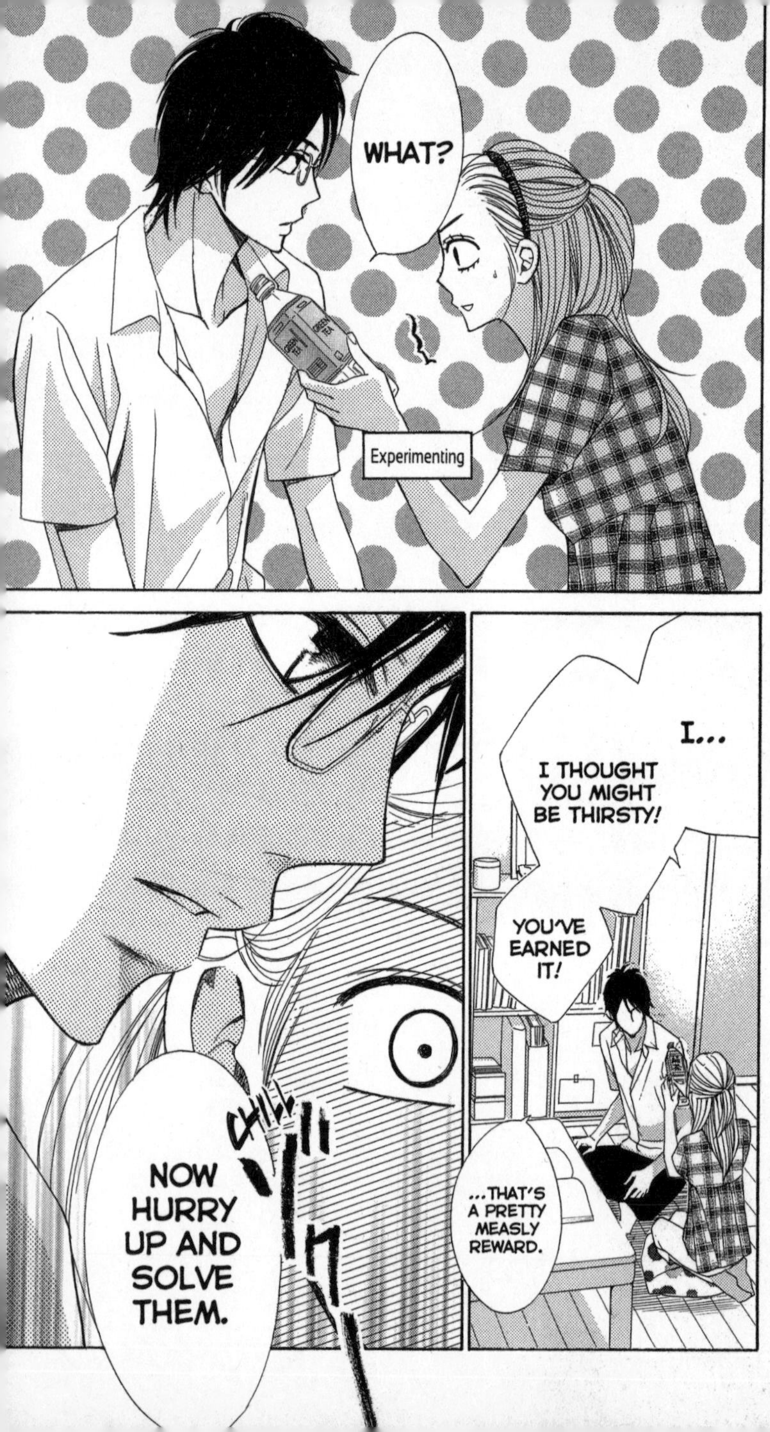
WHAT?
Experimenting
I...
I THOUGHT YOU MIGHT BE THIRSTY!
YOU'VE EARNED IT!
...THAT'S A PRETTY MEASLY REWARD.
NOW HURRY UP AND SOLVE THEM.

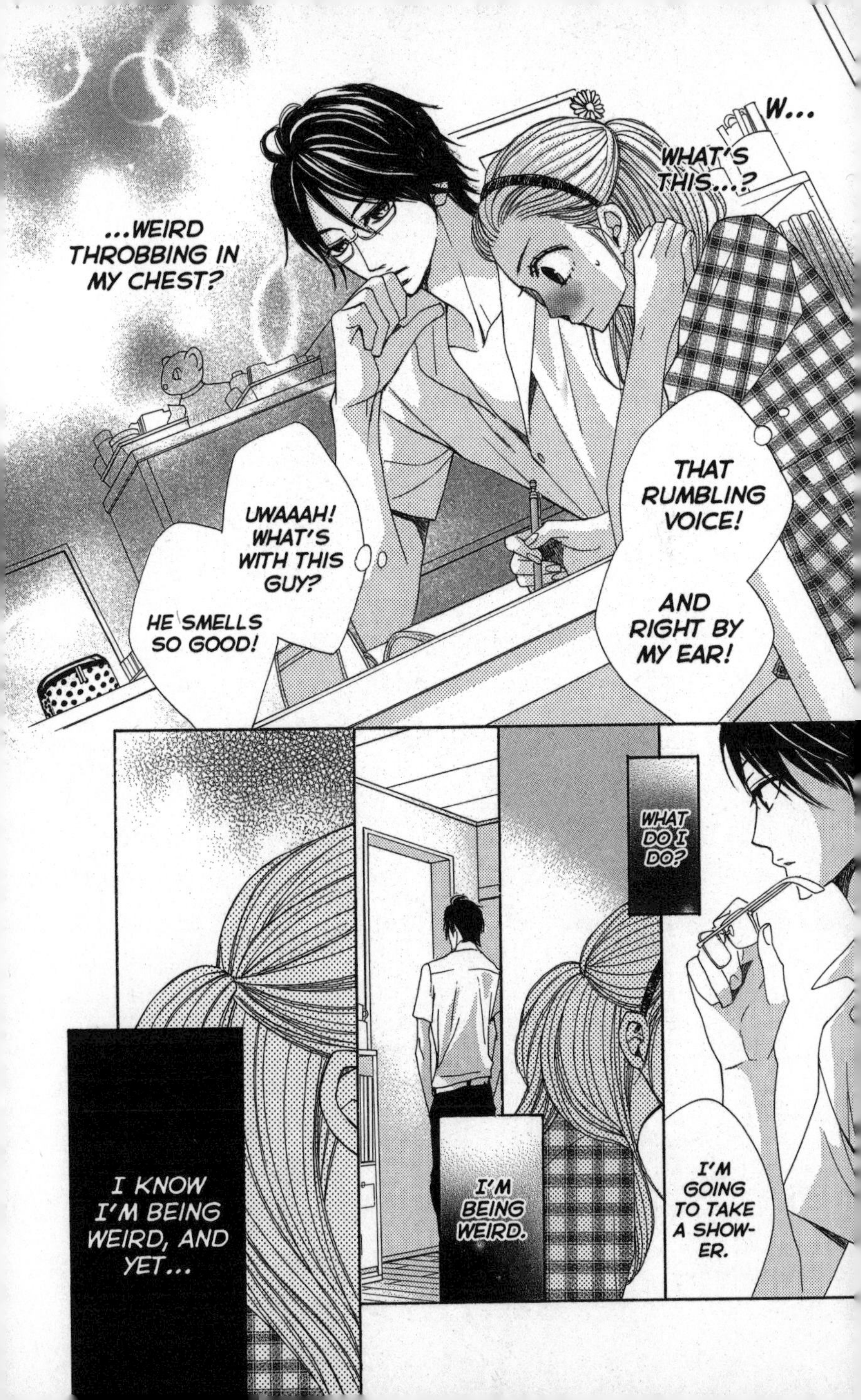
W...
WHAT'S THIS...?
...WEIRD THROBBING IN MY CHEST?
THAT RUMBLING VOICE!
AND RIGHT BY MY EAR!
UWAAAH! WHAT'S WITH THIS GUY?
HE SMELLS SO GOOD!
WHAT DO I DO?
I'M GOING TO TAKE A SHOW-ER.
I'M BEING WEIRD.
I KNOW I'M BEING WEIRD, AND YET...

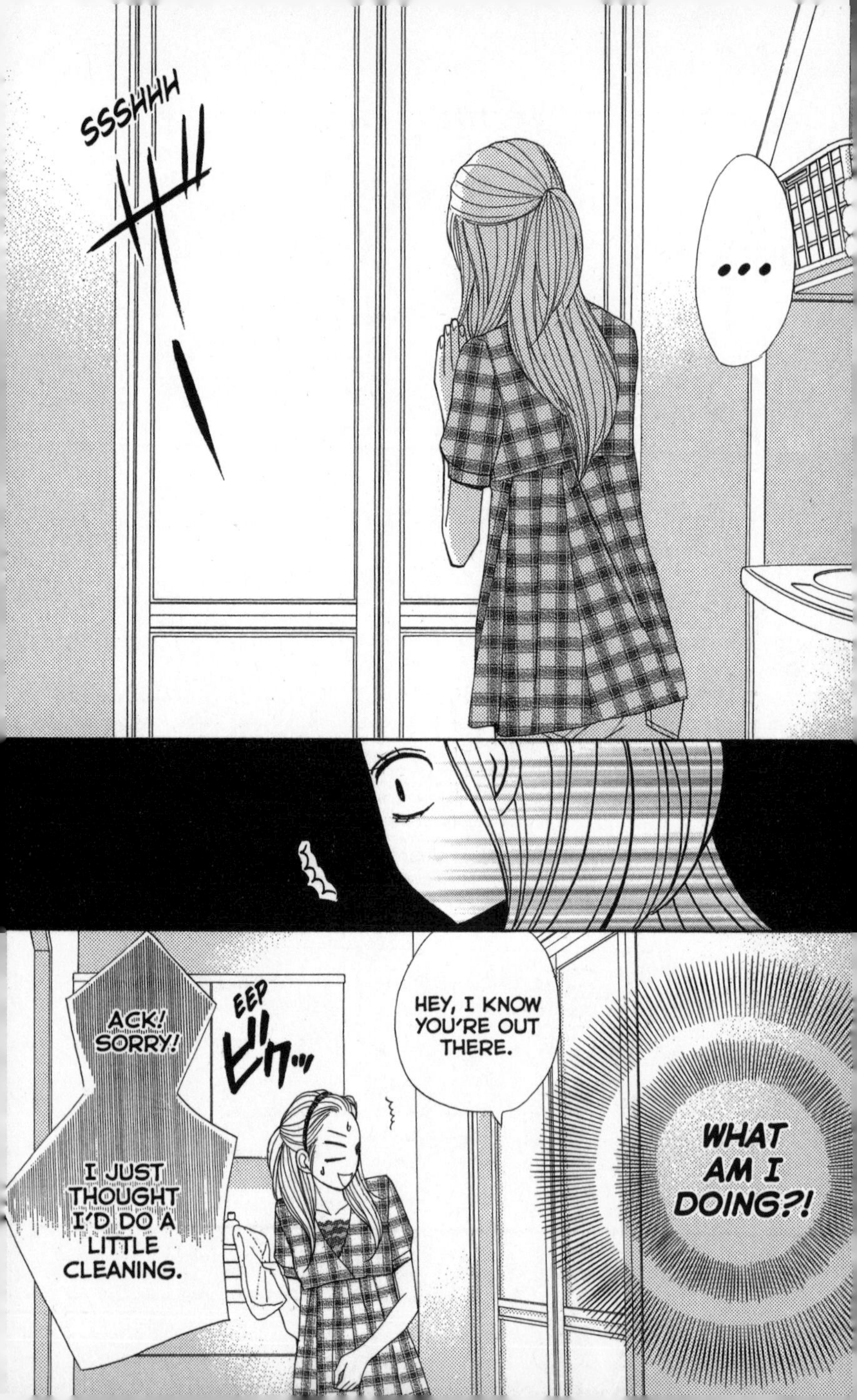
...
SSSHHH
WHAT AM I DOING?!
HEY, I KNOW YOU'RE OUT THERE.
EEP
ビクッ
ACK! SORRY!
I JUST THOUGHT I'D DO A LITTLE CLEANING.

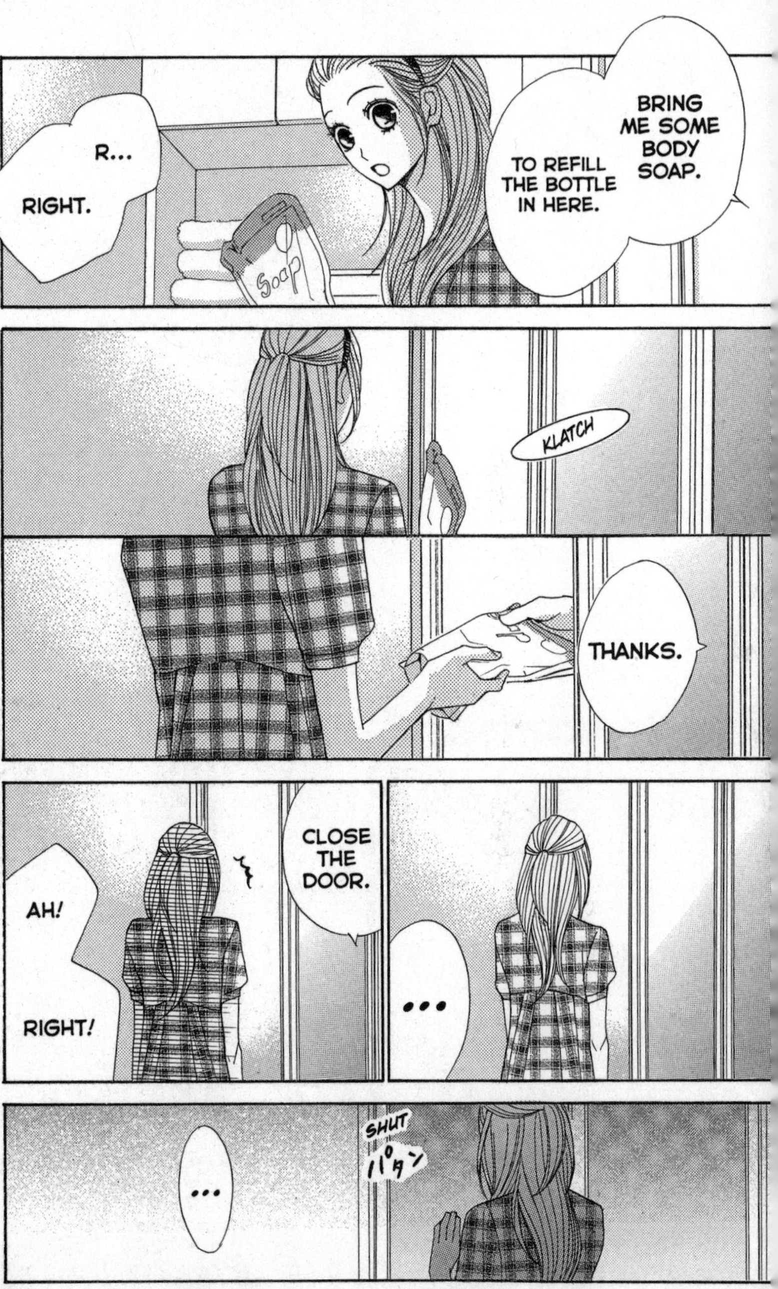
BRING ME SOME BODY SOAP.
TO REFILL THE BOTTLE IN HERE.
R...
RIGHT.
KLATCH
THANKS.
...
CLOSE THE DOOR.
AH!
RIGHT!
SHUT
...

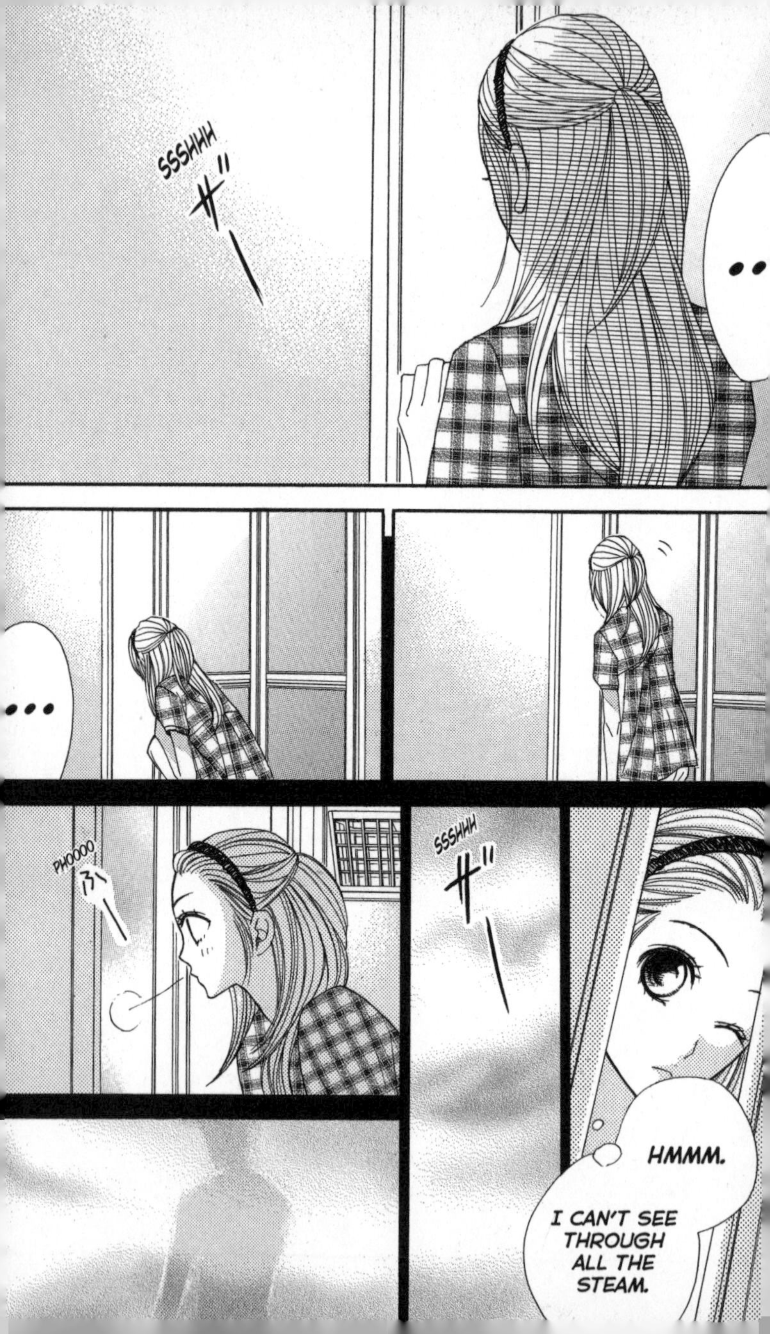

..
SSSHHH
...
HMMM.
I CAN'T SEE THROUGH ALL THE STEAM.
SSSHHH
PHOOOO

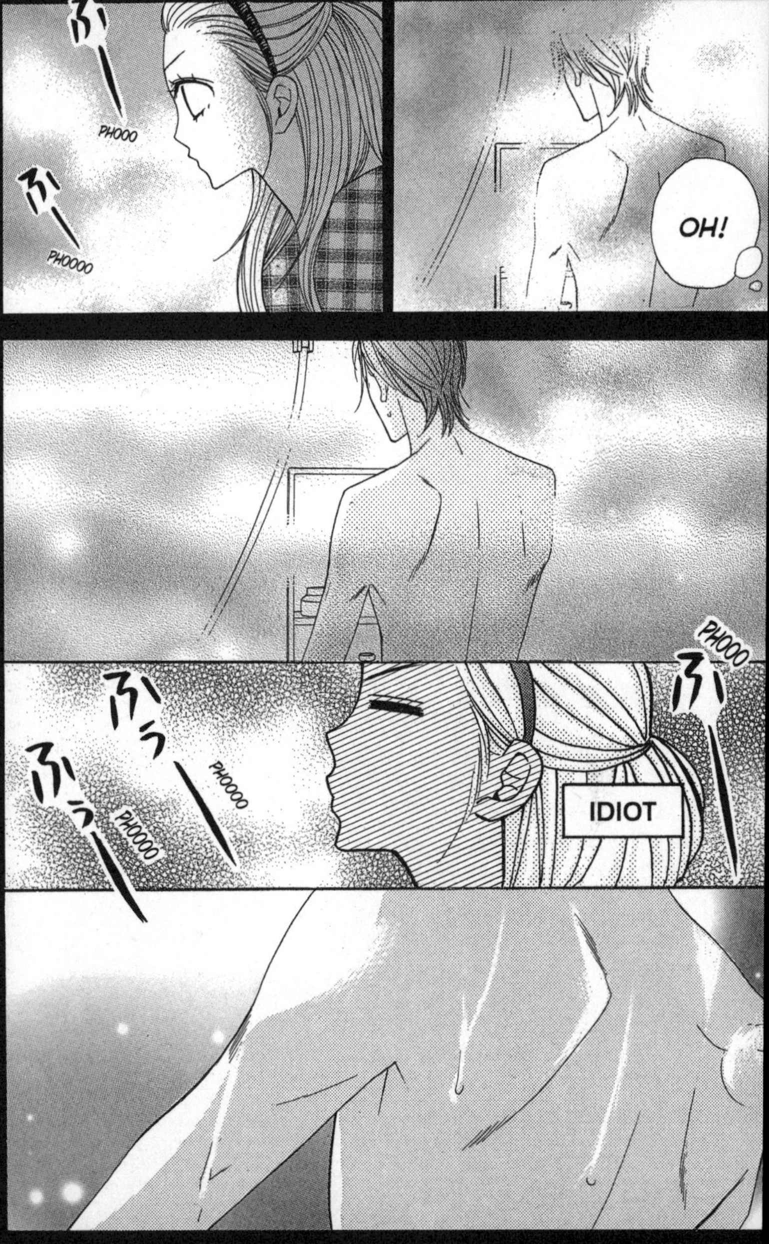
OH!
ふー
PHOOO
ふー
PHOOOO
ふー
PHOOO
IDIOT
ふぅー
PHOOOO
ふぅー
PHOOOOO

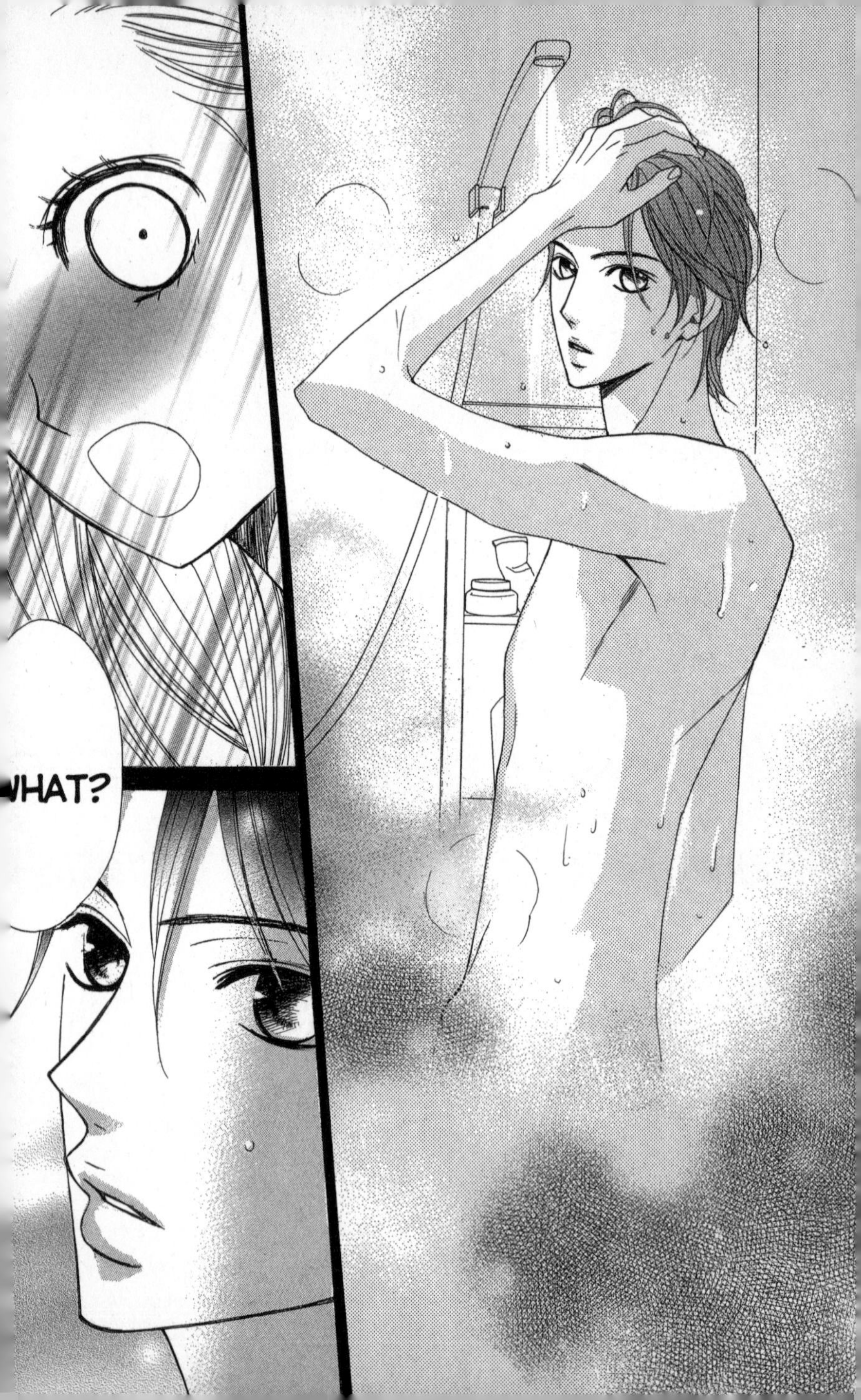
WHAT?

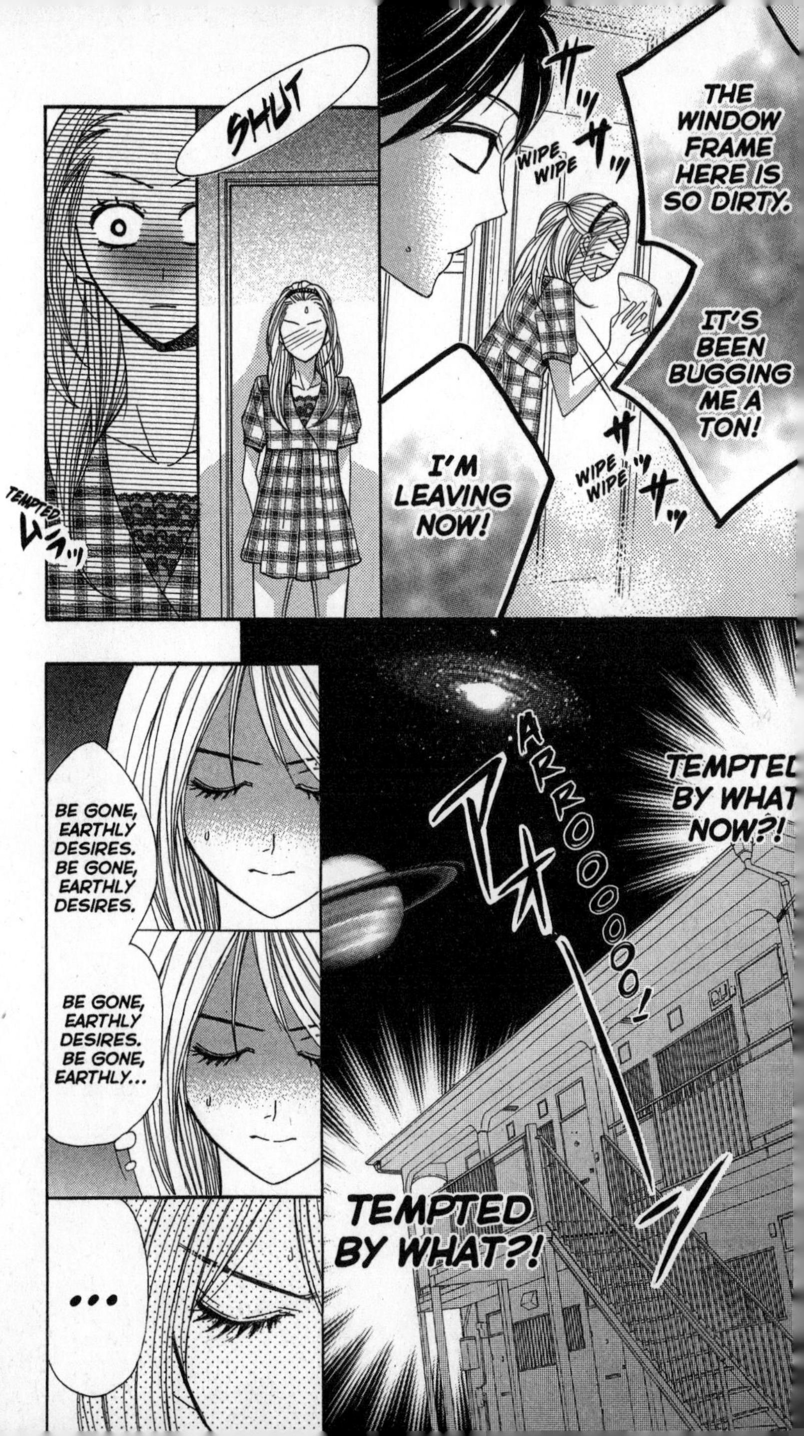
THE WINDOW FRAME HERE IS SO DIRTY.
WIPE WIPE
IT'S BEEN BUGGING ME A TON!
WIPE WIPE
I'M LEAVING NOW!
SHUT
TEMPTED
TEMPTED BY WHAT NOW?!
ARROOOOOOO!
TEMPTED BY WHAT?!
BE GONE, EARTHLY DESIRES. BE GONE, EARTHLY DESIRES.
BE GONE, EARTHLY DESIRES. BE GONE, EARTHLY...
...

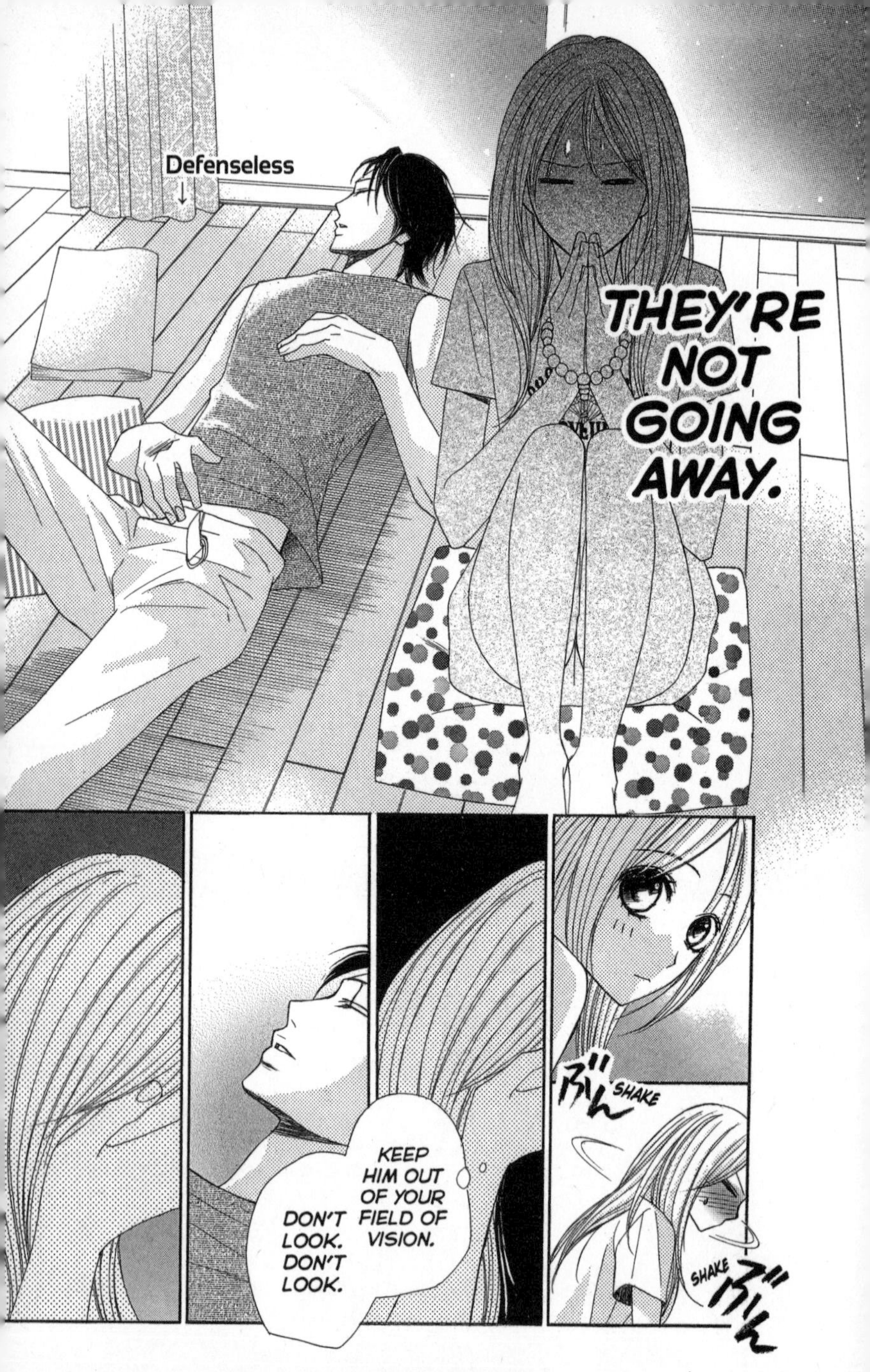
THEY'RE NOT GOING AWAY.
Defenseless
ぶん SHAKE
SHAKE ぶん
KEEP HIM OUT OF YOUR FIELD OF VISION.
DON'T LOOK. DON'T LOOK.

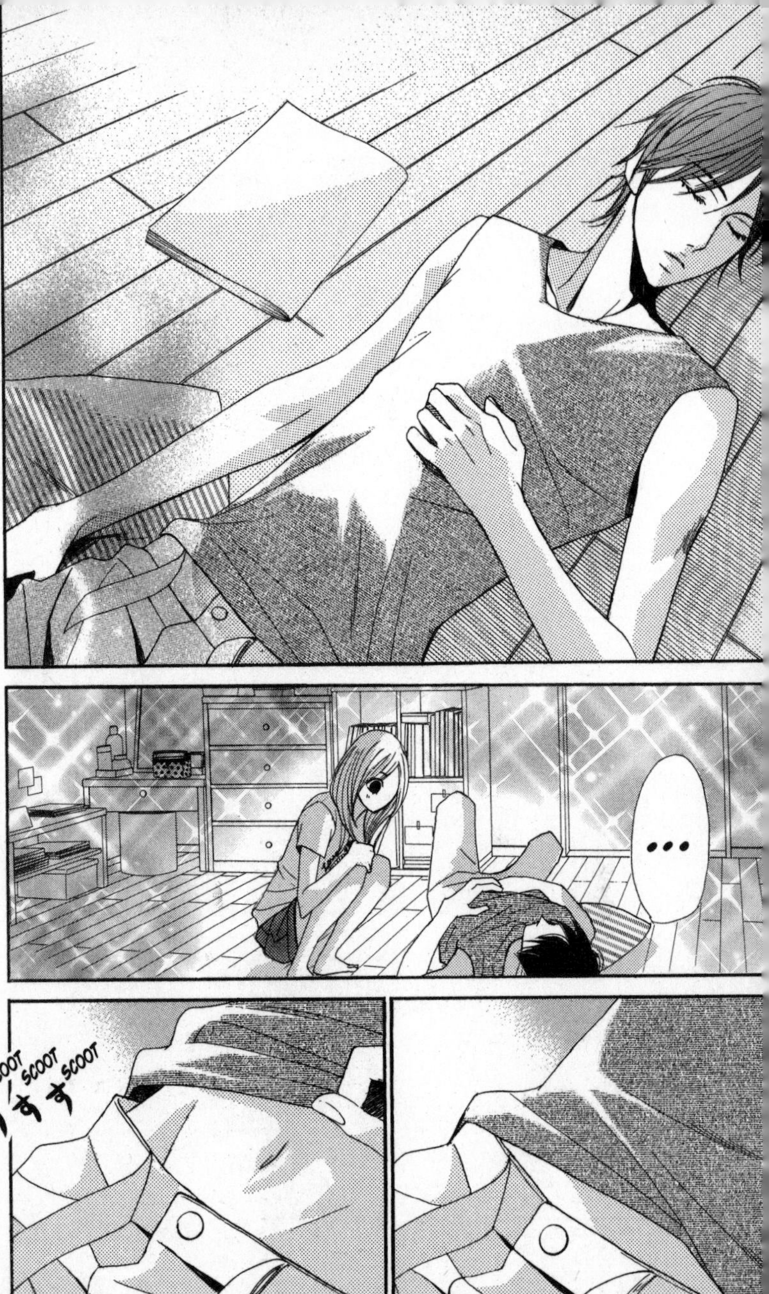
...
すすす
SCOOT SCOOT SCOOT

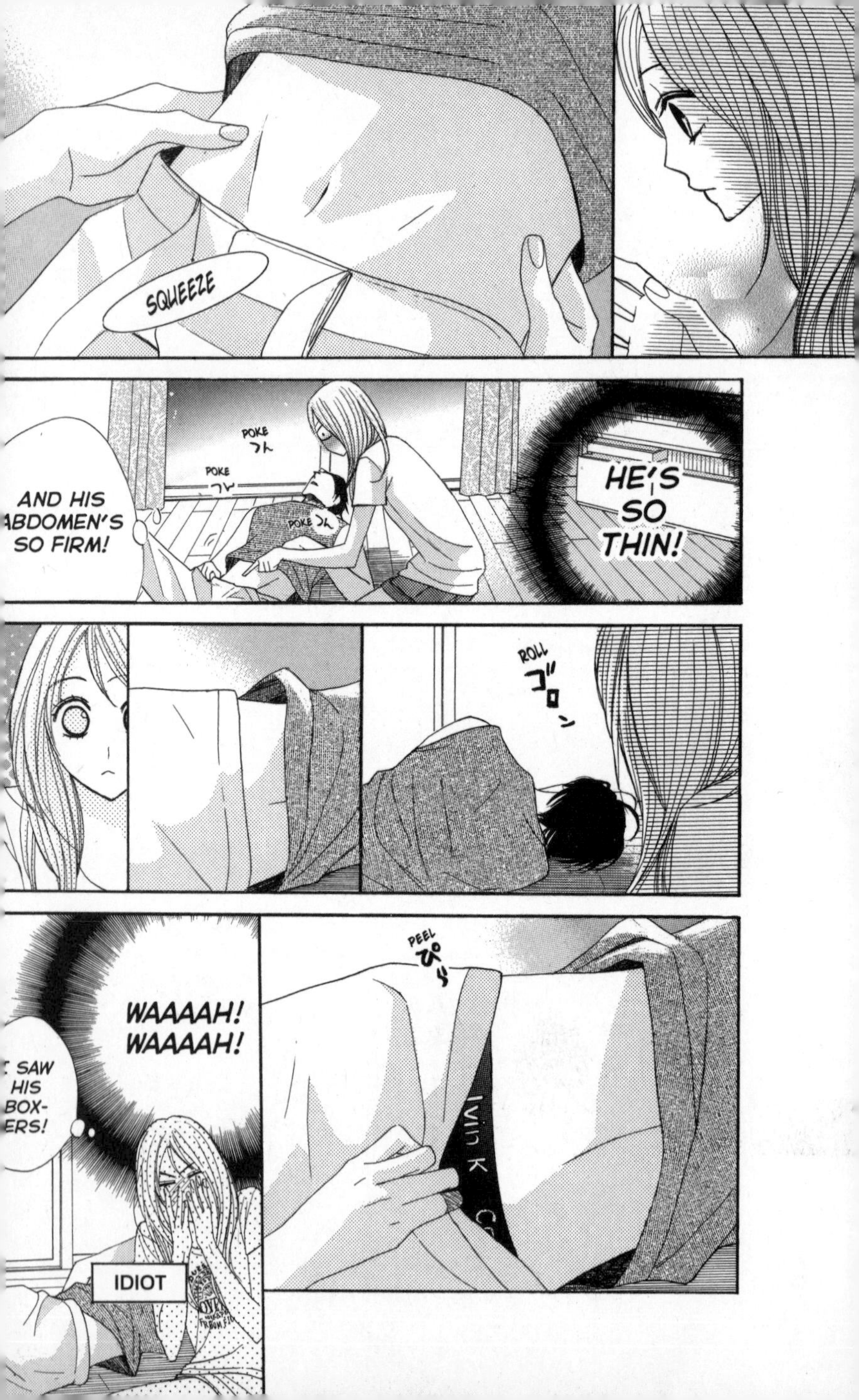
SQUEEZE
HE'S SO THIN!
POKE つん
POKE つん
POKE つん
AND HIS ABDOMEN'S SO FIRM!
ROLL ゴロン
PEEL ぴら
WAAAAH! WAAAAH!
I SAW HIS BOXERS!
IDIOT

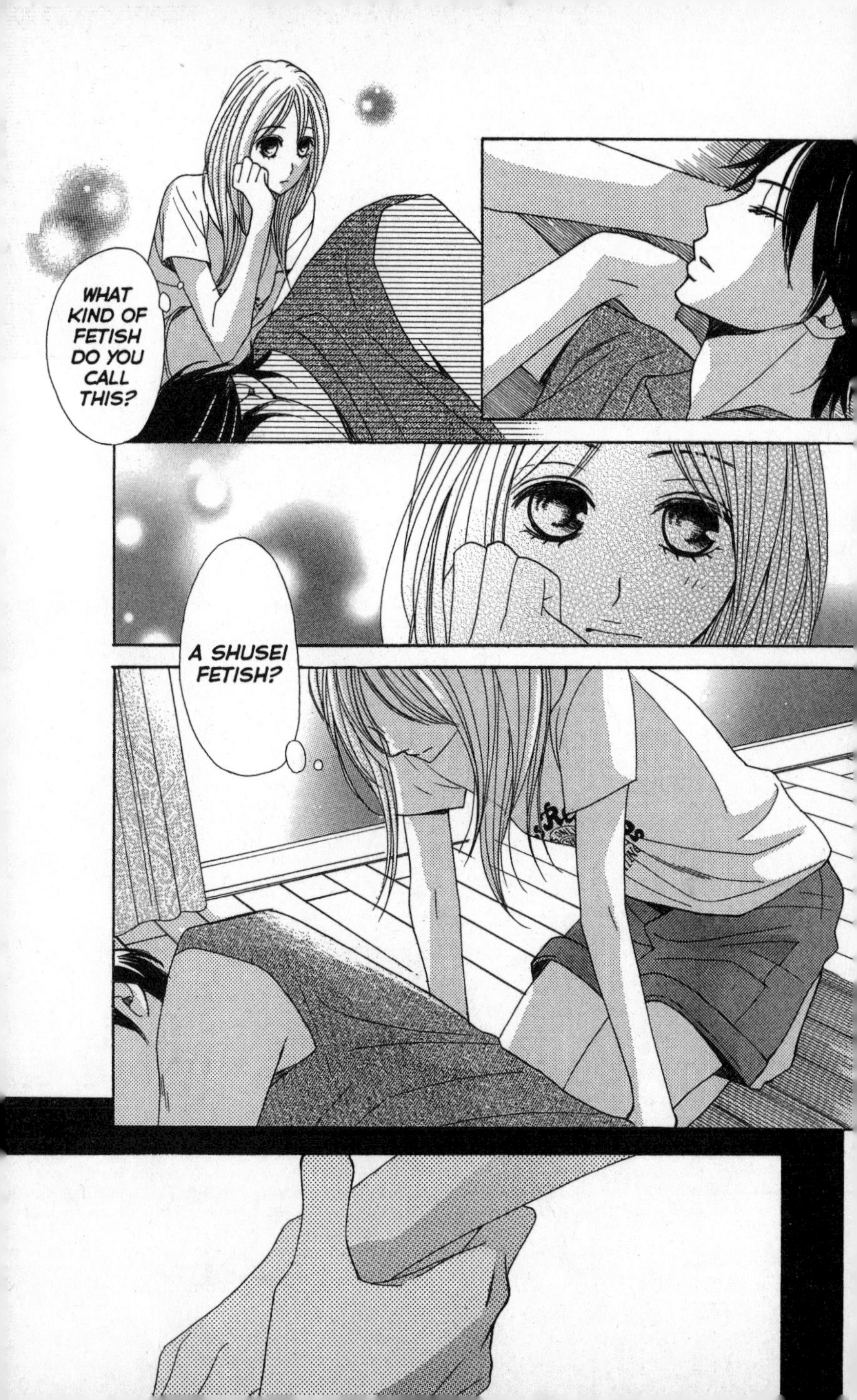
WHAT KIND OF FETISH DO YOU CALL THIS?
A SHUSEI FETISH?

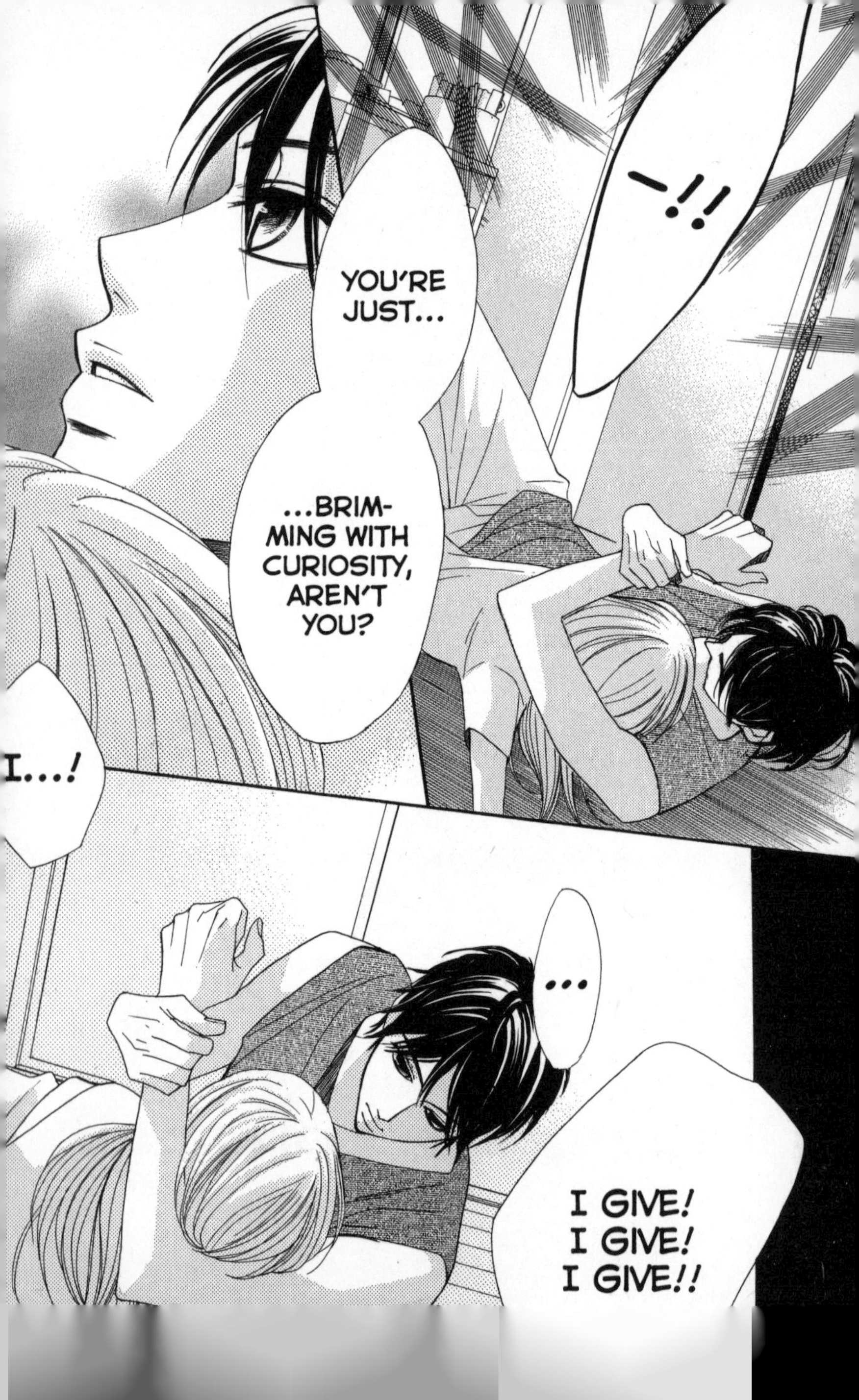
—!!
YOU'RE JUST...
...BRIM- MING WITH CURIOSITY, AREN'T YOU?
I...!
...
I GIVE! I GIVE! I GIVE!!

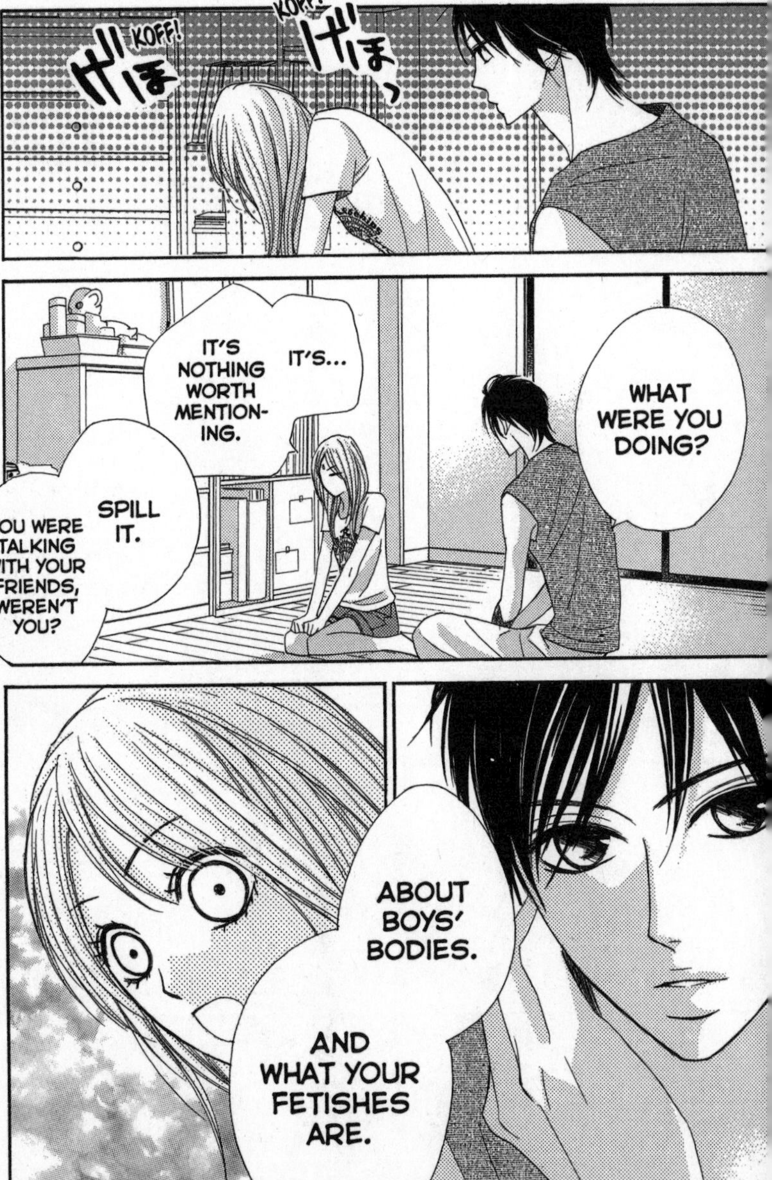
KOFF!
げほっ
KOFF!
げほ
WHAT WERE YOU DOING?
IT'S...
IT'S NOTHING WORTH MENTIONING.
SPILL IT.
YOU WERE TALKING WITH YOUR FRIENDS, WEREN'T YOU?
ABOUT BOYS' BODIES.
AND WHAT YOUR FETISHES ARE.

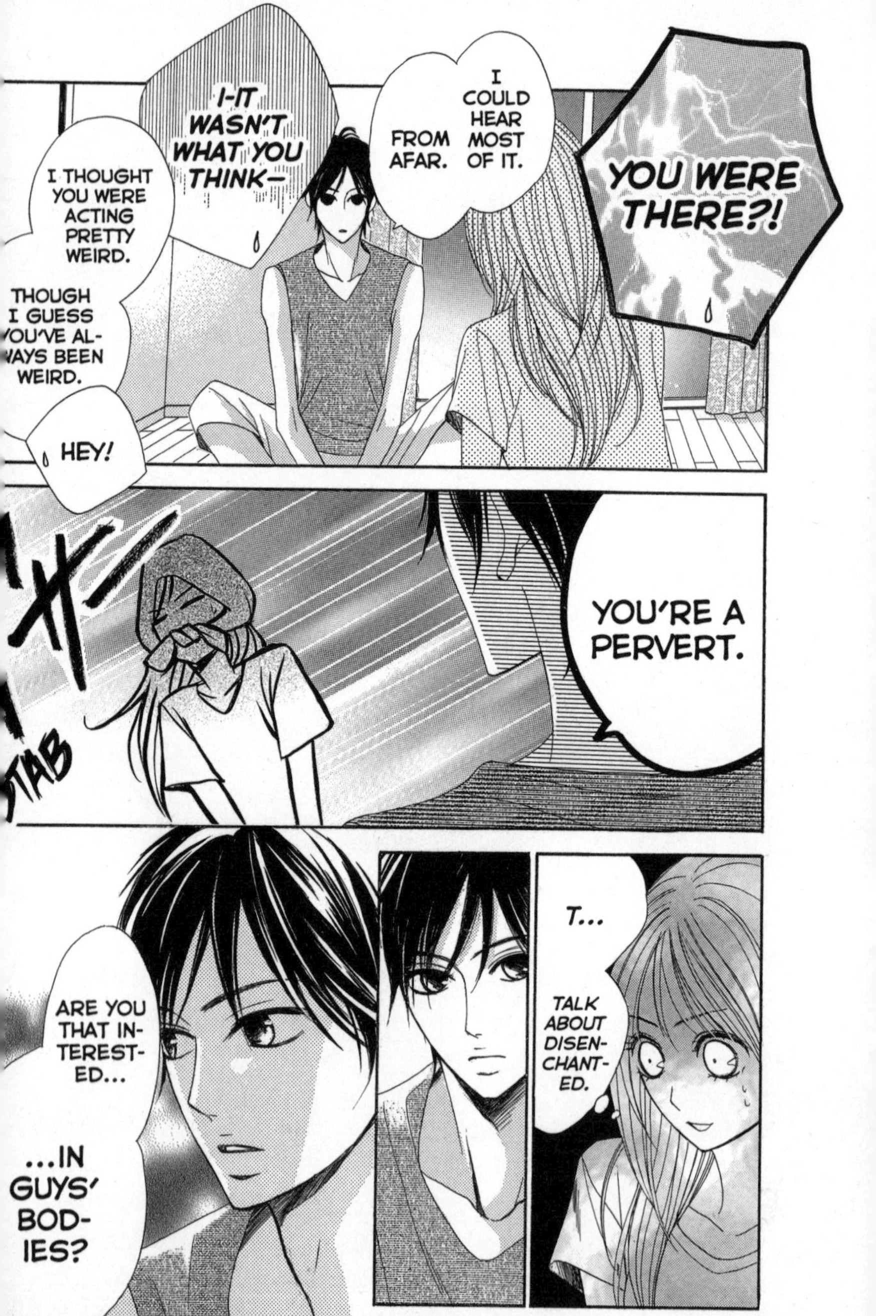
YOU WERE THERE?!
I COULD HEAR MOST OF IT. FROM AFAR.
I-IT WASN'T WHAT YOU THINK—
I THOUGHT YOU WERE ACTING PRETTY WEIRD.
THOUGH I GUESS YOU'VE ALWAYS BEEN WEIRD.
HEY!
YOU'RE A PERVERT.
STAB
T...
TALK ABOUT DISENCHANTED.
ARE YOU THAT INTERESTED...
...IN GUYS' BODIES?

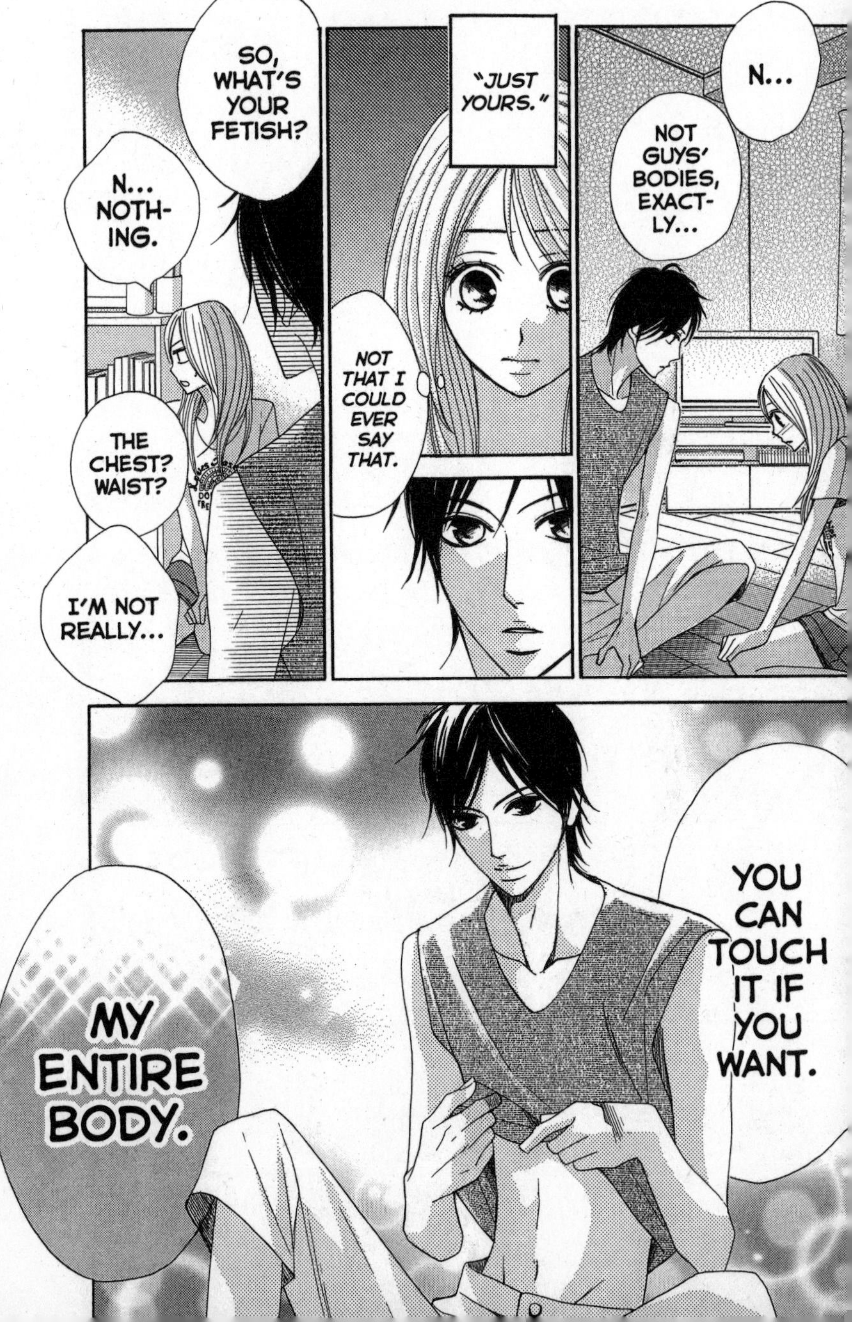
N...
NOT GUYS' BODIES, EXACTLY...
"JUST YOURS."
NOT THAT I COULD EVER SAY THAT.
SO, WHAT'S YOUR FETISH?
N... NOTHING.
THE CHEST? WAIST?
I'M NOT REALLY...
YOU CAN TOUCH IT IF YOU WANT.
MY ENTIRE BODY.

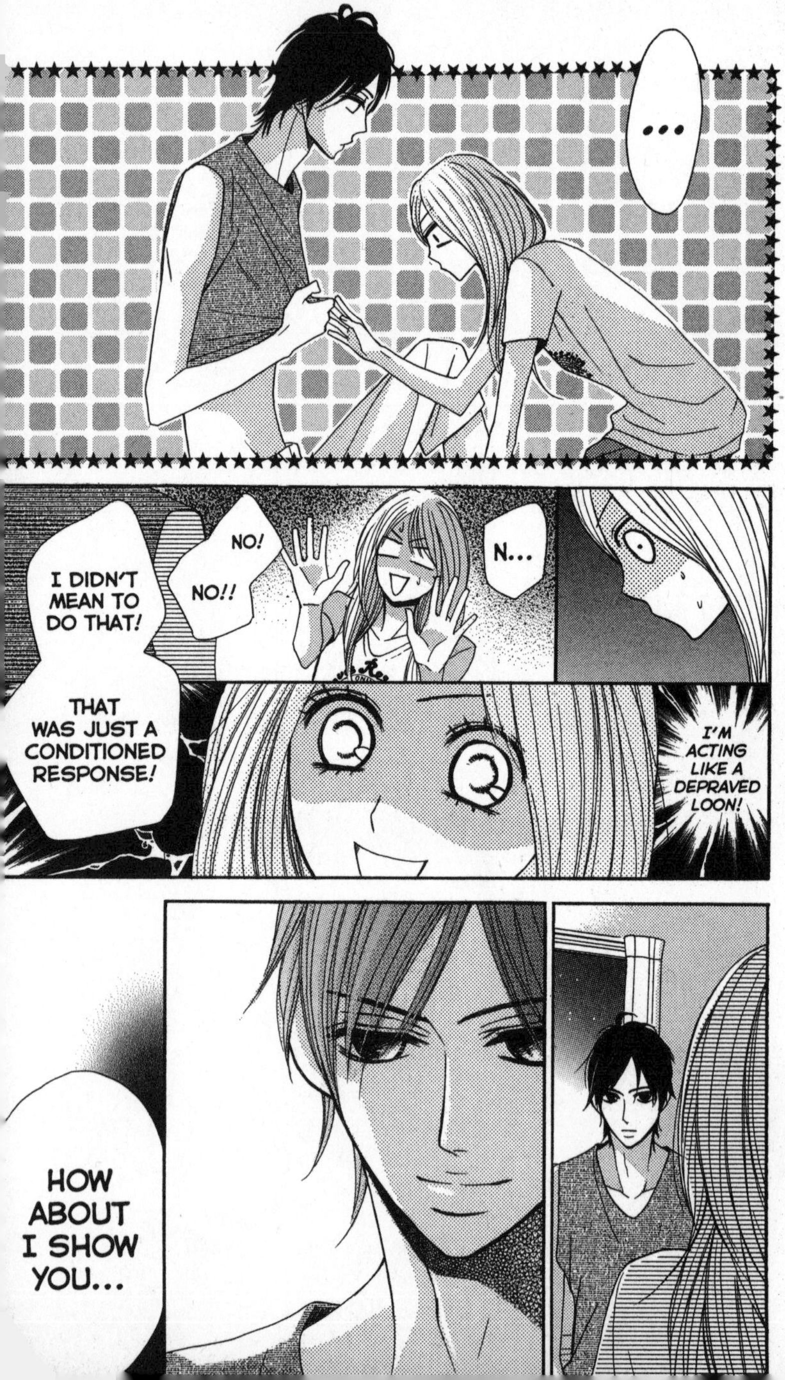
...
N...
NO!
NO!!
I DIDN'T MEAN TO DO THAT!
I'M ACTING LIKE A DEPRAVED LOON!
THAT WAS JUST A CONDITIONED RESPONSE!
HOW ABOUT I SHOW YOU...

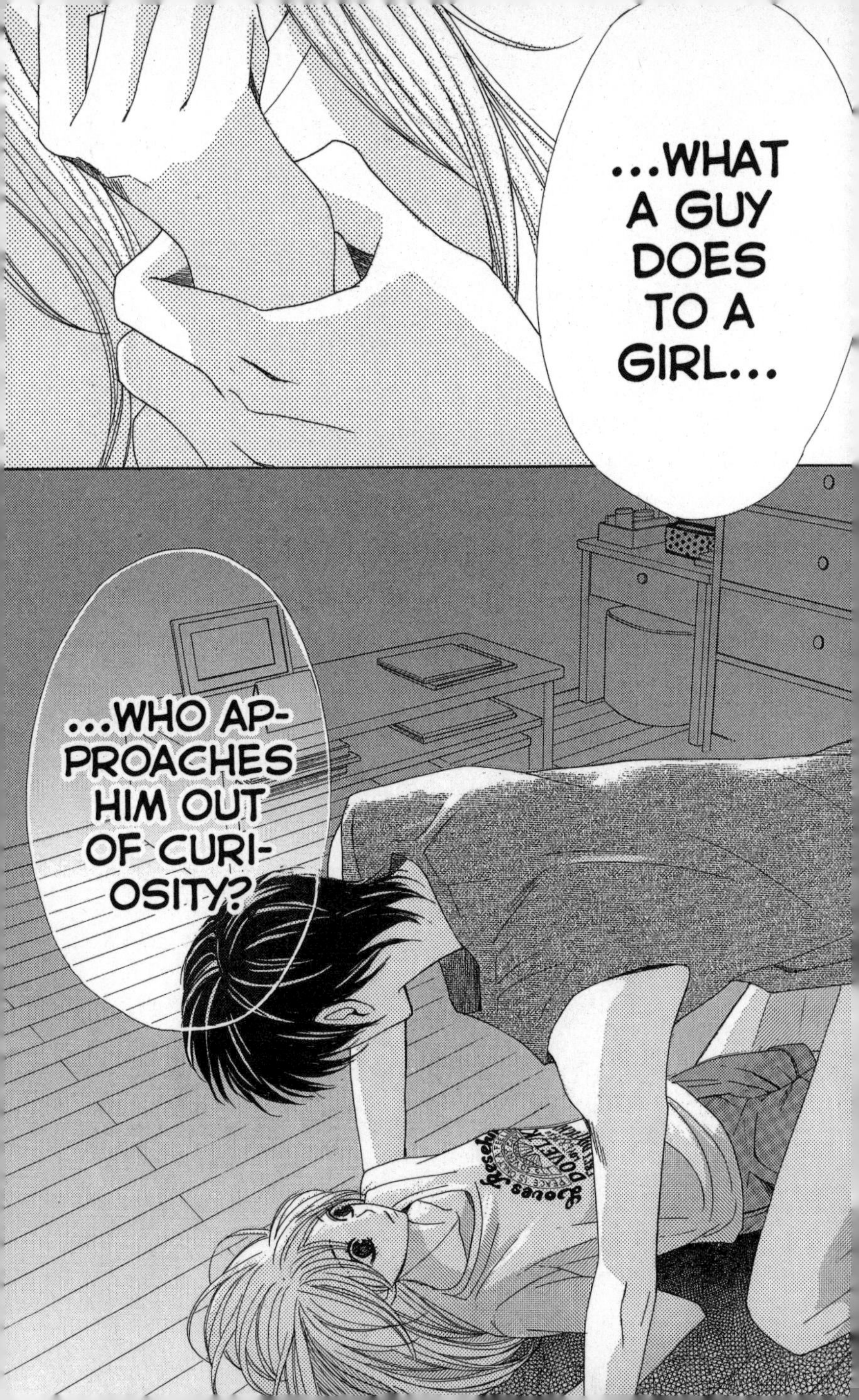
...WHAT A GUY DOES TO A GIRL...
...WHO AP-PROACHES HIM OUT OF CURI-OSITY?

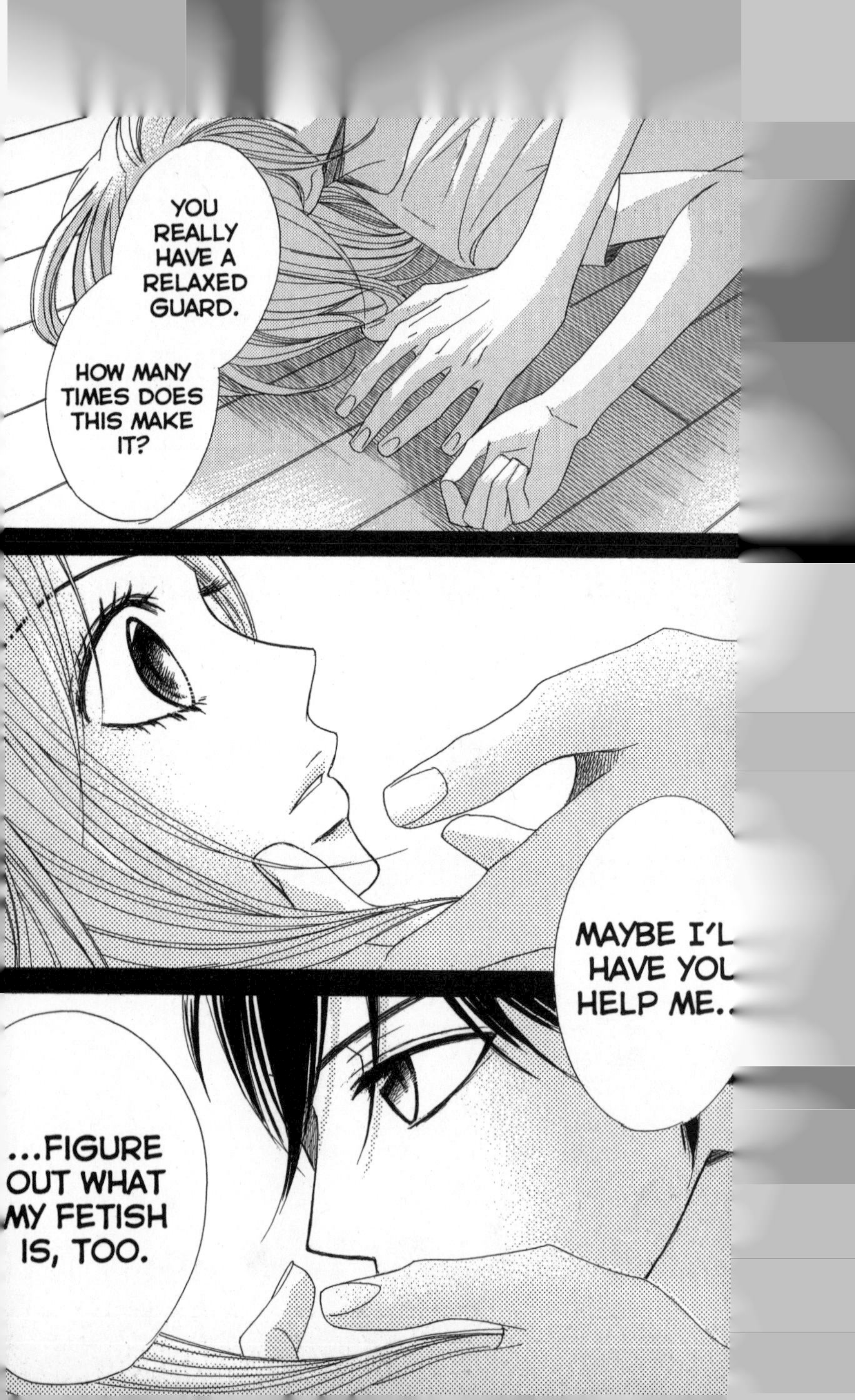
YOU REALLY HAVE A RELAXED GUARD.
HOW MANY TIMES DOES THIS MAKE IT?
MAYBE I'L HAVE YOU HELP ME..
...FIGURE OUT WHAT MY FETISH IS, TOO.

YOUR
ECK'S
O SLEN-
DER.

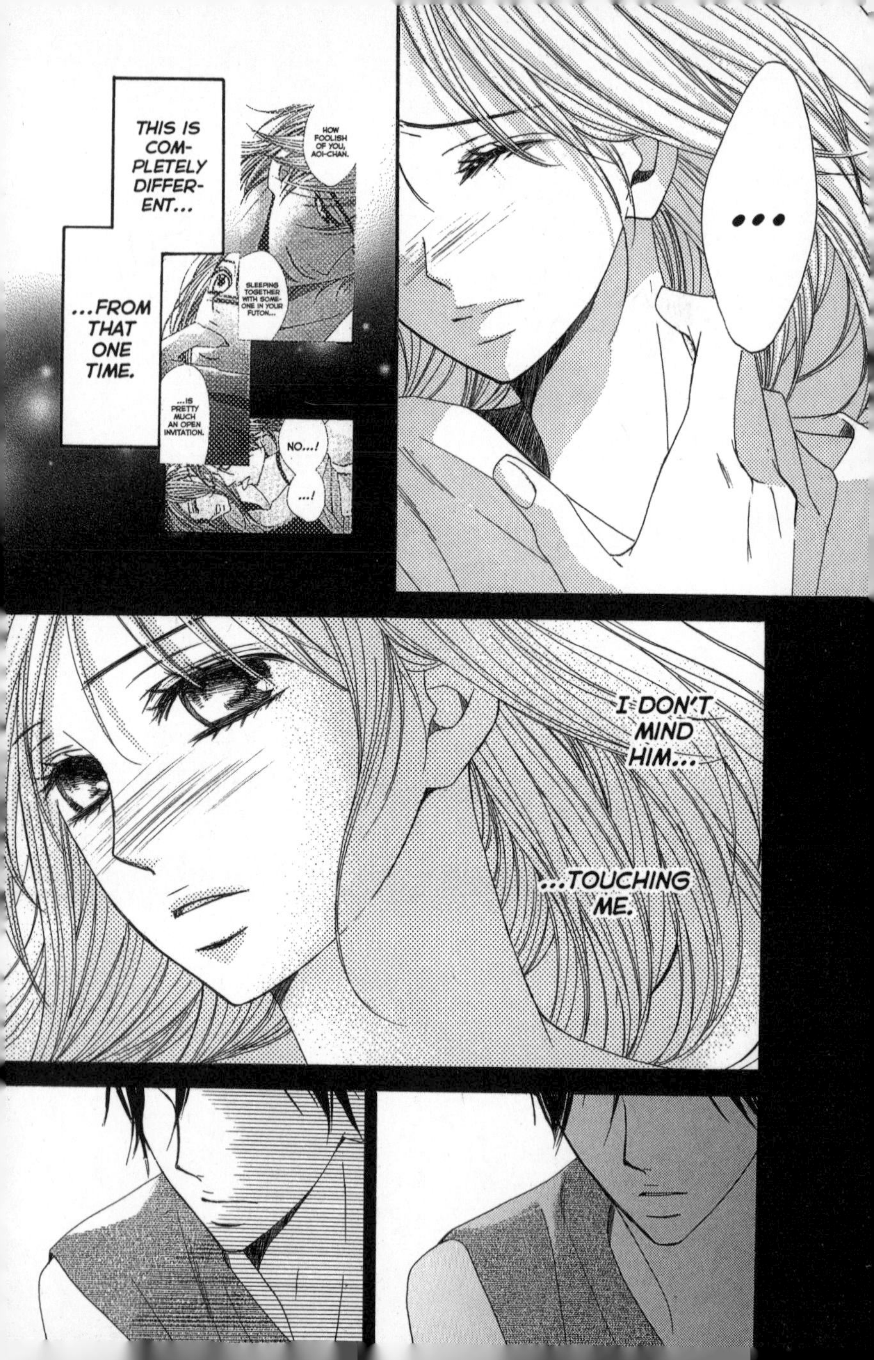
...
HOW FOOLISH OF YOU, AOI-CHAN.
THIS IS COMPLETELY DIFFERENT...
SLEEPING TOGETHER WITH SOMEONE IN YOUR FUTON...
...FROM THAT ONE TIME.
...IS PRETTY MUCH AN OPEN INVITATION.
NO...!
...!
I DON'T MIND HIM...
...TOUCHING ME.

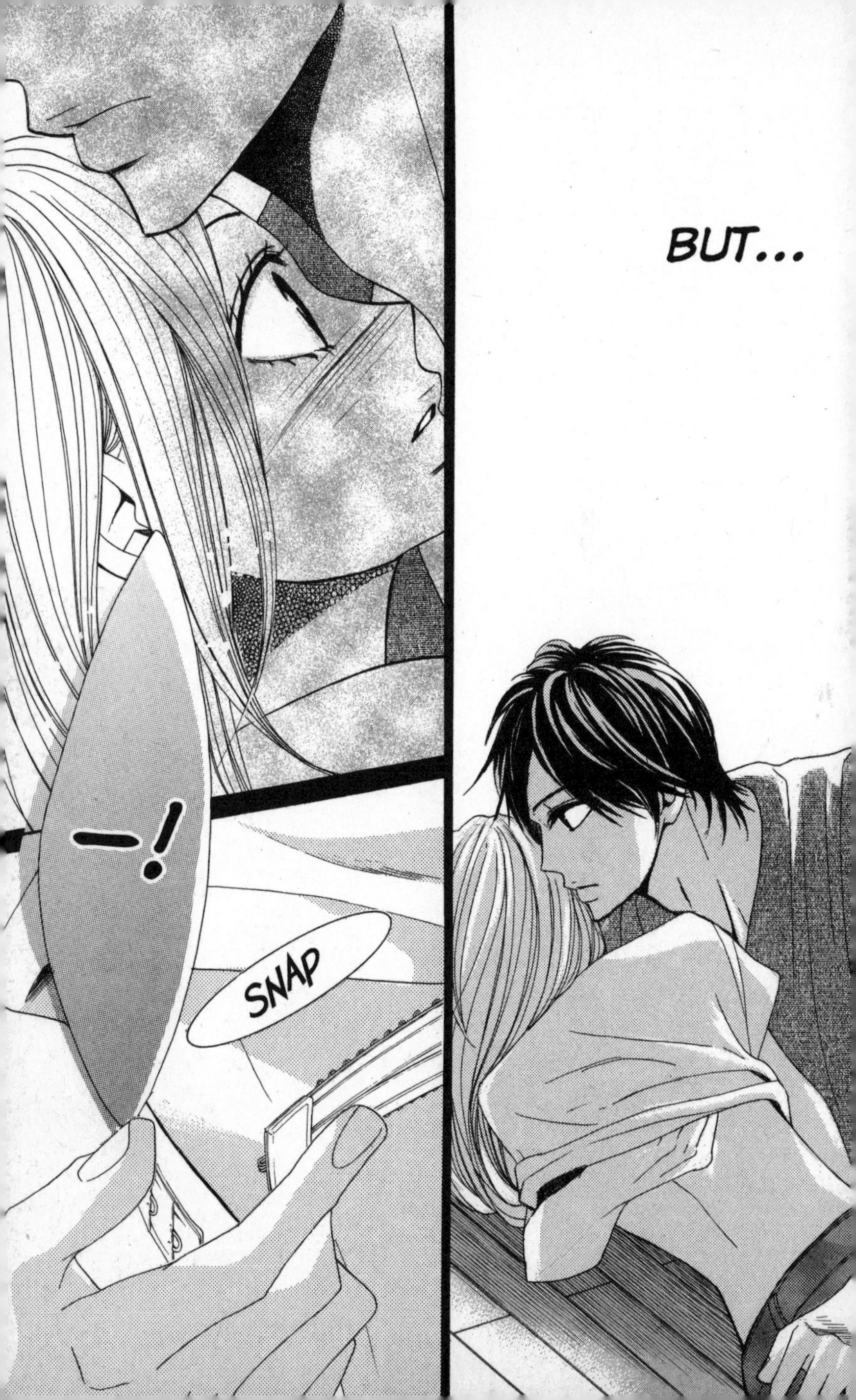
BUT...
—!
SNAP

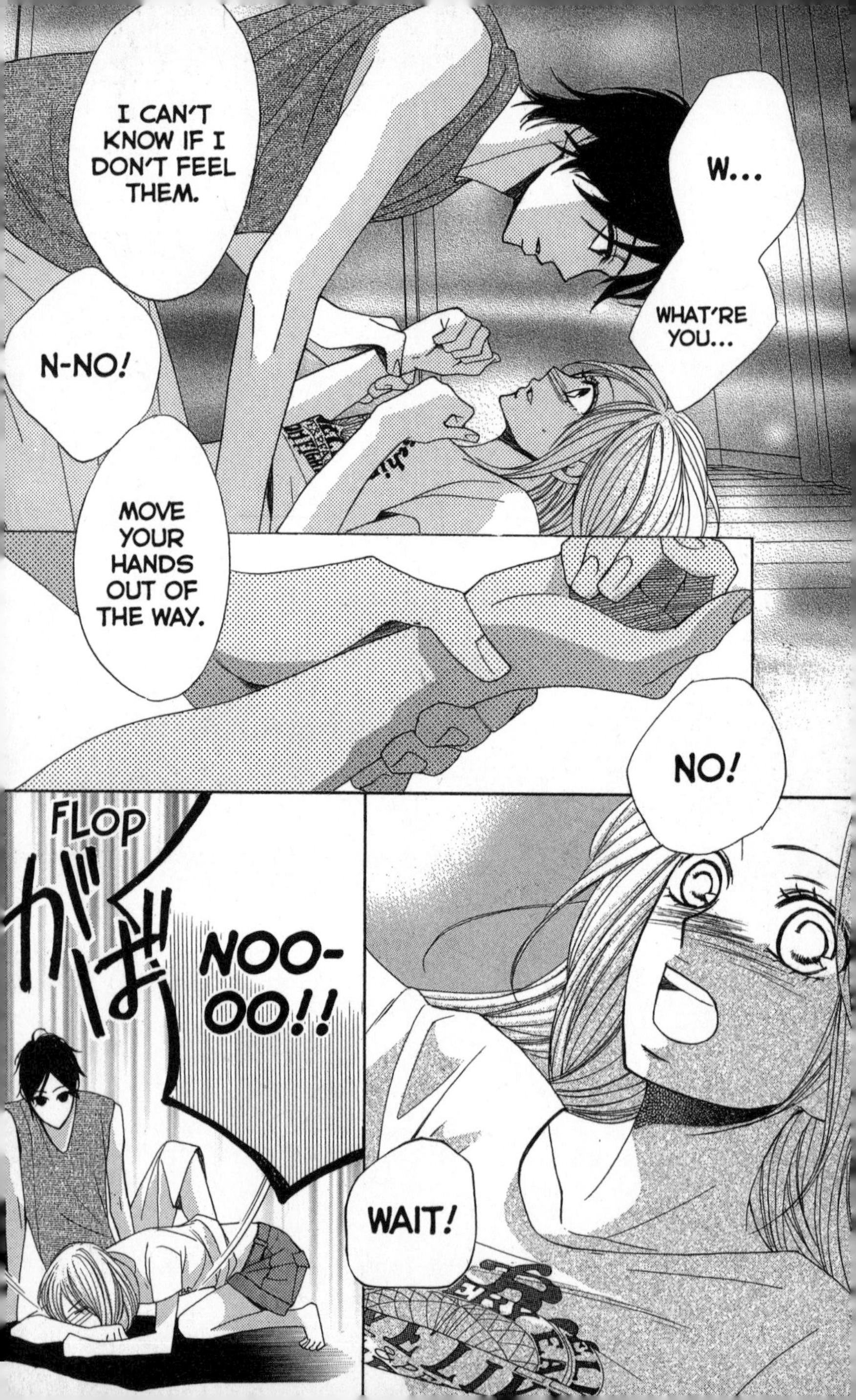
W...
WHAT'RE YOU...
I CAN'T KNOW IF I DON'T FEEL THEM.
N-NO!
MOVE YOUR HANDS OUT OF THE WAY.
NO!
WAIT!
FLOP
がば
NOO-OO!!

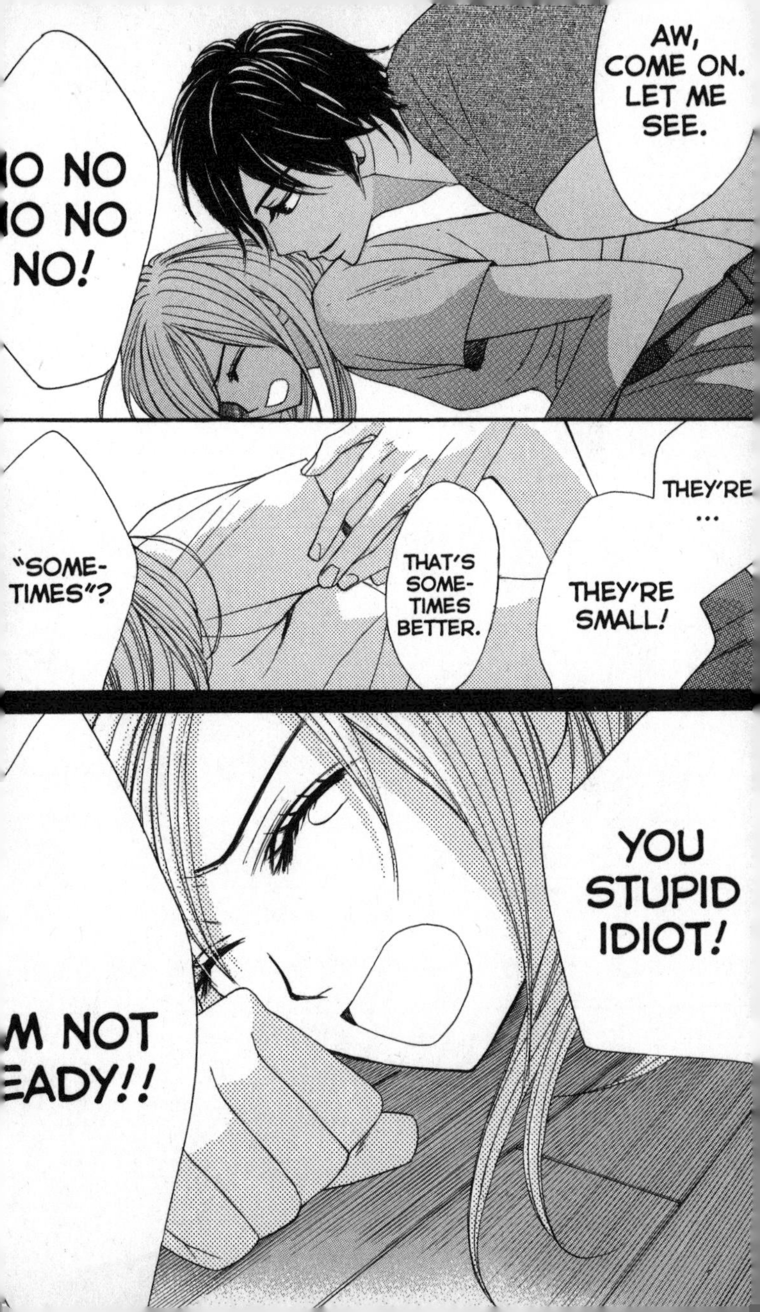
AW, COME ON. LET ME SEE.
O NO O NO NO!
THEY'RE ...
THEY'RE SMALL!
THAT'S SOME-TIMES BETTER.
"SOME-TIMES"?
YOU STUPID IDIOT!
M NOT EADY!!

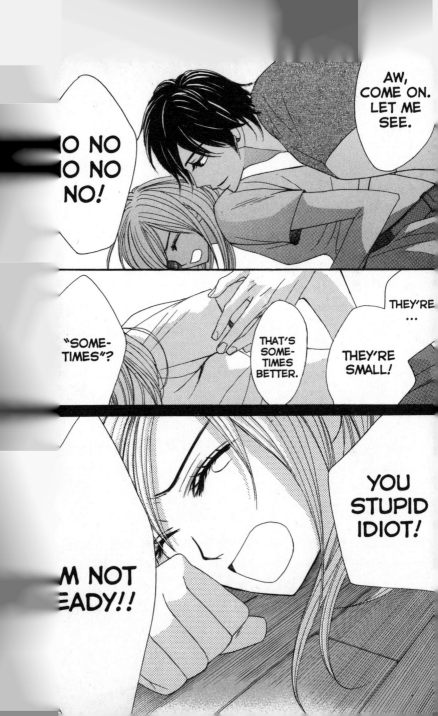

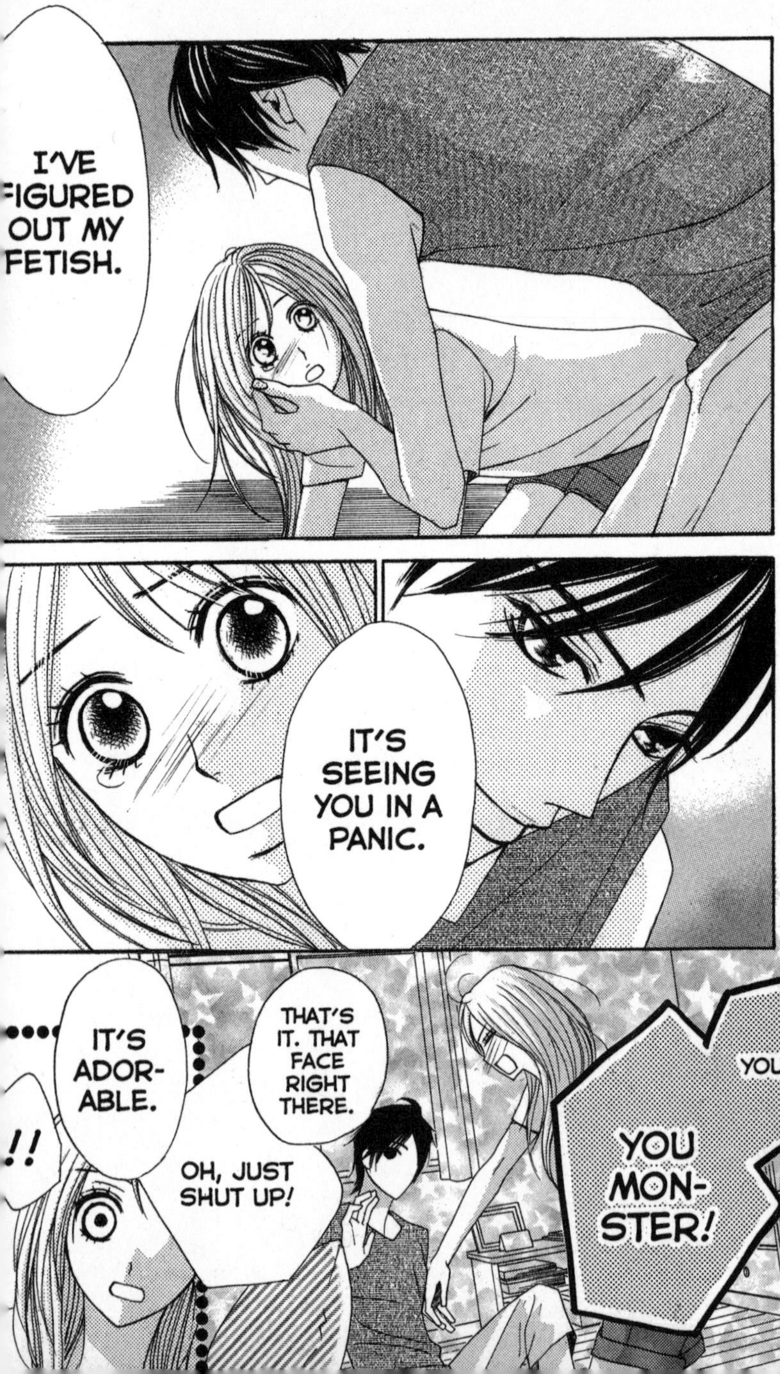
I'VE FIGURED OUT MY FETISH.
IT'S SEEING YOU IN A PANIC.
YOU...
YOU MONSTER!
THAT'S IT. THAT FACE RIGHT THERE.
IT'S ADORABLE.
!!
OH, JUST SHUT UP!

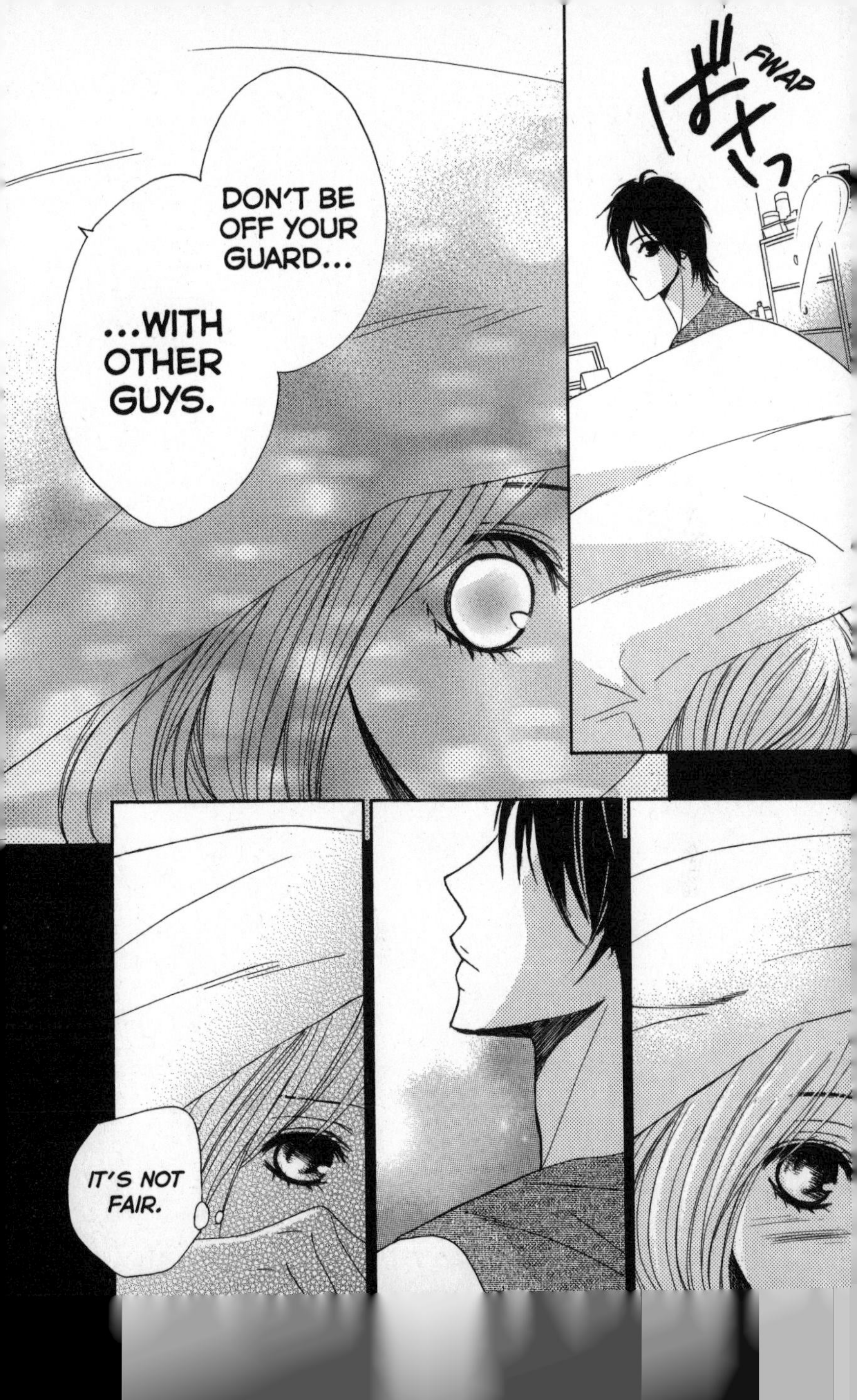
ばさっ
FWAP
DON'T BE OFF YOUR GUARD...
...WITH OTHER GUYS.
IT'S NOT FAIR.

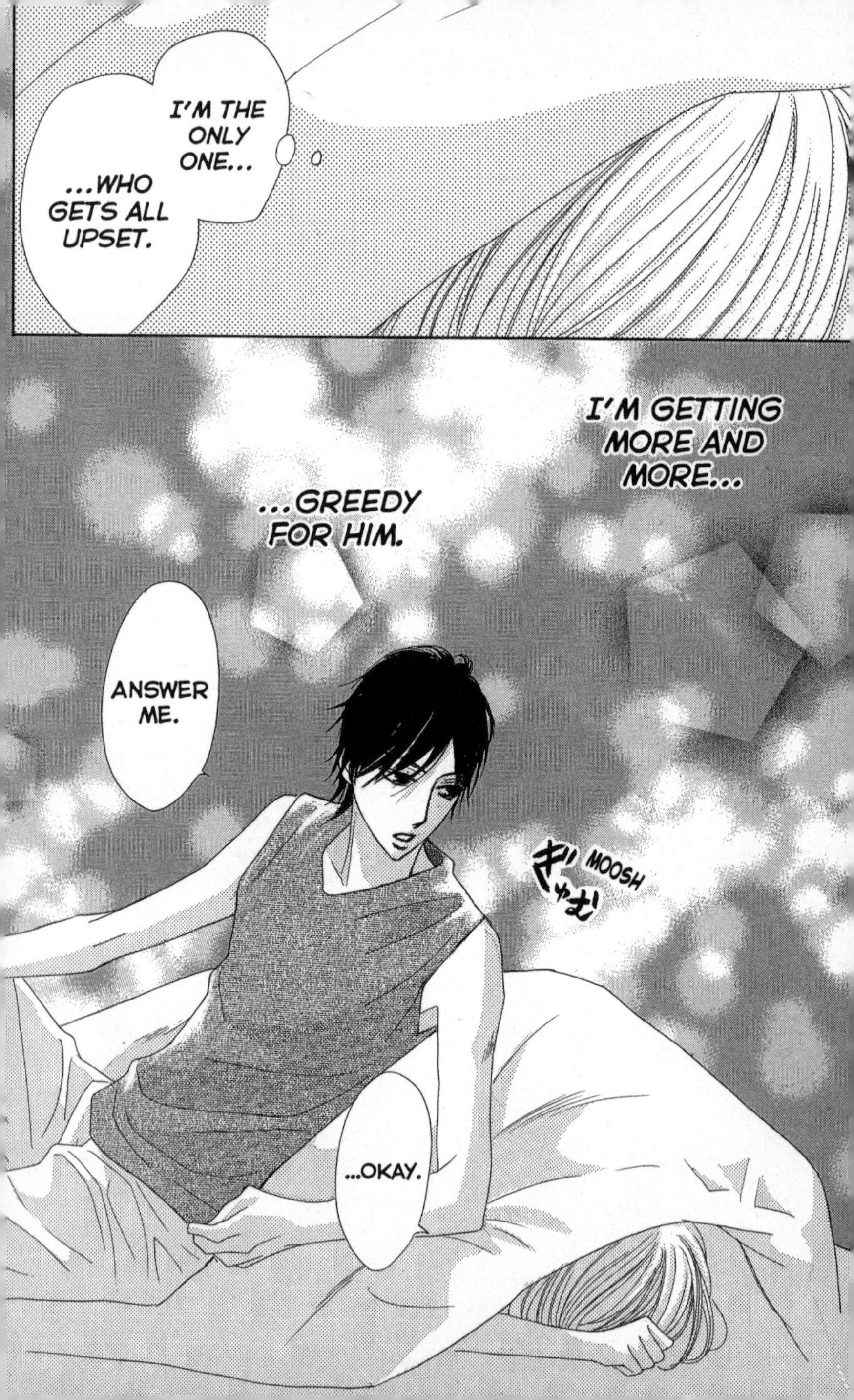
I'M THE ONLY ONE...
...WHO GETS ALL UPSET.
I'M GETTING MORE AND MORE...
...GREEDY FOR HIM.
ぎゅむ MOOSH
ANSWER ME.
...OKAY.

L♥DK

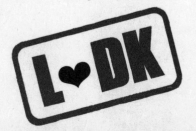

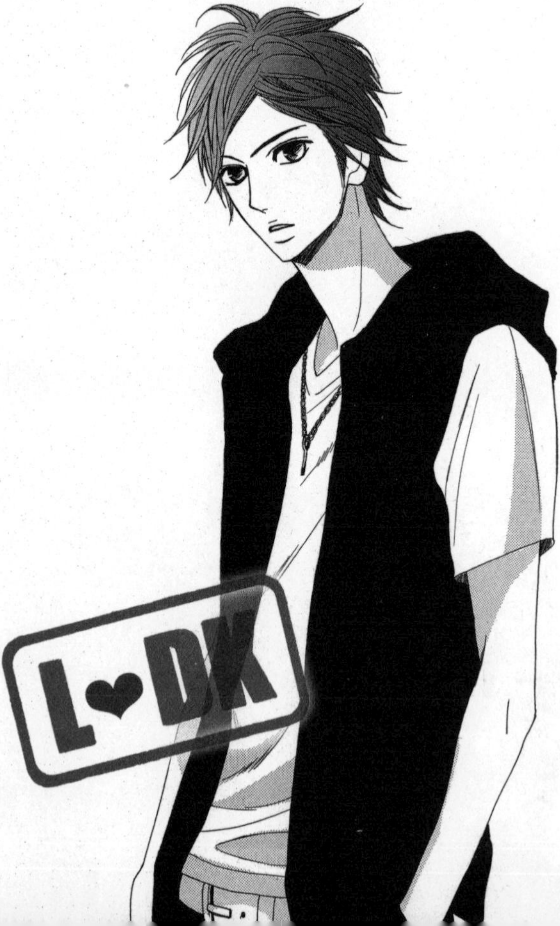
L♥DK

#15 Momo-colored Crush

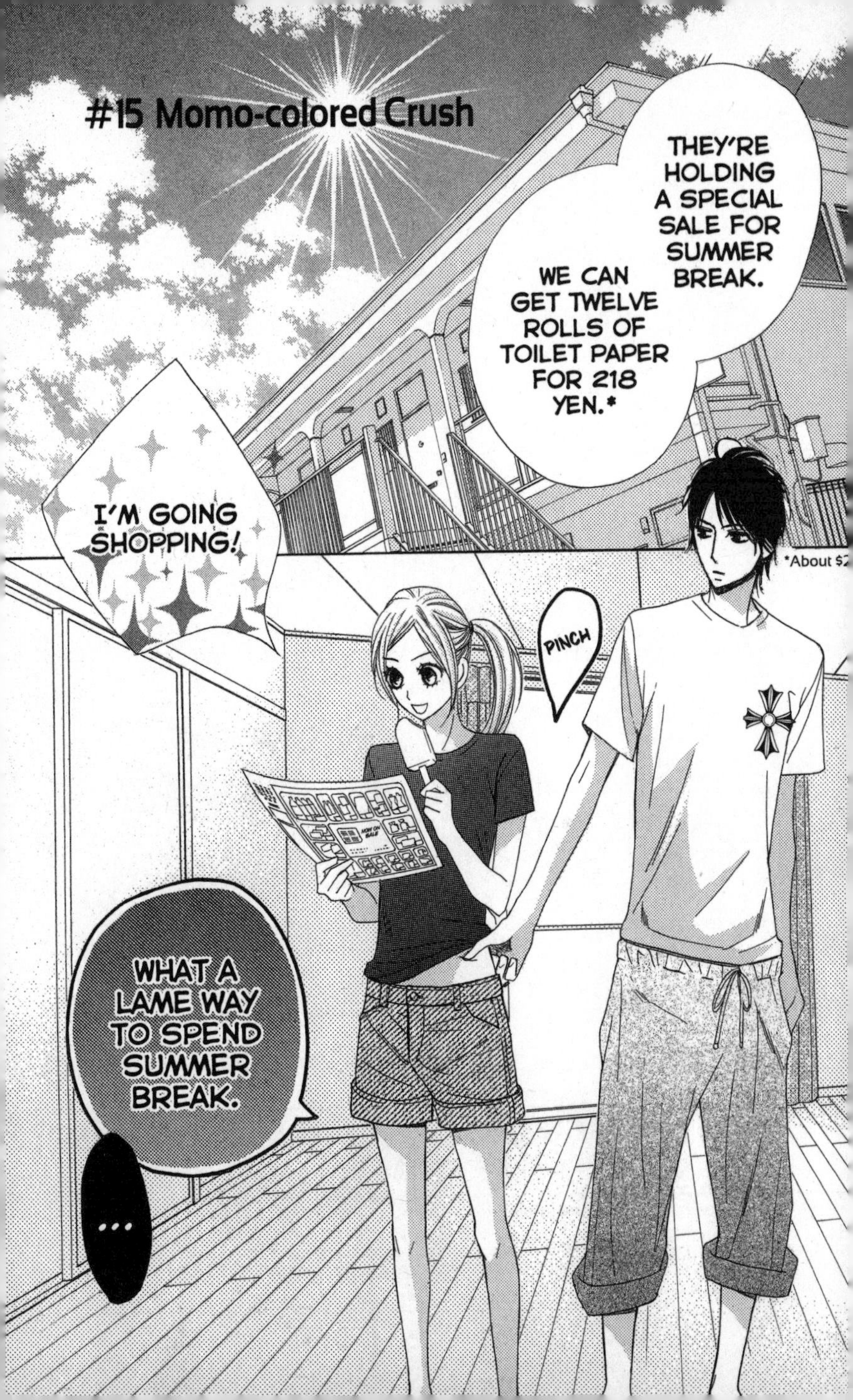
THEY'RE HOLDING A SPECIAL SALE FOR SUMMER BREAK.
WE CAN GET TWELVE ROLLS OF TOILET PAPER FOR 218 YEN.*
I'M GOING SHOPPING!
PINCH
WHAT A LAME WAY TO SPEND SUMMER BREAK.
...

*About $2

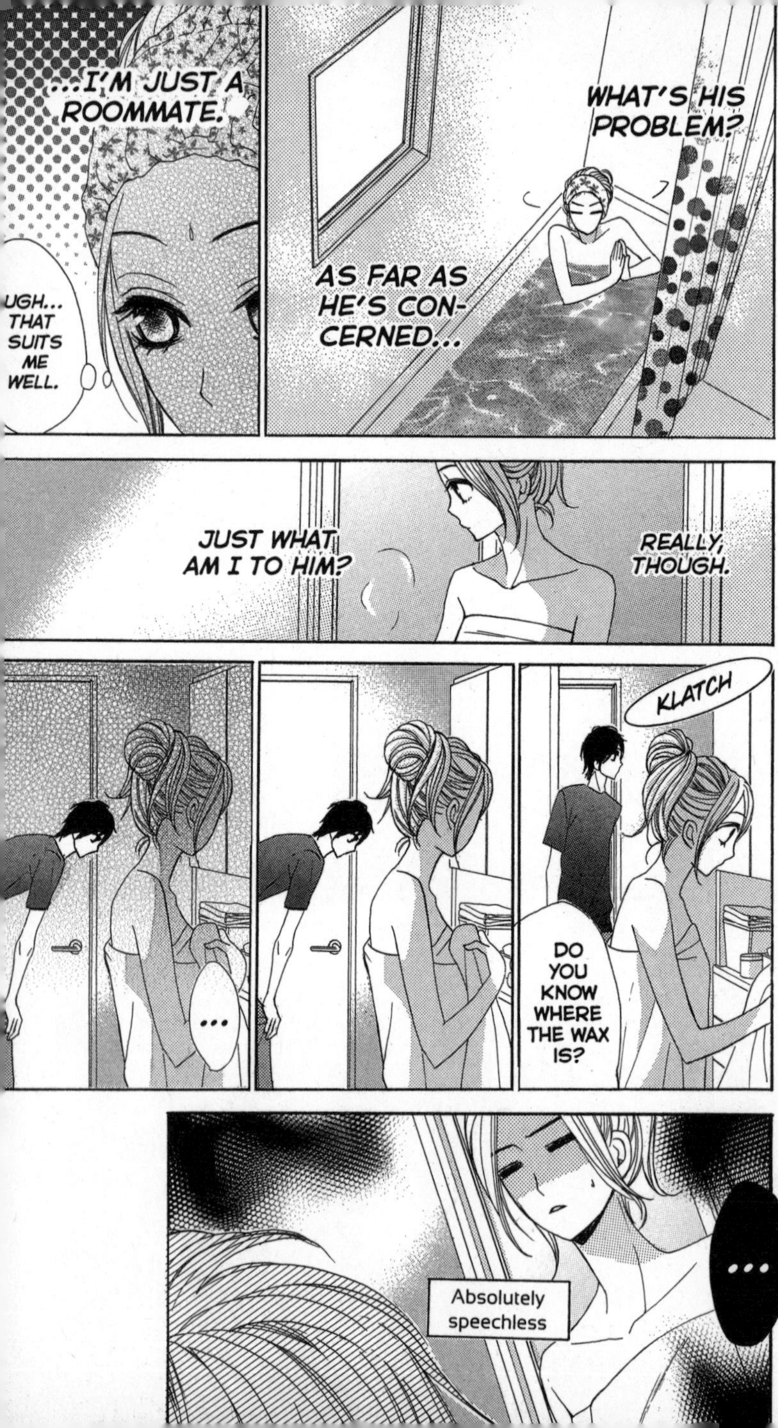
WHAT'S HIS PROBLEM?
AS FAR AS HE'S CON-CERNED...
...I'M JUST A ROOMMATE.
UGH... THAT SUITS ME WELL.
REALLY, THOUGH.
JUST WHAT AM I TO HIM?
KLATCH
DO YOU KNOW WHERE THE WAX IS?
...
...
Absolutely speechless

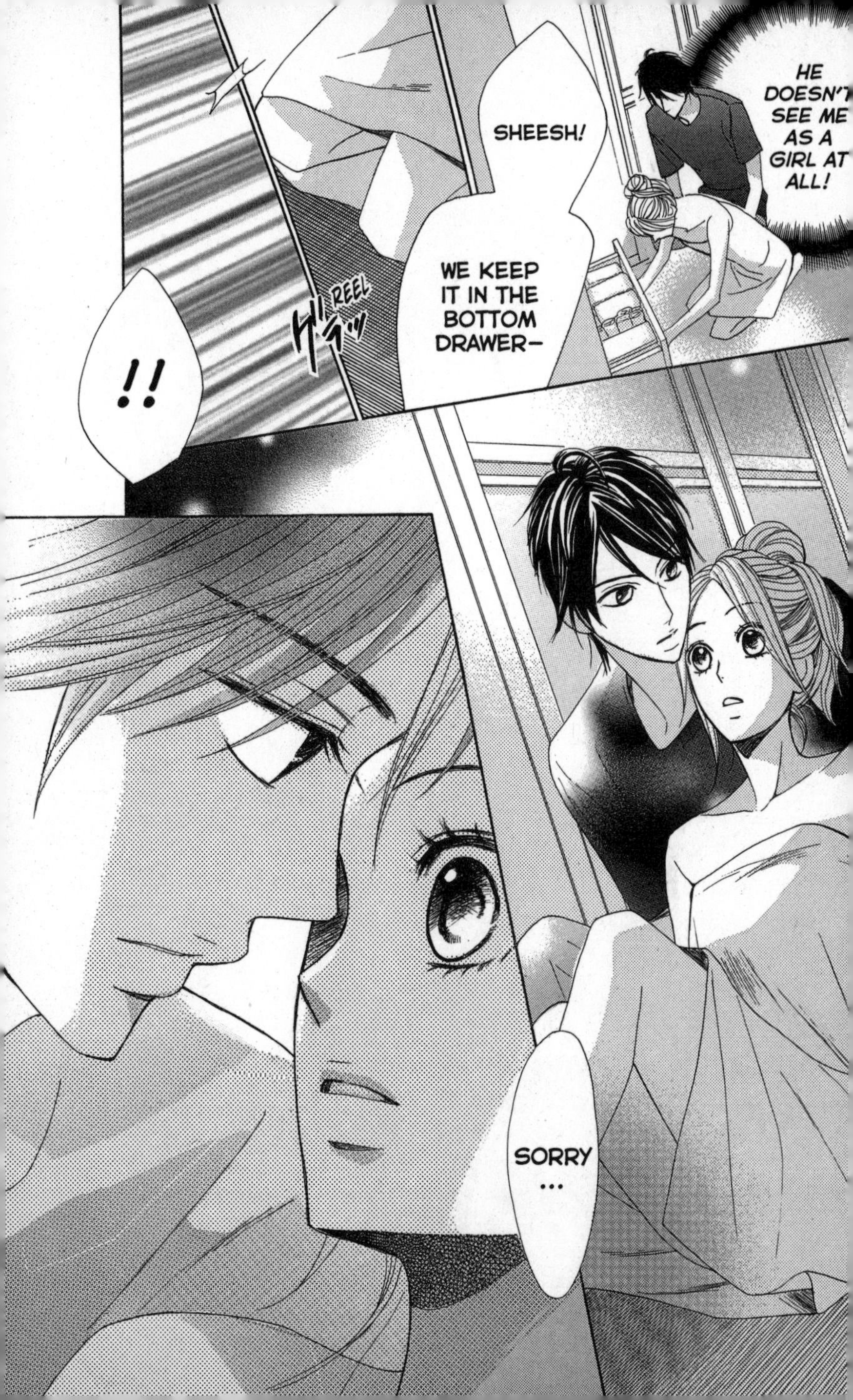
HE DOESN'T SEE ME AS A GIRL AT ALL!
SHEESH!
WE KEEP IT IN THE BOTTOM DRAWER—
REEL
!!
SORRY ...

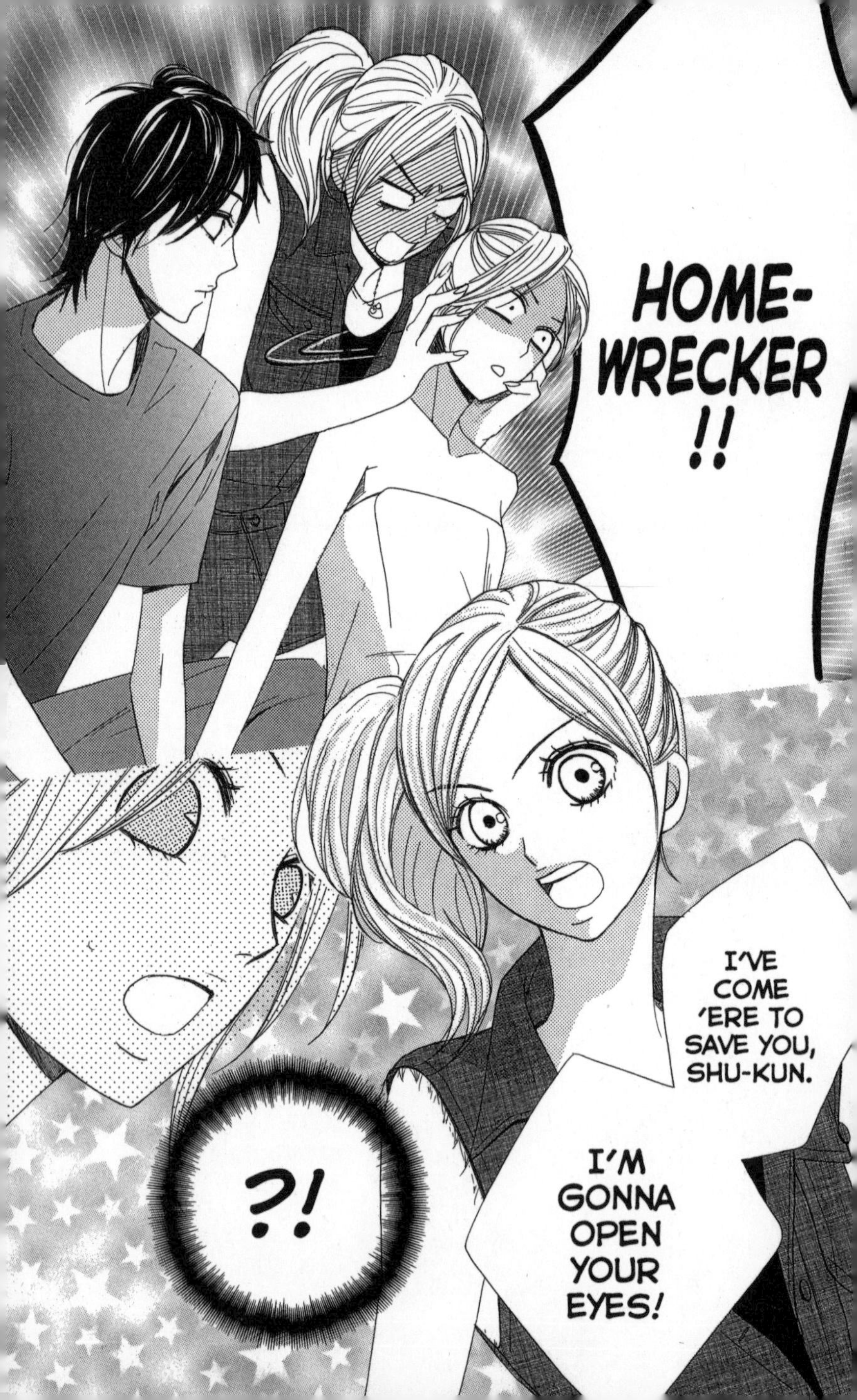
HOME-WRECKER!!
I'VE COME 'ERE TO SAVE YOU, SHU-KUN.
I'M GONNA OPEN YOUR EYES!
?!

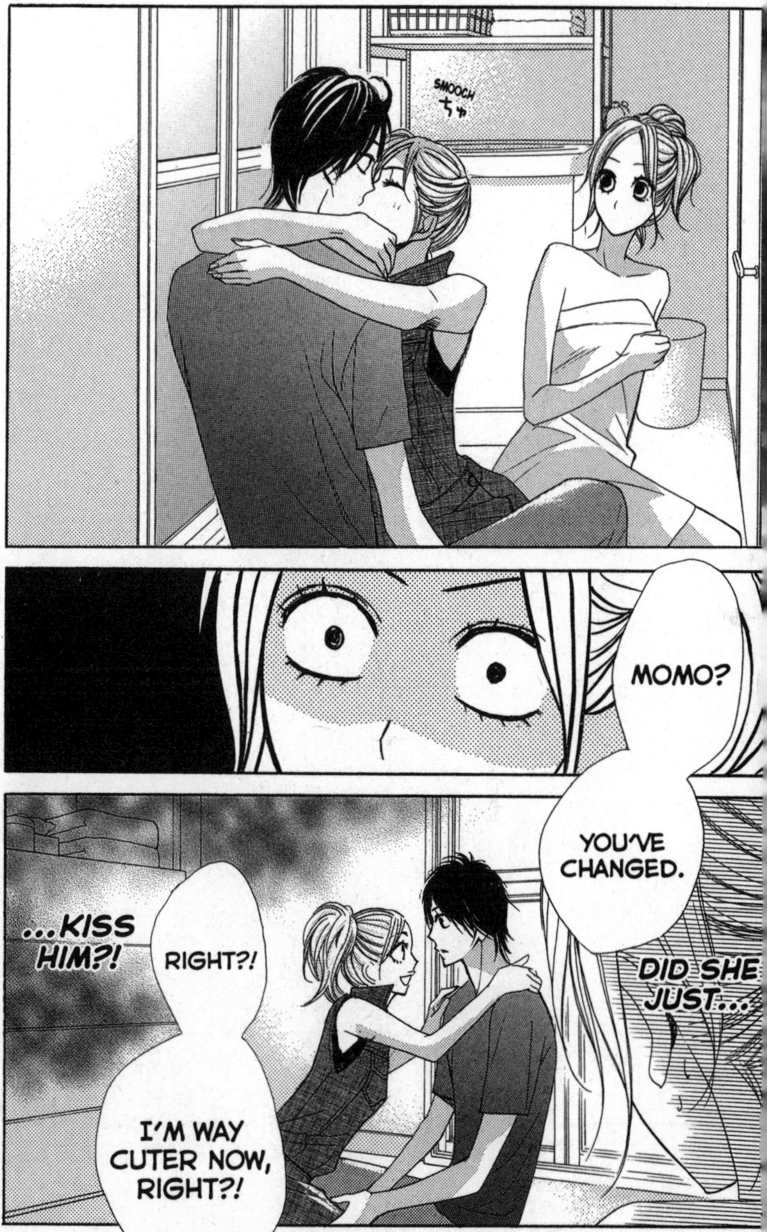
SMOOCH
ちゅ
MOMO?
YOU'VE CHANGED.
DID SHE JUST...
...KISS HIM?!
RIGHT?!
I'M WAY CUTER NOW, RIGHT?!

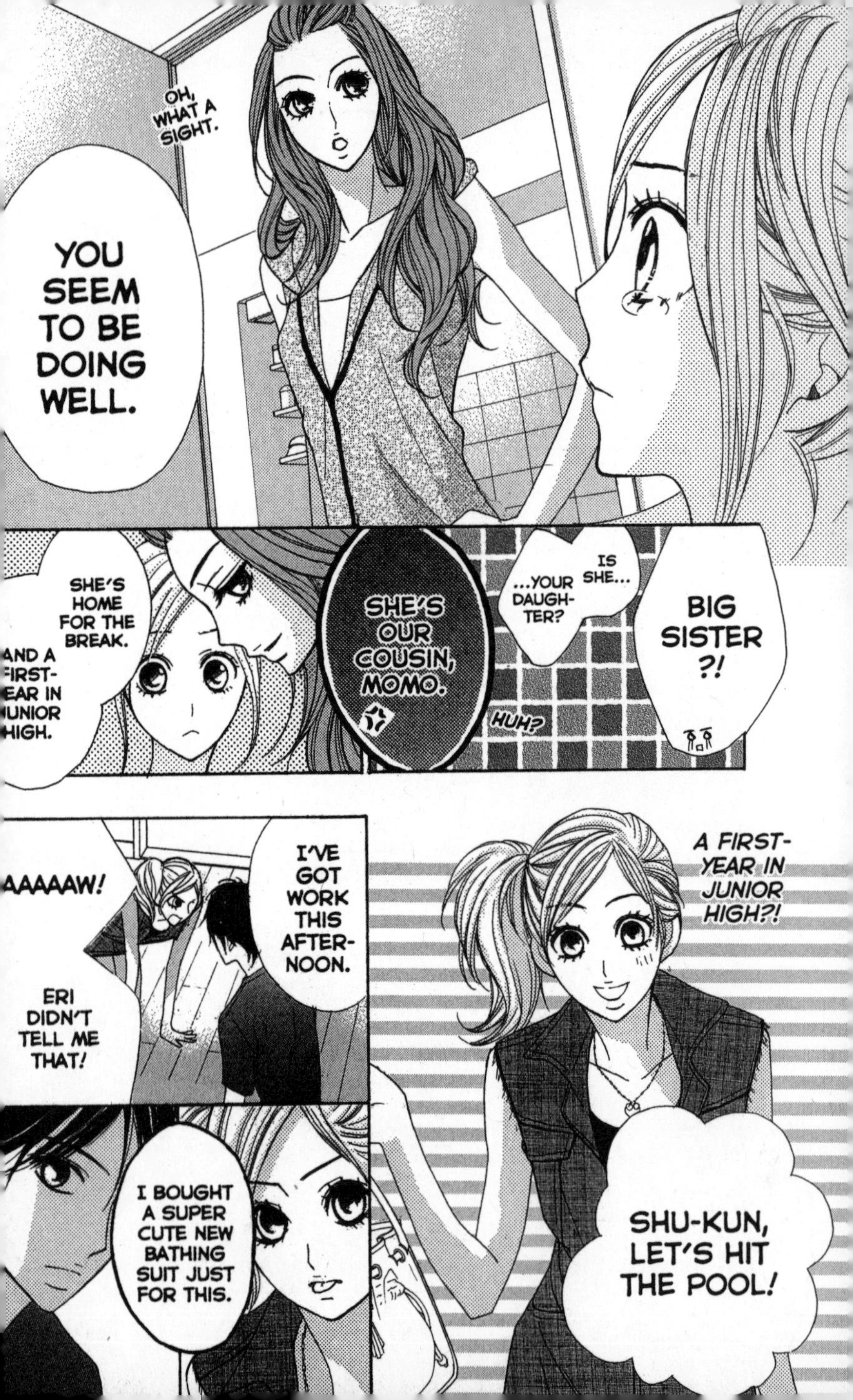
OH, WHAT A SIGHT.
YOU SEEM TO BE DOING WELL.
BIG SISTER ?!
IS SHE...
...YOUR DAUGHTER?
HUH?
SHE'S OUR COUSIN, MOMO.
SHE'S HOME FOR THE BREAK.
AND A FIRST-EAR IN UNIOR HIGH.
A FIRST-YEAR IN JUNIOR HIGH?!
SHU-KUN, LET'S HIT THE POOL!
I'VE GOT WORK THIS AFTERNOON.
AAAAAW!
ERI DIDN'T TELL ME THAT!
I BOUGHT A SUPER CUTE NEW BATHING SUIT JUST FOR THIS.

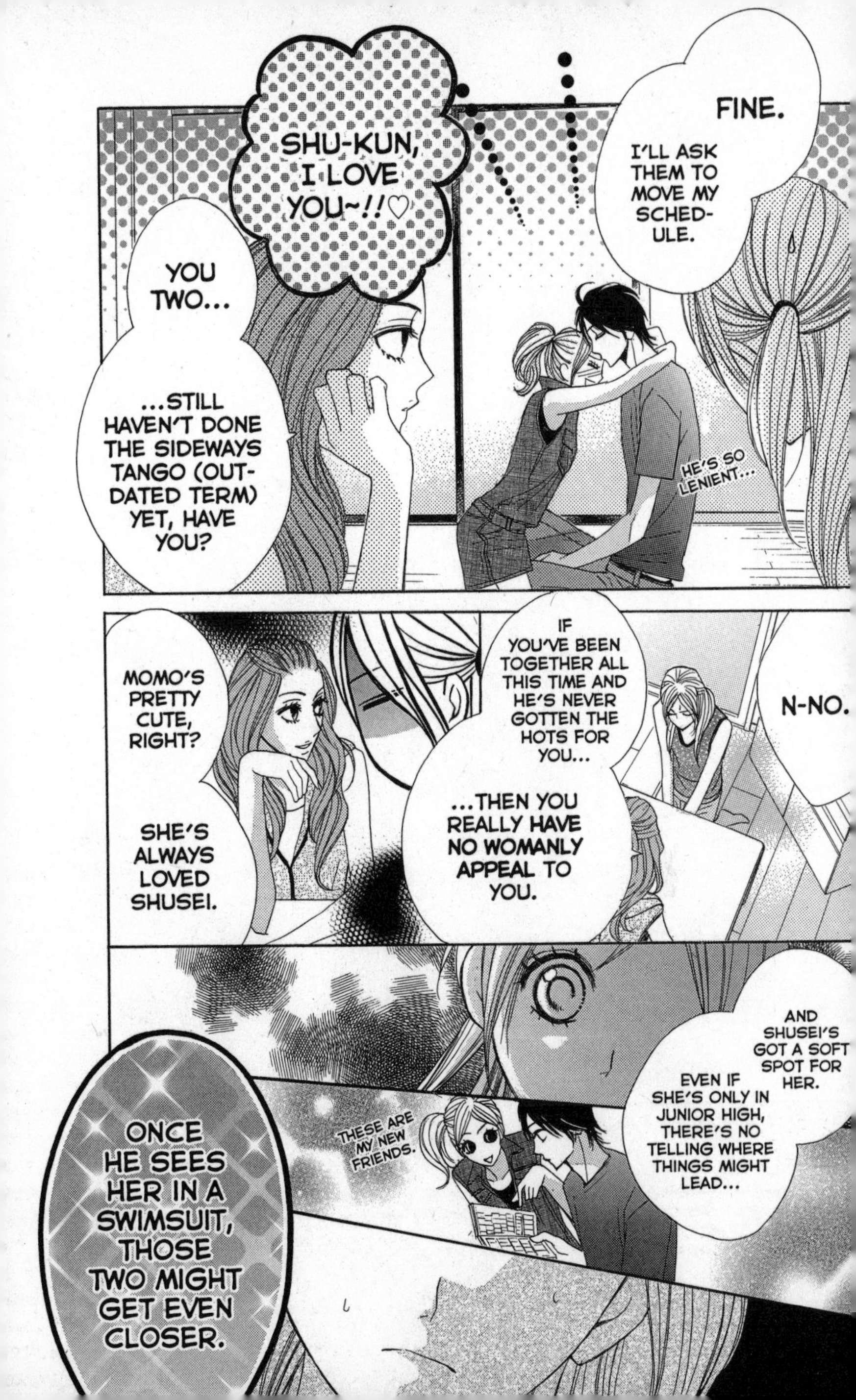
FINE.
I'LL ASK THEM TO MOVE MY SCHED-ULE.
SHU-KUN, I LOVE YOU~!!♡
HE'S SO LENIENT...
YOU TWO...
...STILL HAVEN'T DONE THE SIDEWAYS TANGO (OUT-DATED TERM) YET, HAVE YOU?
N-NO.
IF YOU'VE BEEN TOGETHER ALL THIS TIME AND HE'S NEVER GOTTEN THE HOTS FOR YOU...
...THEN YOU REALLY HAVE NO WOMANLY APPEAL TO YOU.
MOMO'S PRETTY CUTE, RIGHT?
SHE'S ALWAYS LOVED SHUSEI.
AND SHUSEI'S GOT A SOFT SPOT FOR HER.
EVEN IF SHE'S ONLY IN JUNIOR HIGH, THERE'S NO TELLING WHERE THINGS MIGHT LEAD...
THESE ARE MY NEW FRIENDS.
ONCE HE SEES HER IN A SWIMSUIT, THOSE TWO MIGHT GET EVEN CLOSER.

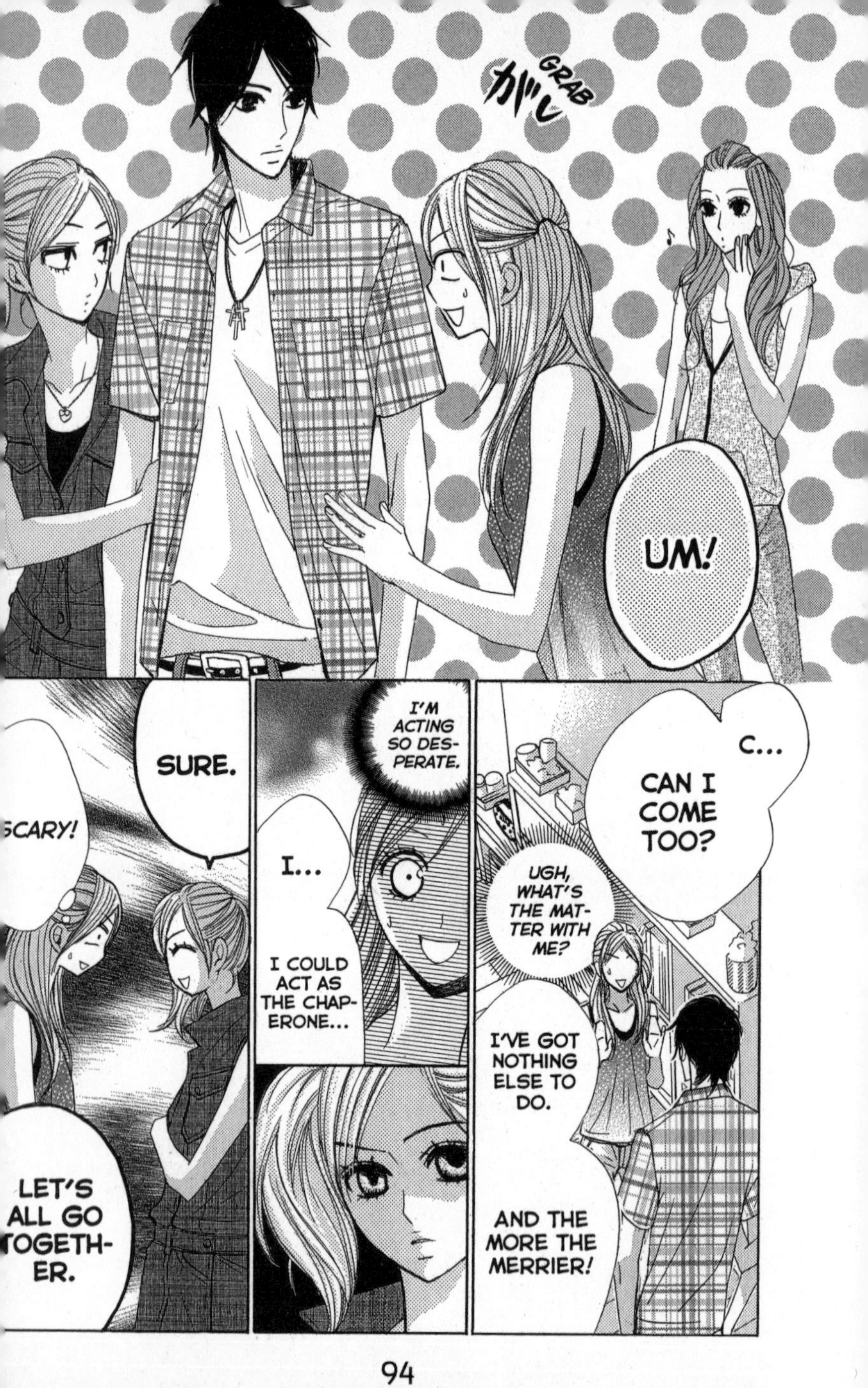
GRAB
UM!
C... CAN I COME TOO?
UGH, WHAT'S THE MATTER WITH ME?
I'VE GOT NOTHING ELSE TO DO.
AND THE MORE THE MERRIER!
I'M ACTING SO DES-PERATE.
I...
I COULD ACT AS THE CHAP-ERONE...
SURE.
SCARY!
LET'S ALL GO TOGETH-ER.

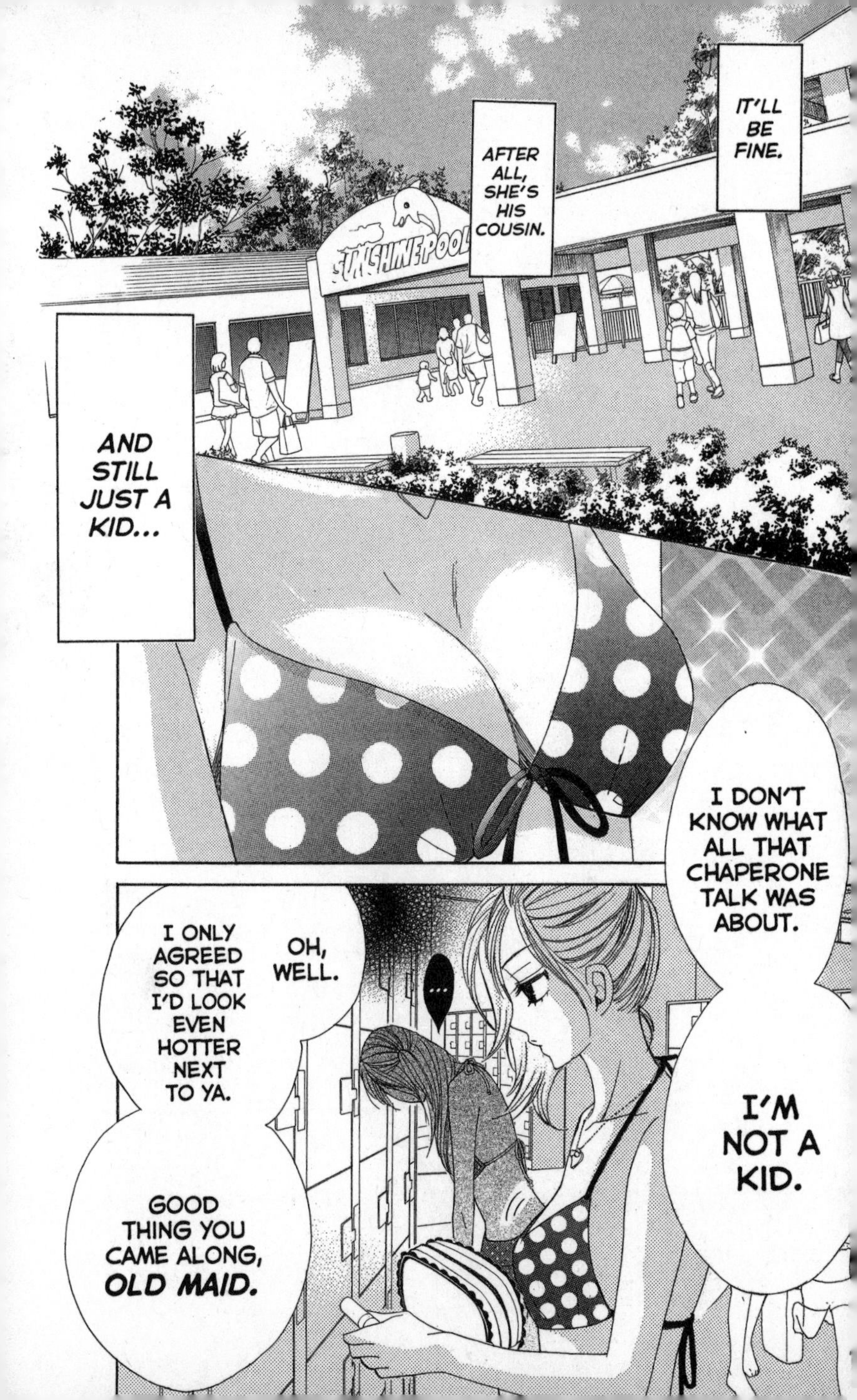

IT'LL BE FINE.
AFTER ALL, SHE'S HIS COUSIN.
SUNSHINE POOL
AND STILL JUST A KID...
I DON'T KNOW WHAT ALL THAT CHAPERONE TALK WAS ABOUT.
I'M NOT A KID.
...
OH, WELL.
I ONLY AGREED SO THAT I'D LOOK EVEN HOTTER NEXT TO YA.
GOOD THING YOU CAME ALONG, **OLD MAID.**

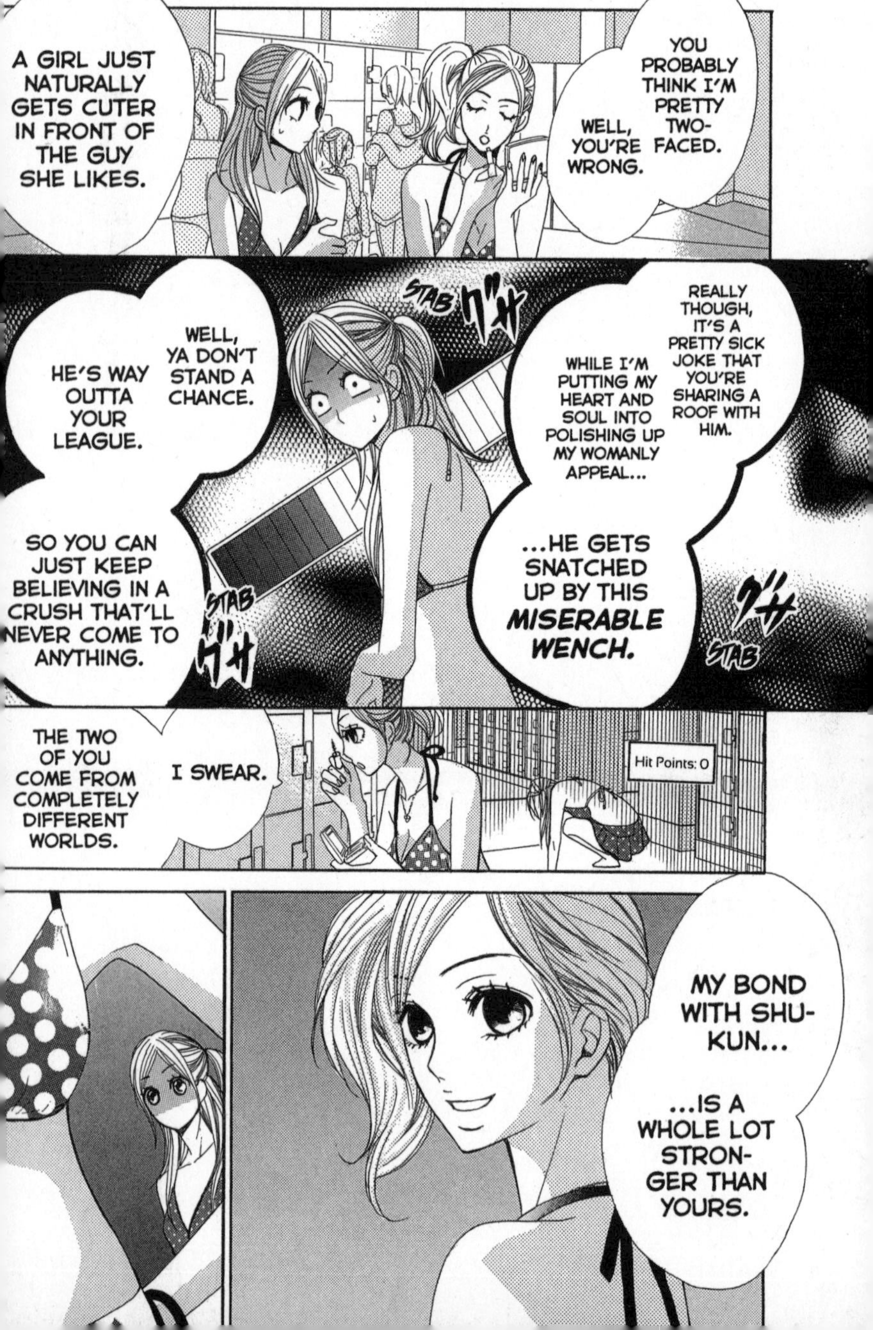
YOU PROBABLY THINK I'M PRETTY TWO-FACED.
WELL, YOU'RE WRONG.
A GIRL JUST NATURALLY GETS CUTER IN FRONT OF THE GUY SHE LIKES.
STAB グサ
REALLY THOUGH, IT'S A PRETTY SICK JOKE THAT YOU'RE SHARING A ROOF WITH HIM.
WHILE I'M PUTTING MY HEART AND SOUL INTO POLISHING UP MY WOMANLY APPEAL...
...HE GETS SNATCHED UP BY THIS *MISERABLE WENCH.*
グサ STAB
WELL, YA DON'T STAND A CHANCE.
HE'S WAY OUTTA YOUR LEAGUE.
SO YOU CAN JUST KEEP BELIEVING IN A CRUSH THAT'LL NEVER COME TO ANYTHING.
STAB グサ
Hit Points: 0
I SWEAR.
THE TWO OF YOU COME FROM COMPLETELY DIFFERENT WORLDS.
MY BOND WITH SHU-KUN...
...IS A WHOLE LOT STRONGER THAN YOURS.

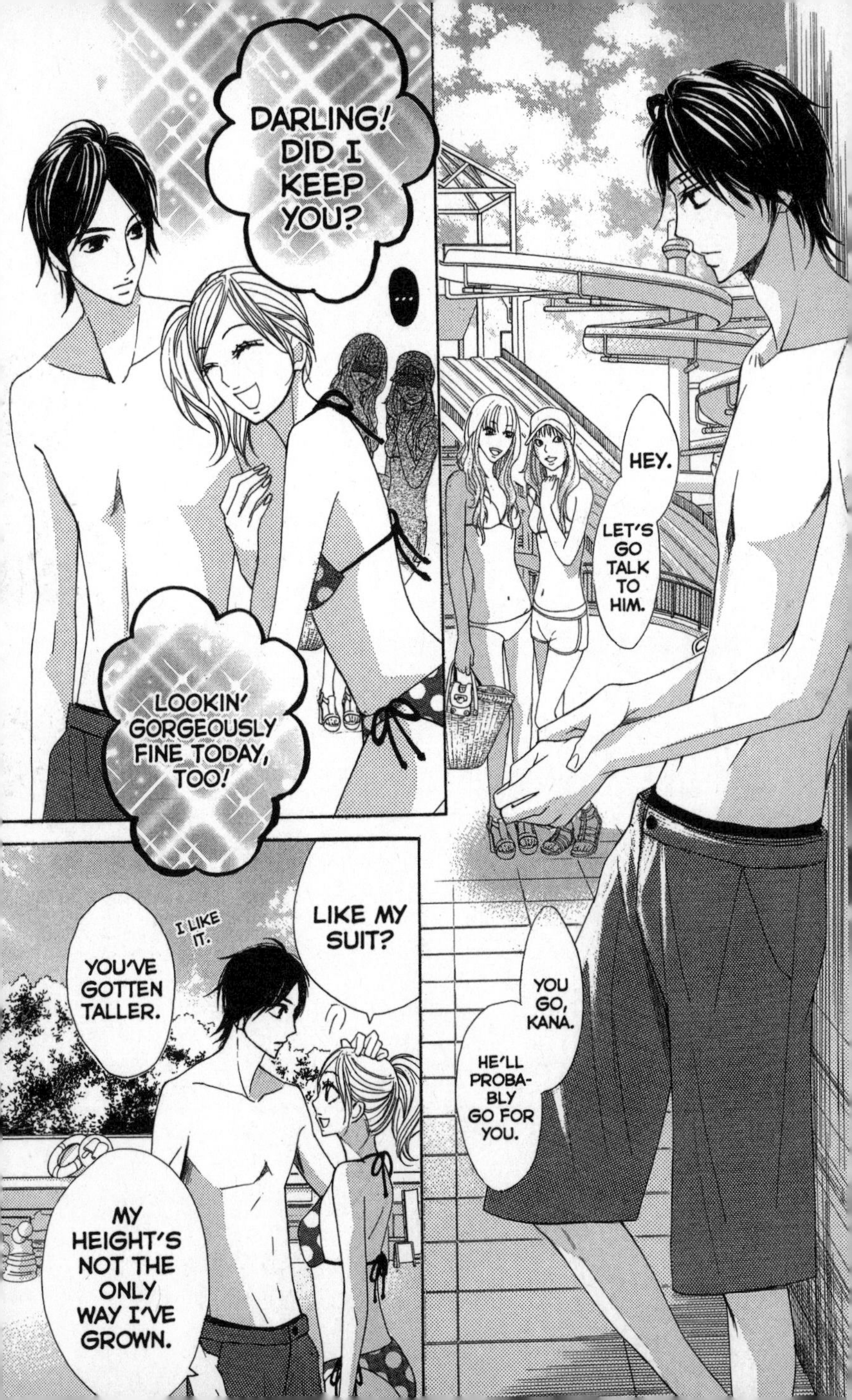
HEY.
LET'S GO TALK TO HIM.
YOU GO, KANA.
HE'LL PROBA-BLY GO FOR YOU.
DARLING! DID I KEEP YOU?
...
LOOKIN' GORGEOUSLY FINE TODAY, TOO!
LIKE MY SUIT?
I LIKE IT.
YOU'VE GOTTEN TALLER.
MY HEIGHT'S NOT THE ONLY WAY I'VE GROWN.

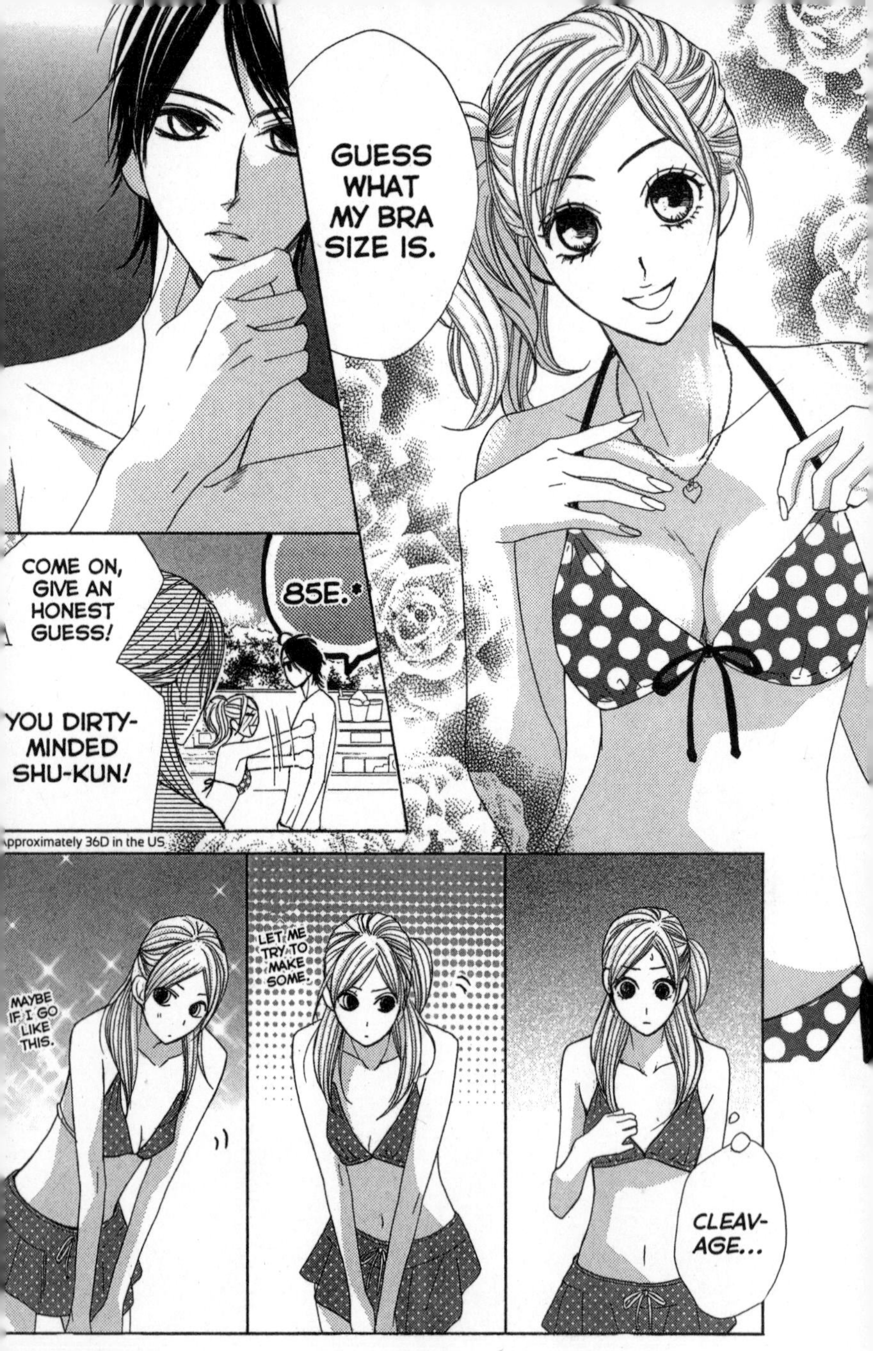
GUESS WHAT MY BRA SIZE IS.
85E.*
COME ON, GIVE AN HONEST GUESS!
YOU DIRTY-MINDED SHU-KUN!
CLEAV-AGE...
LET ME TRY TO MAKE SOME.
MAYBE IF I GO LIKE THIS.

*Approximately 36D in the US.

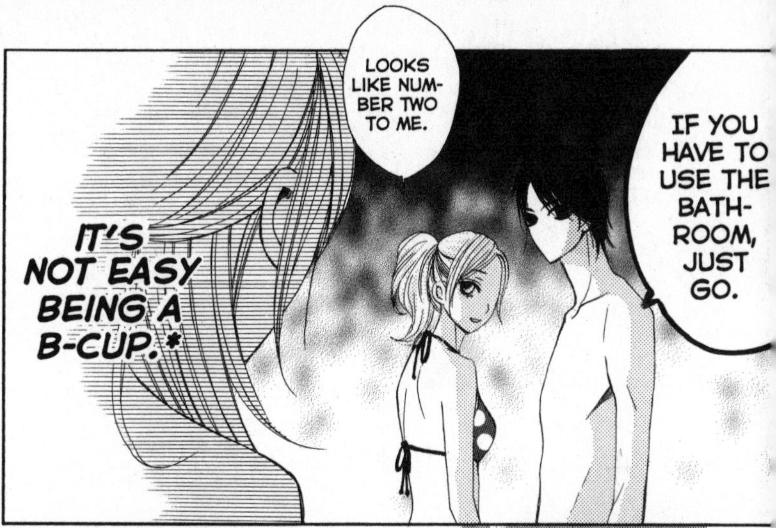
IF YOU HAVE TO USE THE BATH-ROOM, JUST GO.
LOOKS LIKE NUM-BER TWO TO ME.
IT'S NOT EASY BEING A B-CUP.*

*An A-cup in the US.

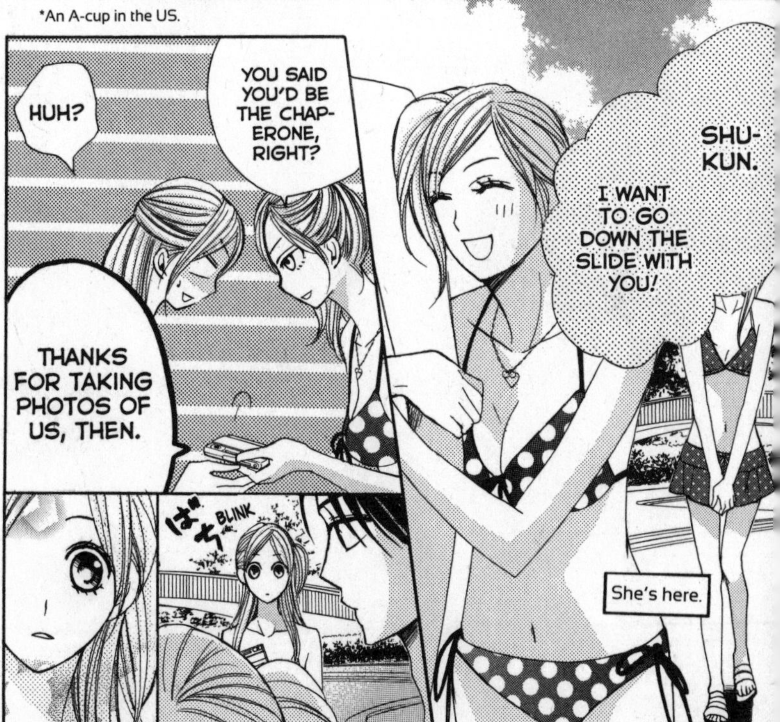
SHU-KUN.
I WANT TO GO DOWN THE SLIDE WITH YOU!
She's here.
YOU SAID YOU'D BE THE CHAP-ERONE, RIGHT?
HUH?
THANKS FOR TAKING PHOTOS OF US, THEN.
ぱち BLINK

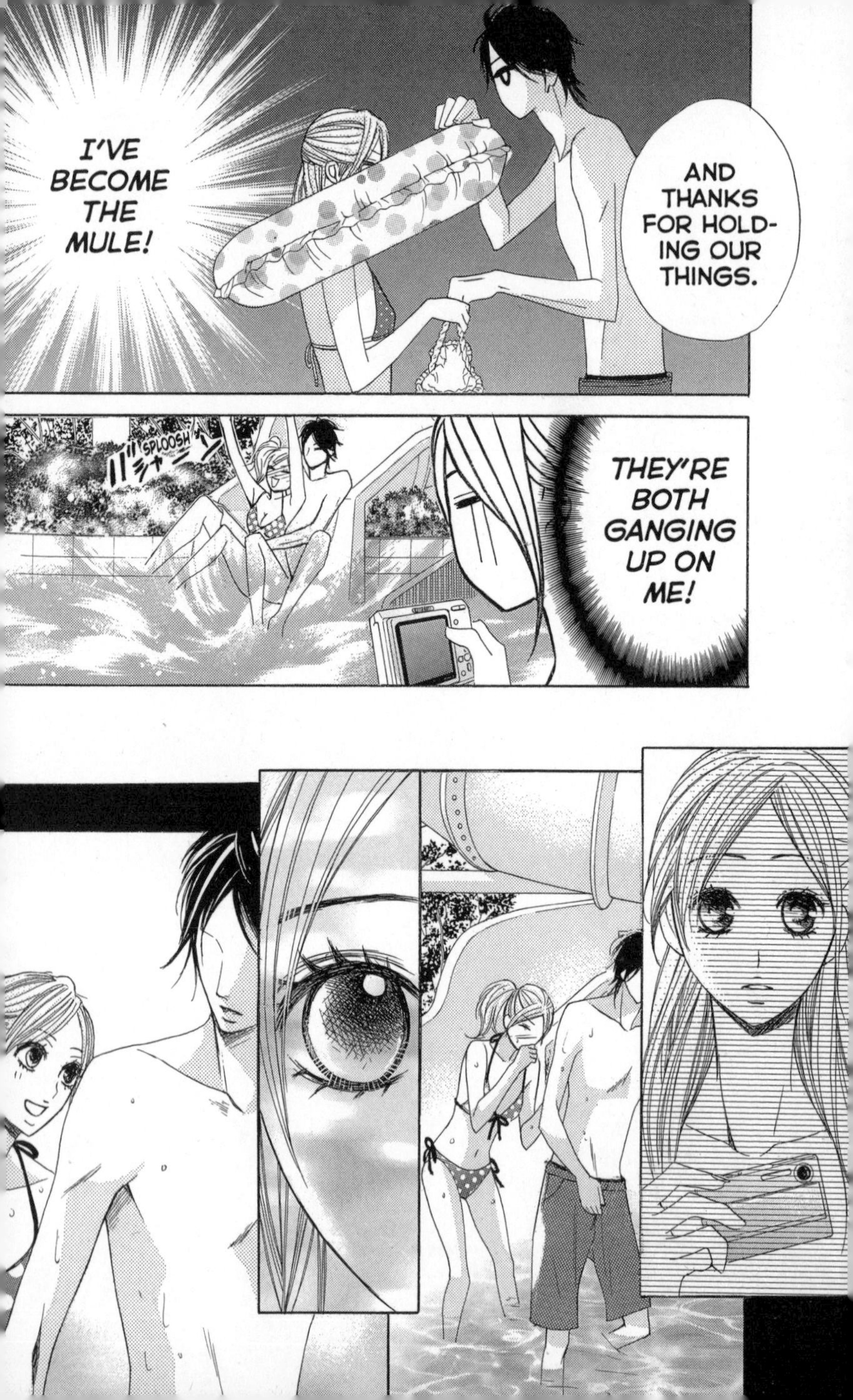
AND THANKS FOR HOLDING OUR THINGS.
I'VE BECOME THE MULE!
THEY'RE BOTH GANGING UP ON ME!
SPLOOSH

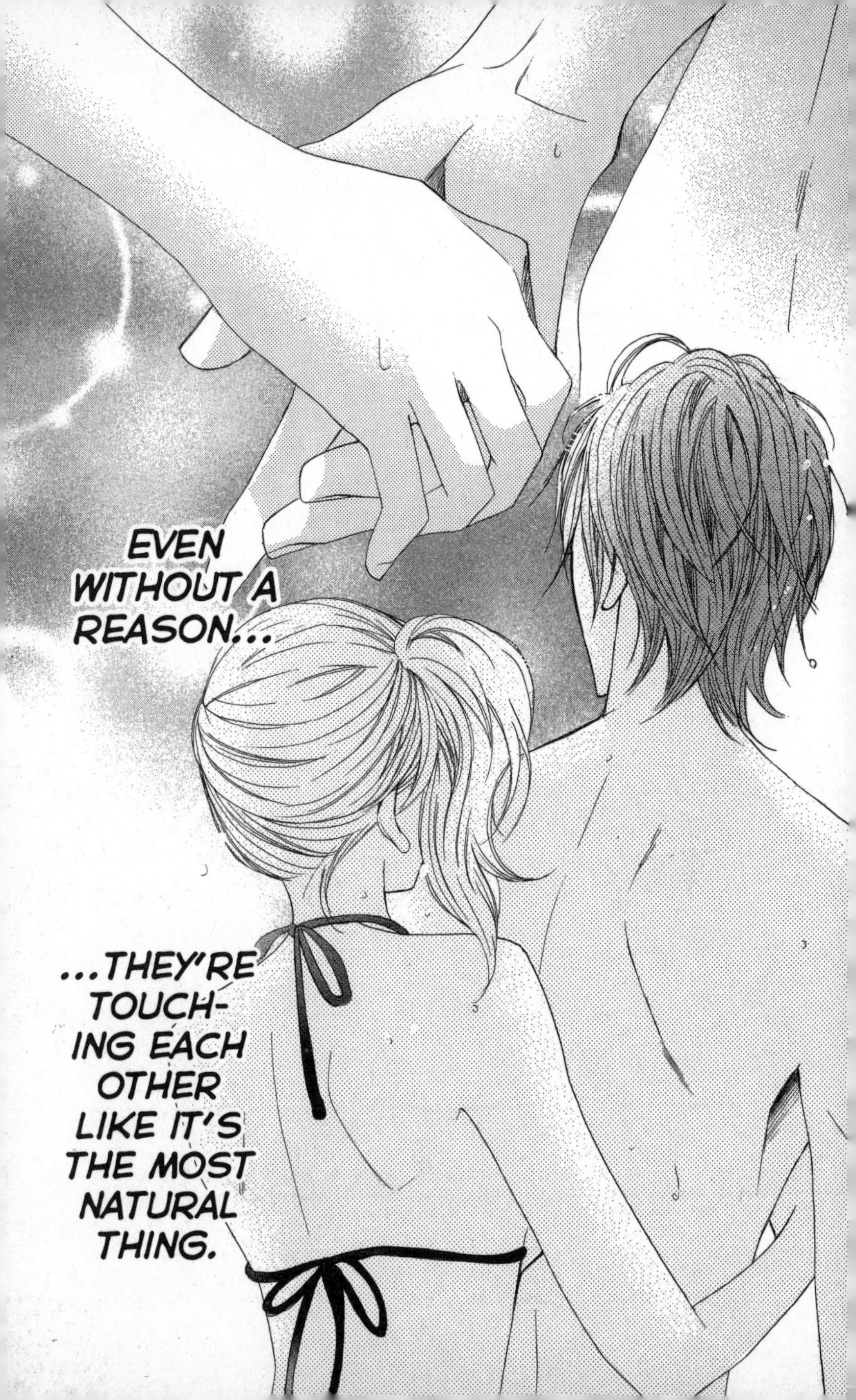
EVEN WITHOUT A REASON...
...THEY'RE TOUCH-ING EACH OTHER LIKE IT'S THE MOST NATURAL THING.

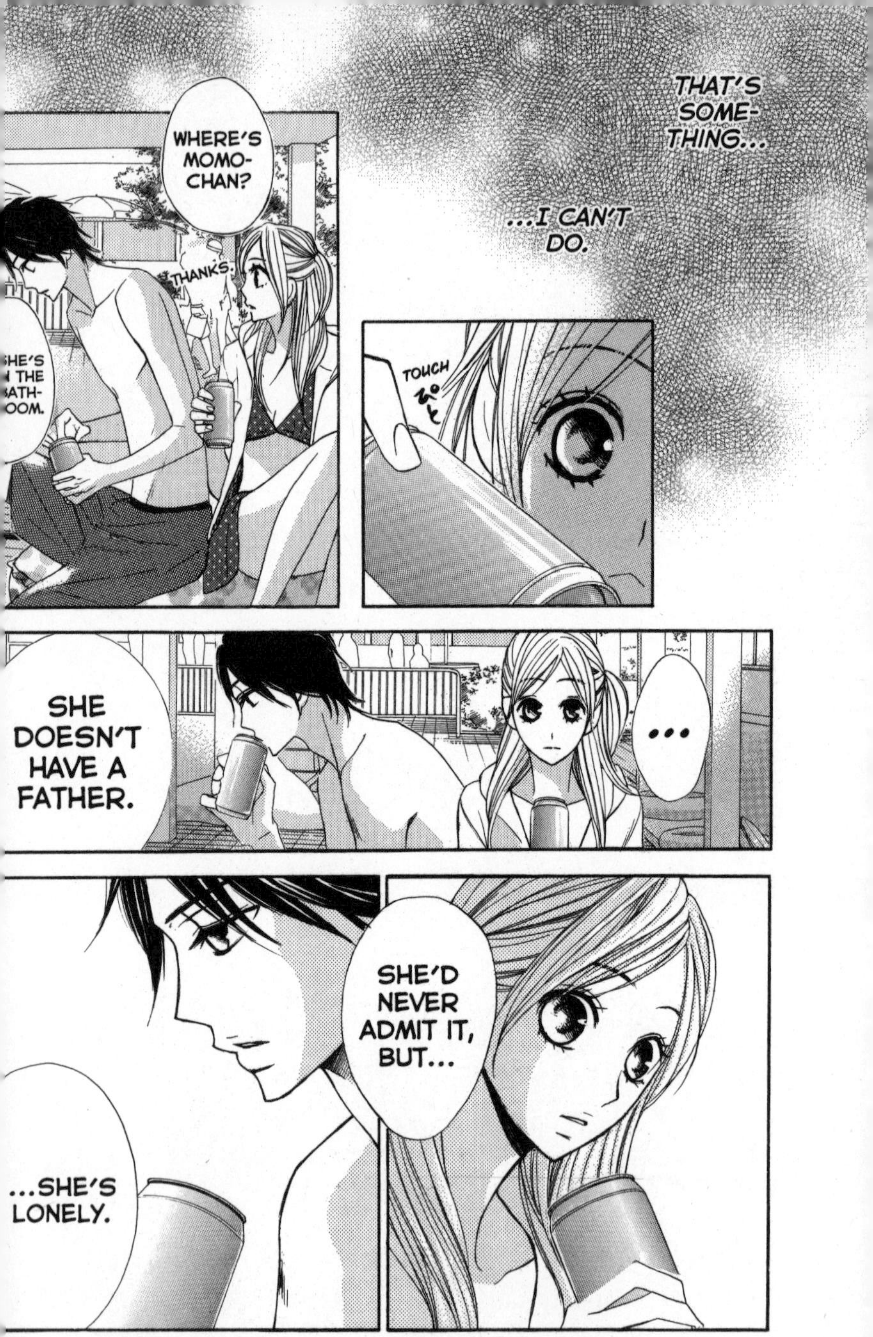
THAT'S SOMETHING...
...I CAN'T DO.
TOUCH
ぴと
WHERE'S MOMO-CHAN?
THANKS.
HE'S N THE ATH-OOM.
...
SHE DOESN'T HAVE A FATHER.
SHE'D NEVER ADMIT IT, BUT...
...SHE'S LONELY.

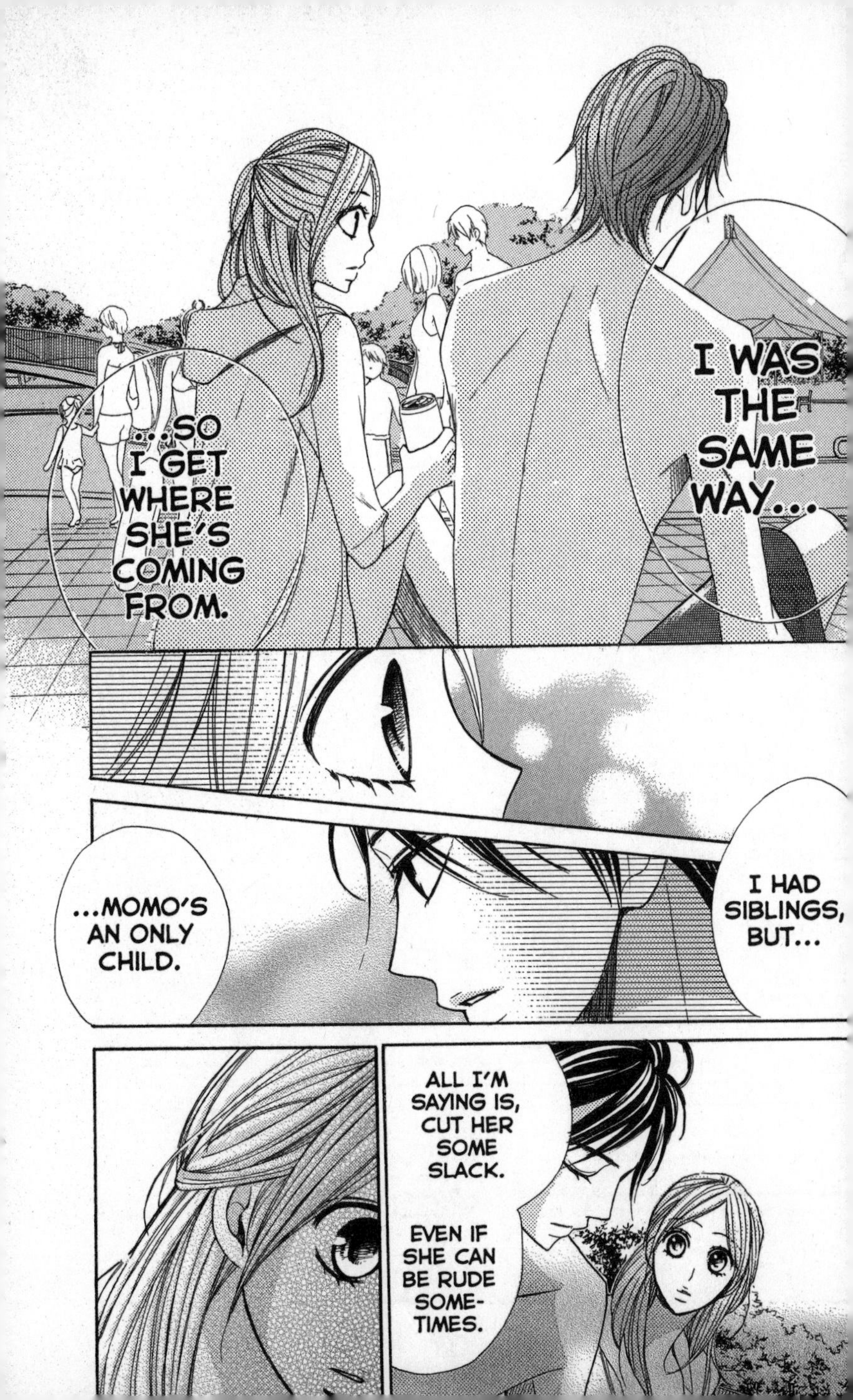
I WAS THE SAME WAY...
...SO I GET WHERE SHE'S COMING FROM.
I HAD SIBLINGS, BUT...
...MOMO'S AN ONLY CHILD.
ALL I'M SAYING IS, CUT HER SOME SLACK.
EVEN IF SHE CAN BE RUDE SOME-TIMES.

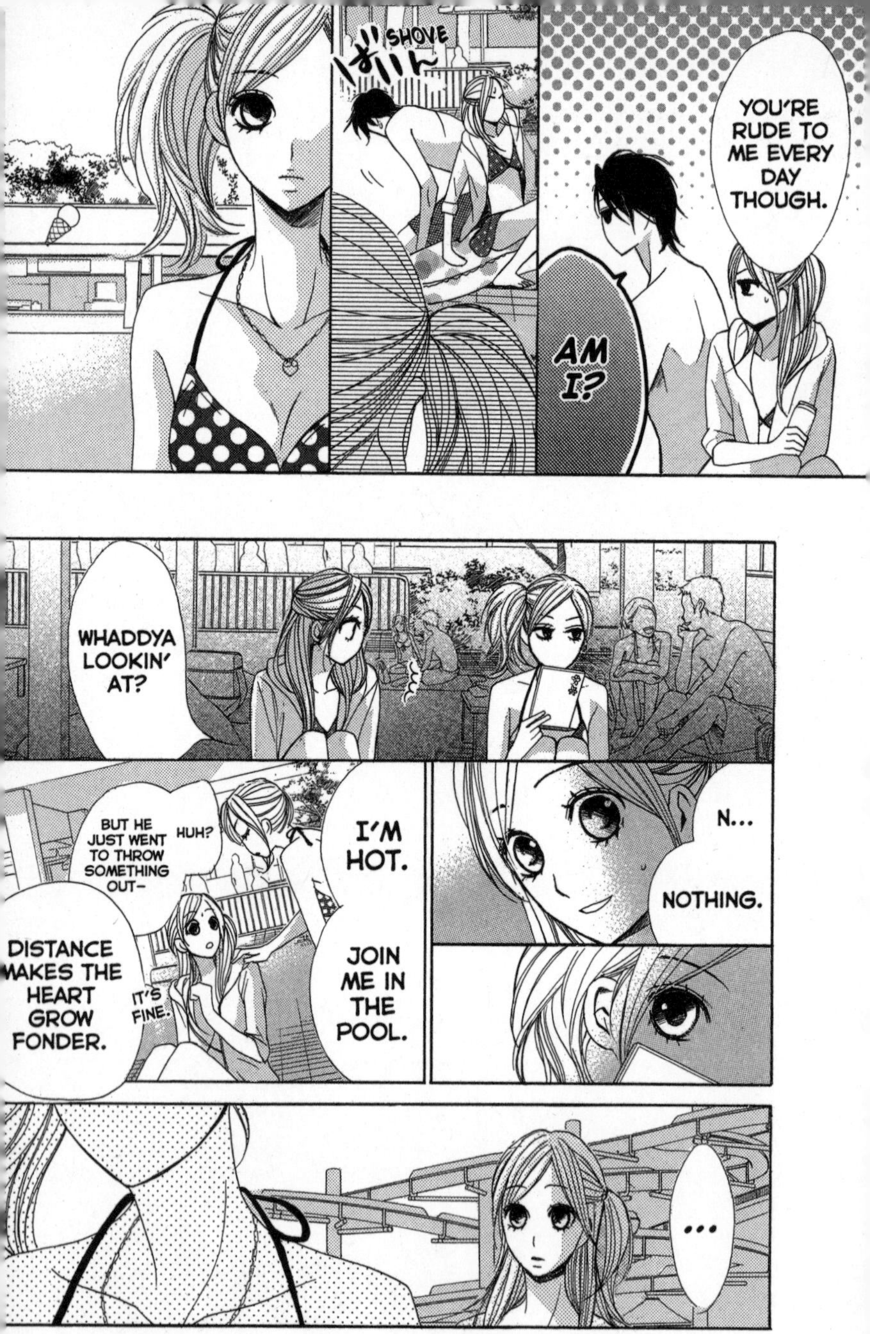
YOU'RE RUDE TO ME EVERY DAY THOUGH.
AM I?
SHOVE
WHADDYA LOOKIN' AT?
N...
NOTHING.
I'M HOT.
JOIN ME IN THE POOL.
HUH?
BUT HE JUST WENT TO THROW SOMETHING OUT—
IT'S FINE.
DISTANCE MAKES THE HEART GROW FONDER.
...

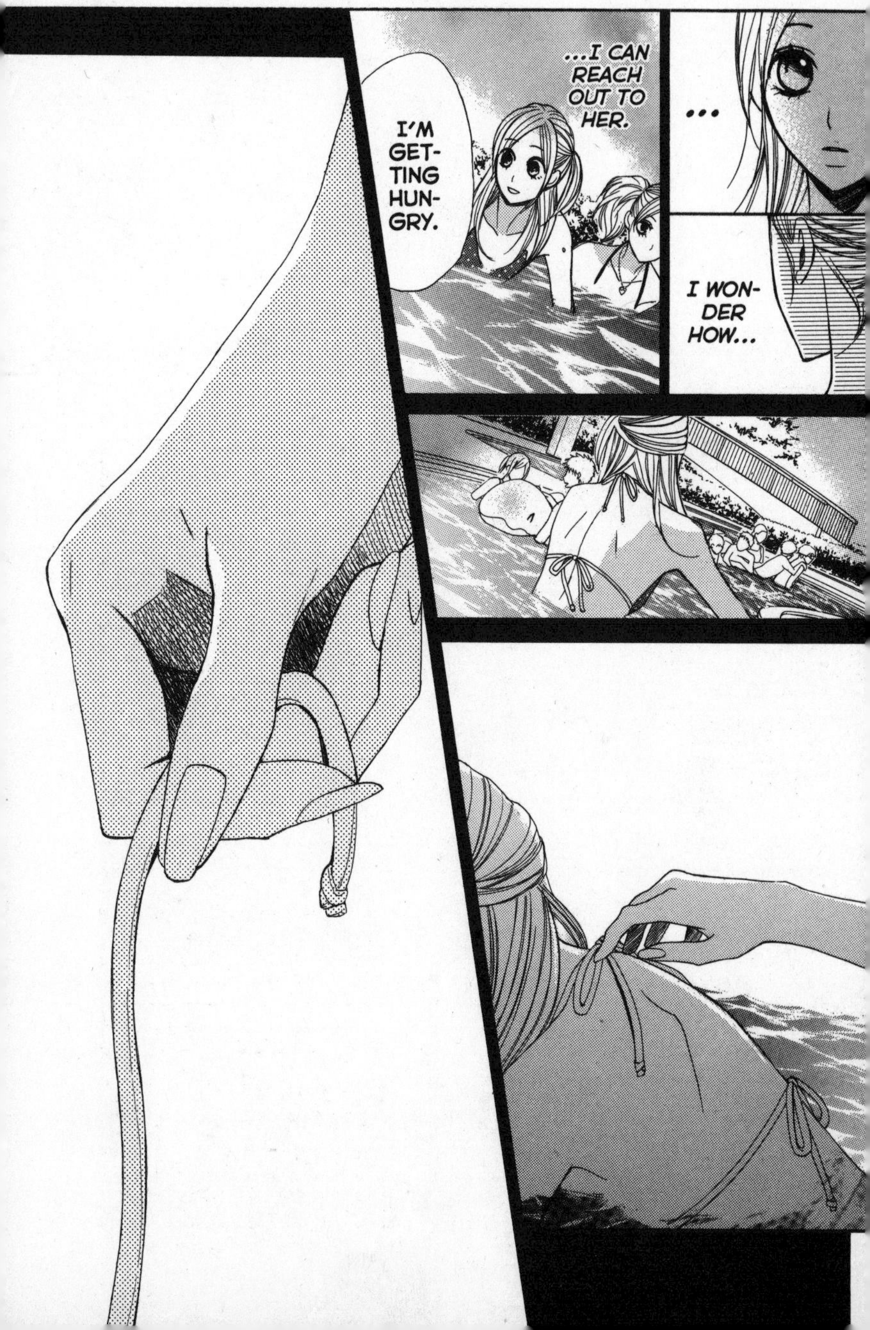
...
I WONDER HOW...
...I CAN REACH OUT TO HER.
I'M GETTING HUNGRY.

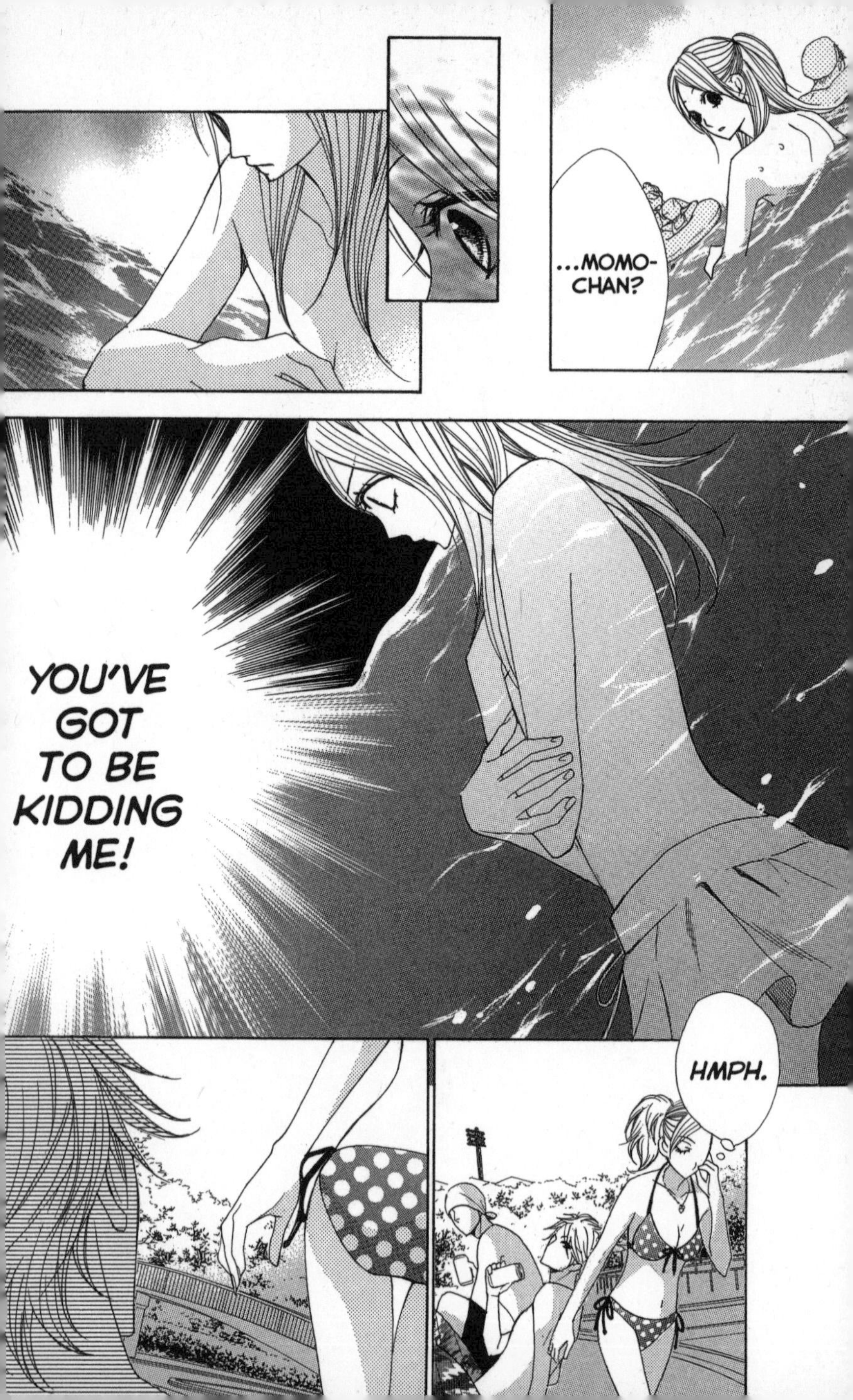
...MOMO-CHAN?
YOU'VE GOT TO BE KIDDING ME!
HMPH.

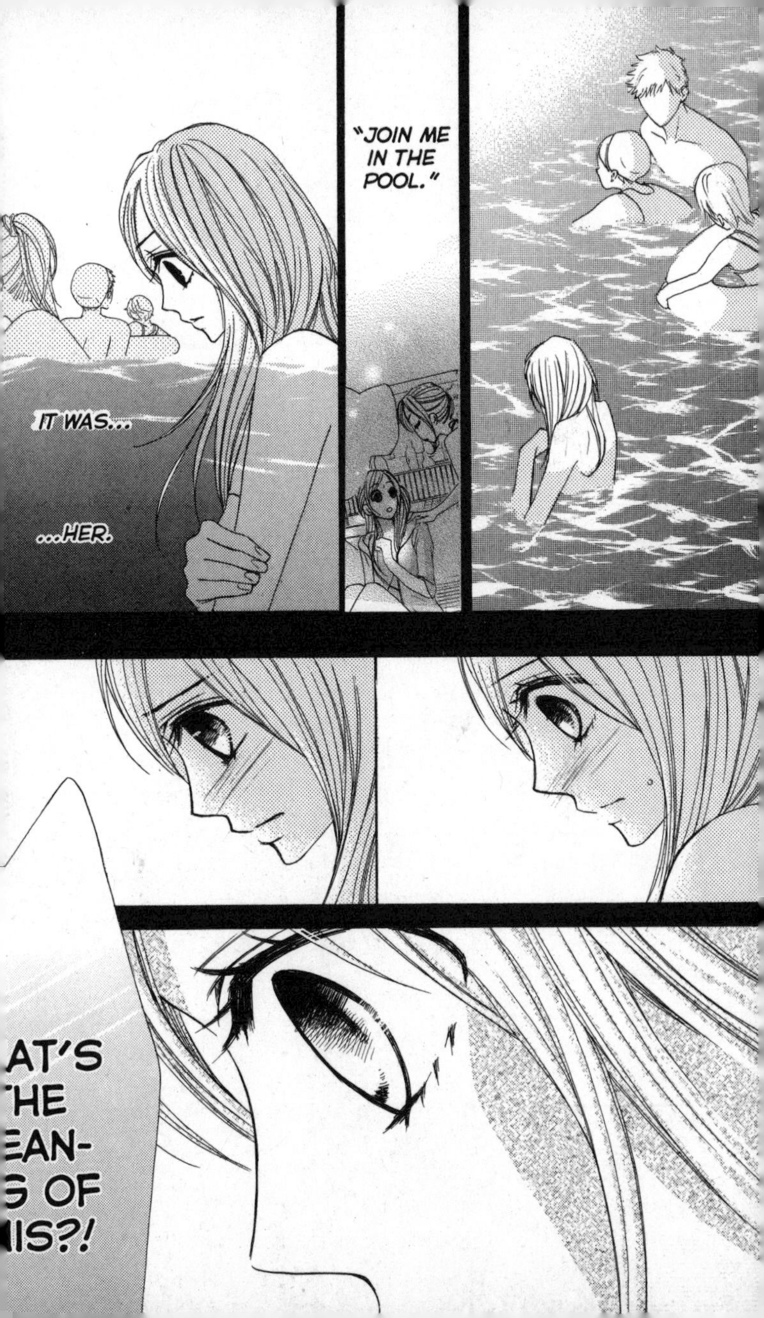
"JOIN ME IN THE POOL."
IT WAS...
...HER.
AT'S THE EAN- G OF IS?!

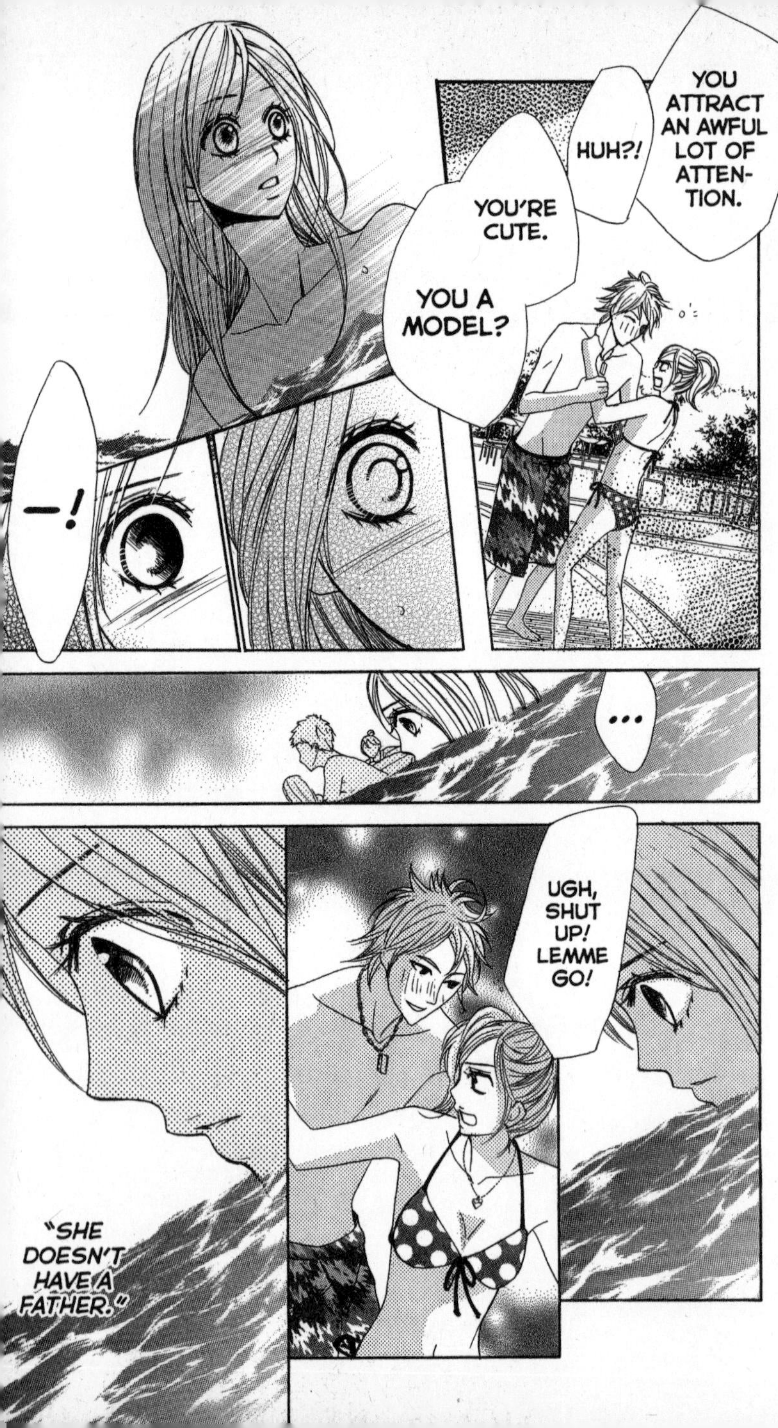
YOU ATTRACT AN AWFUL LOT OF ATTEN-TION.
HUH?!
YOU'RE CUTE.
YOU A MODEL?
—!
...
UGH, SHUT UP! LEMME GO!
"SHE DOESN'T HAVE A FATHER."

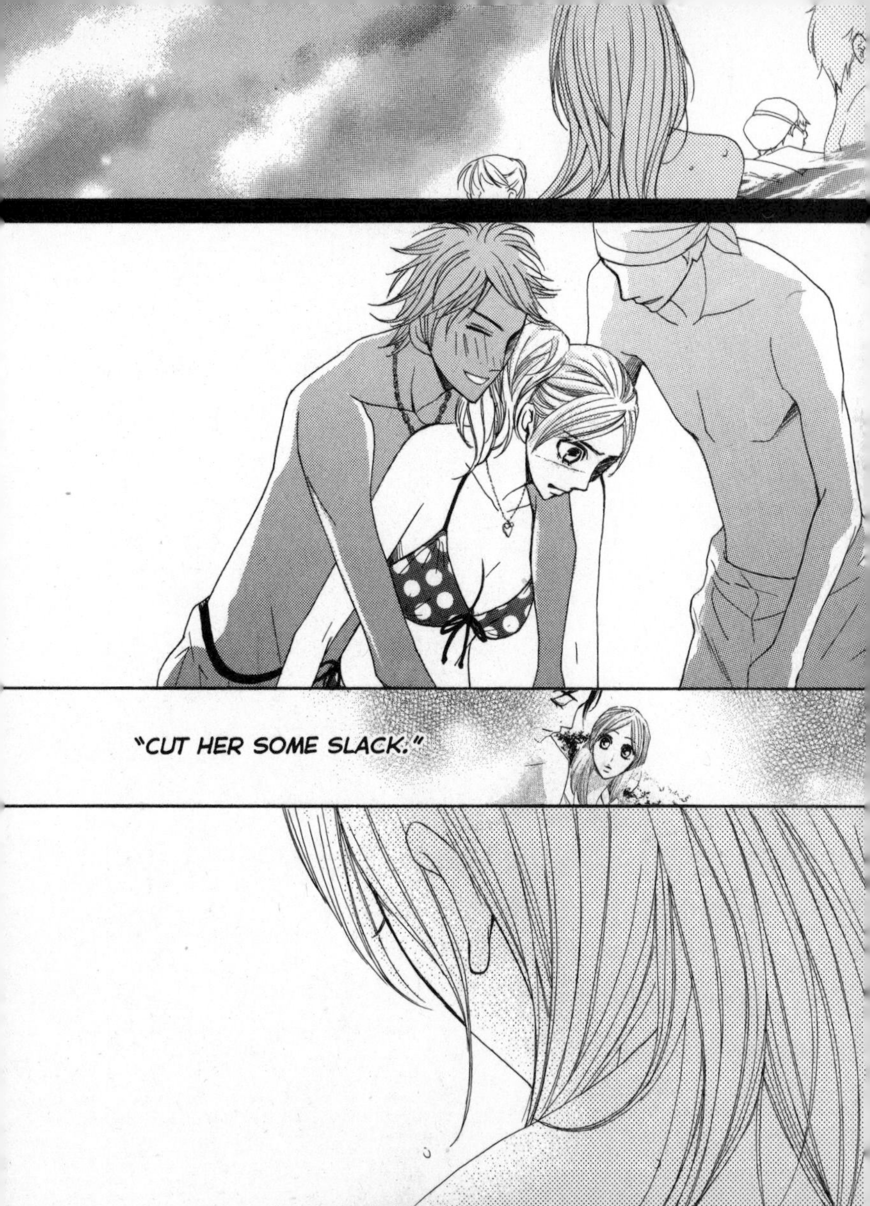
"CUT HER SOME SLACK."

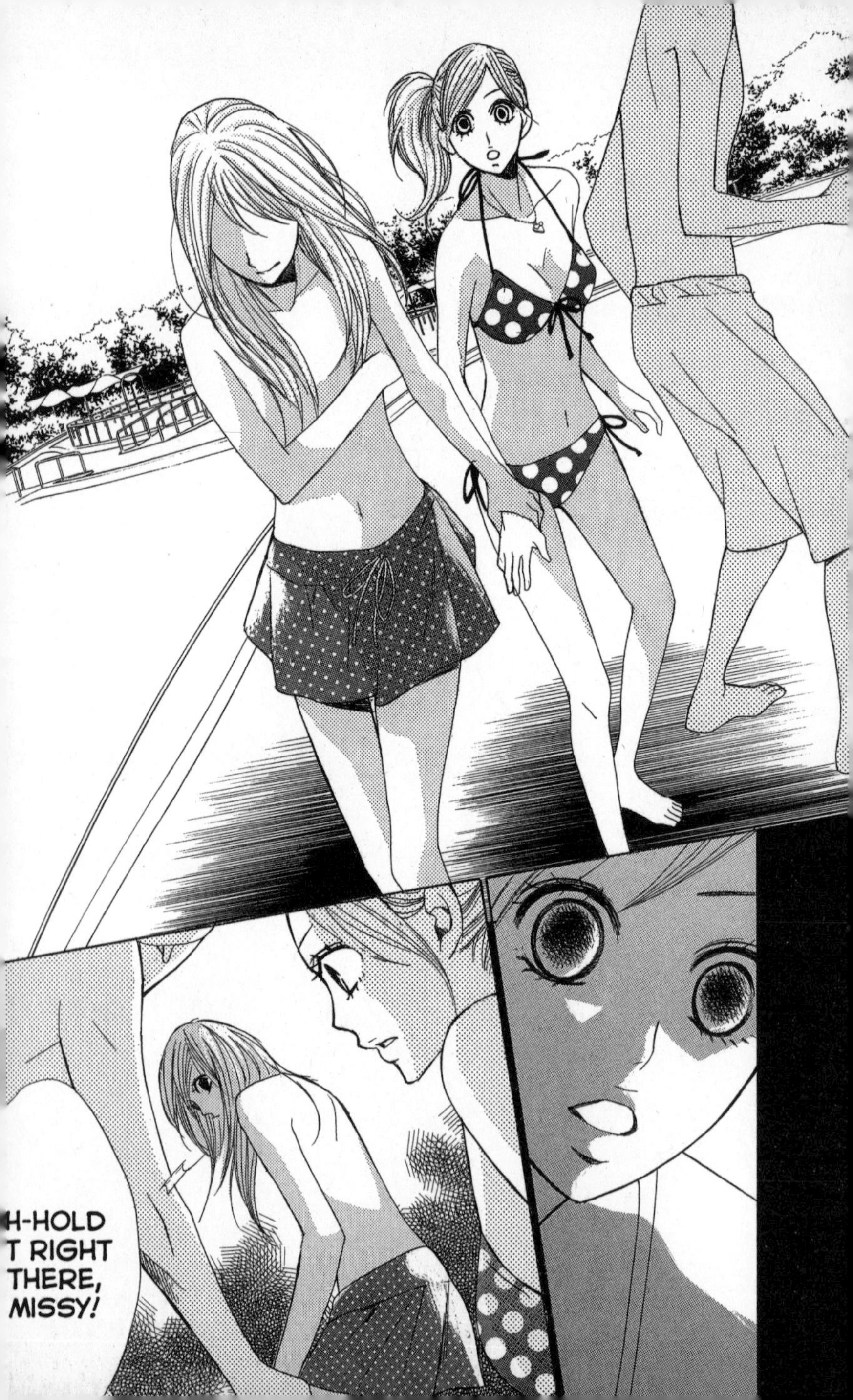

H-HOLD
T RIGHT
THERE,
MISSY!

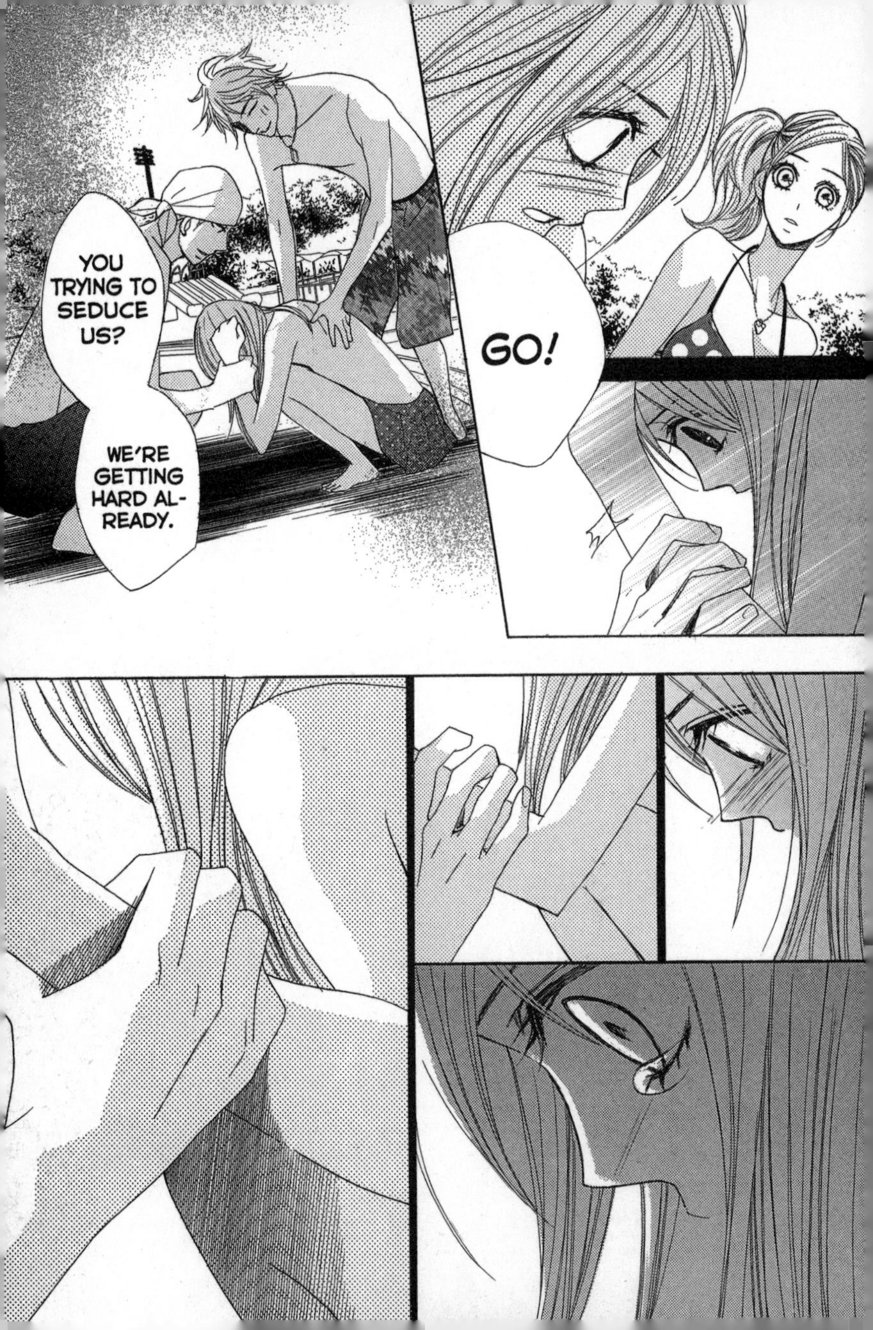
GO!
YOU TRYING TO SEDUCE US?
WE'RE GETTING HARD AL-READY.

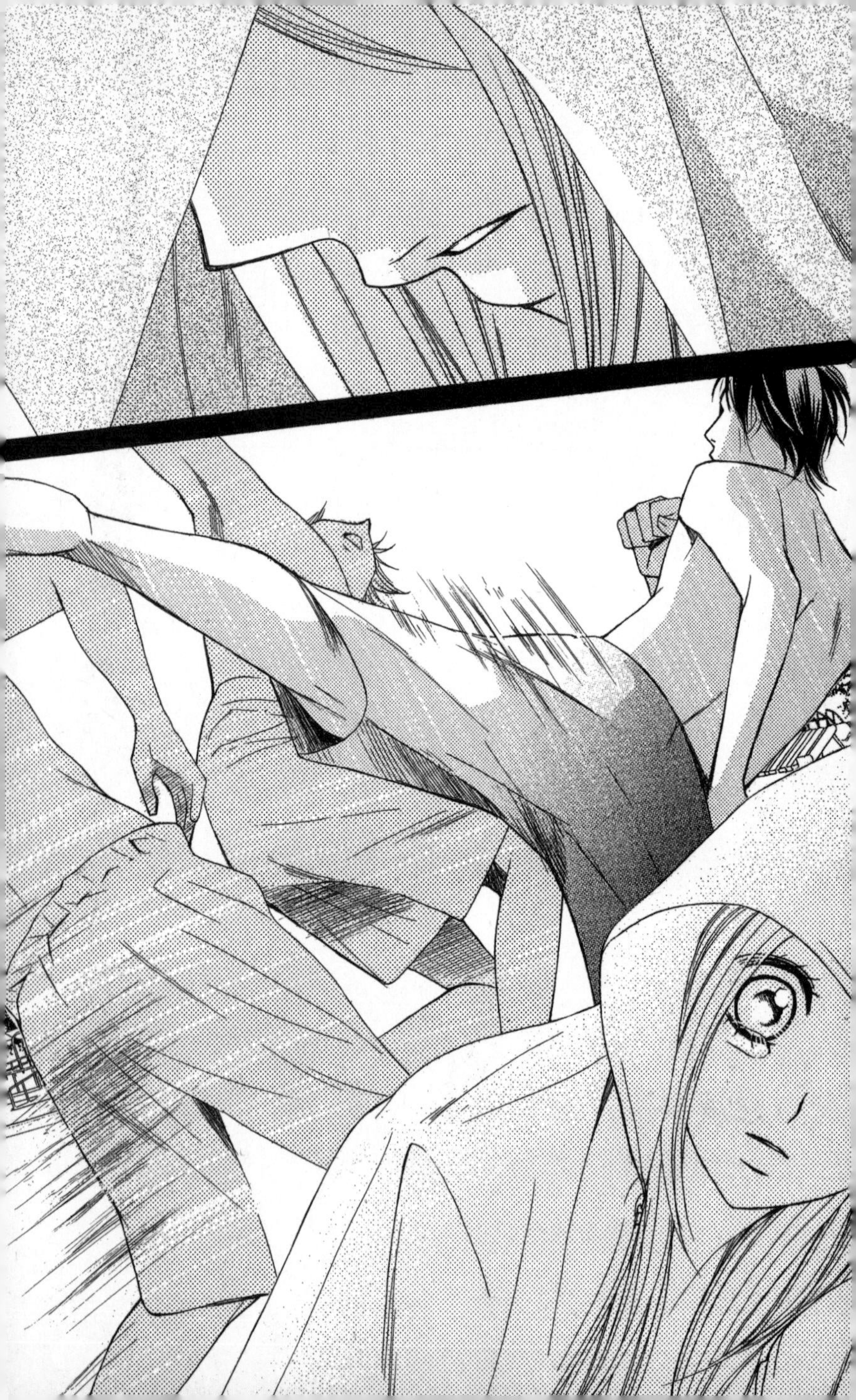

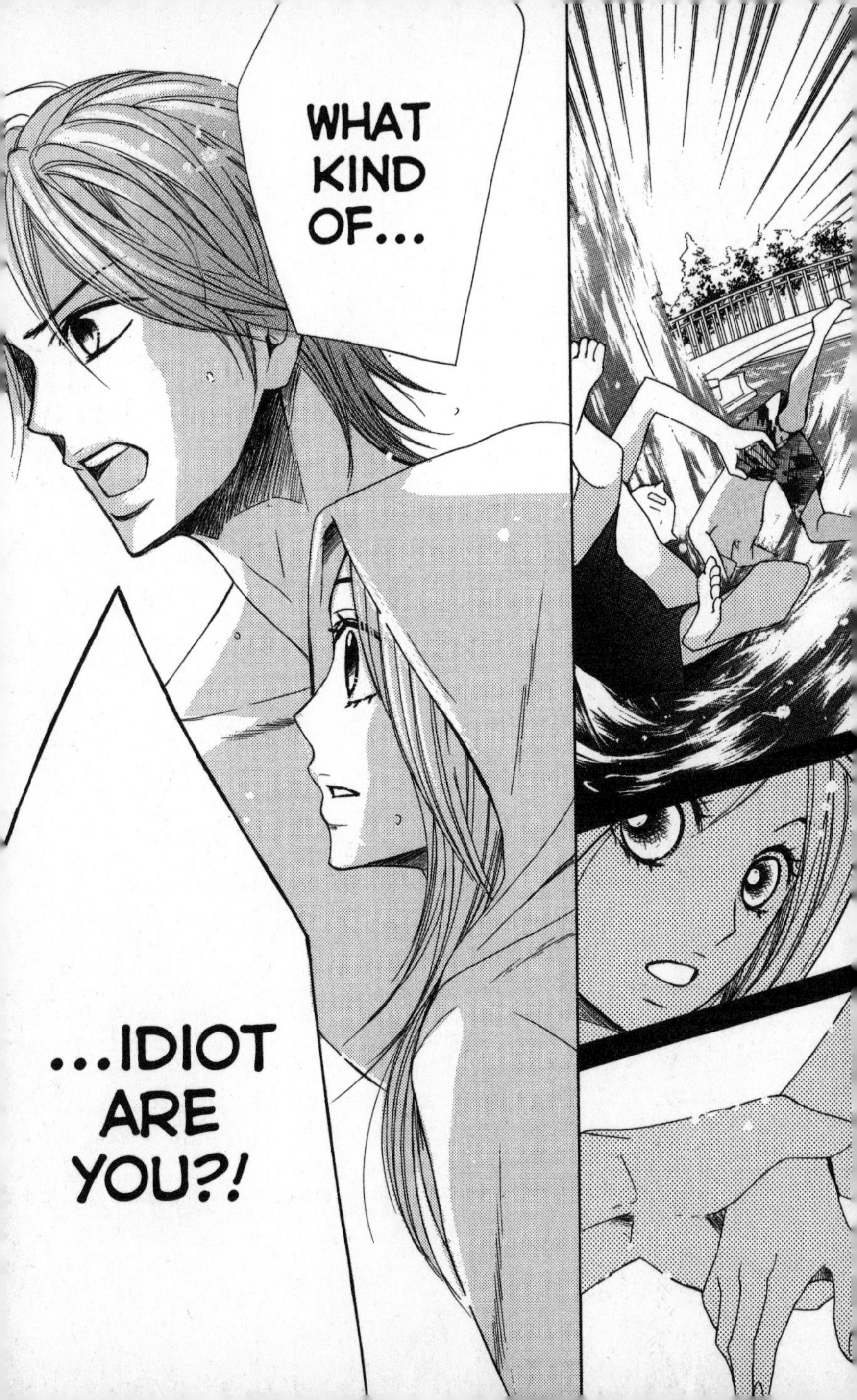
WHAT KIND OF...
...IDIOT ARE YOU?!

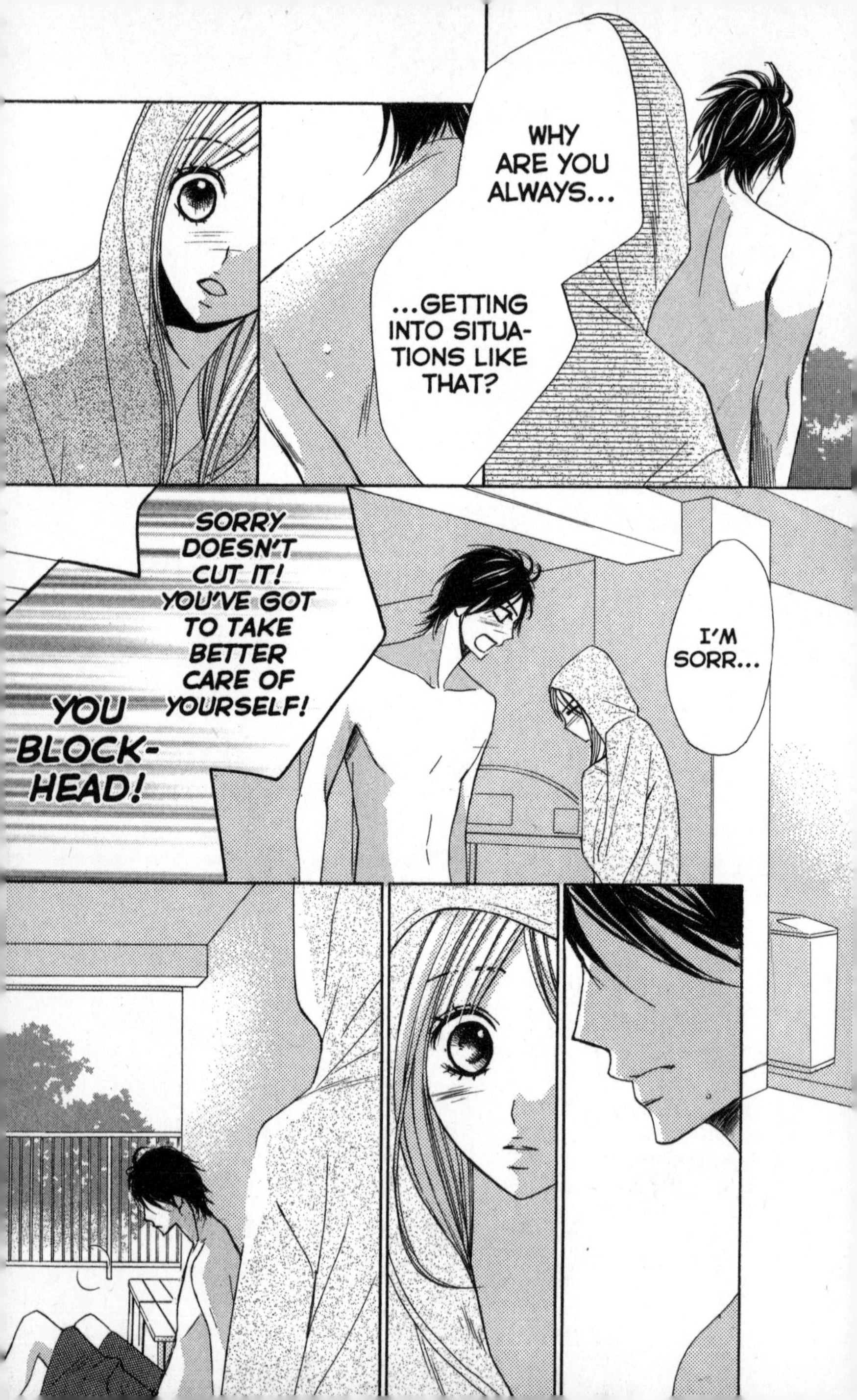
WHY ARE YOU ALWAYS...
...GETTING INTO SITUATIONS LIKE THAT?
I'M SORR...
SORRY DOESN'T CUT IT! YOU'VE GOT TO TAKE BETTER CARE OF YOURSELF!
YOU BLOCKHEAD!

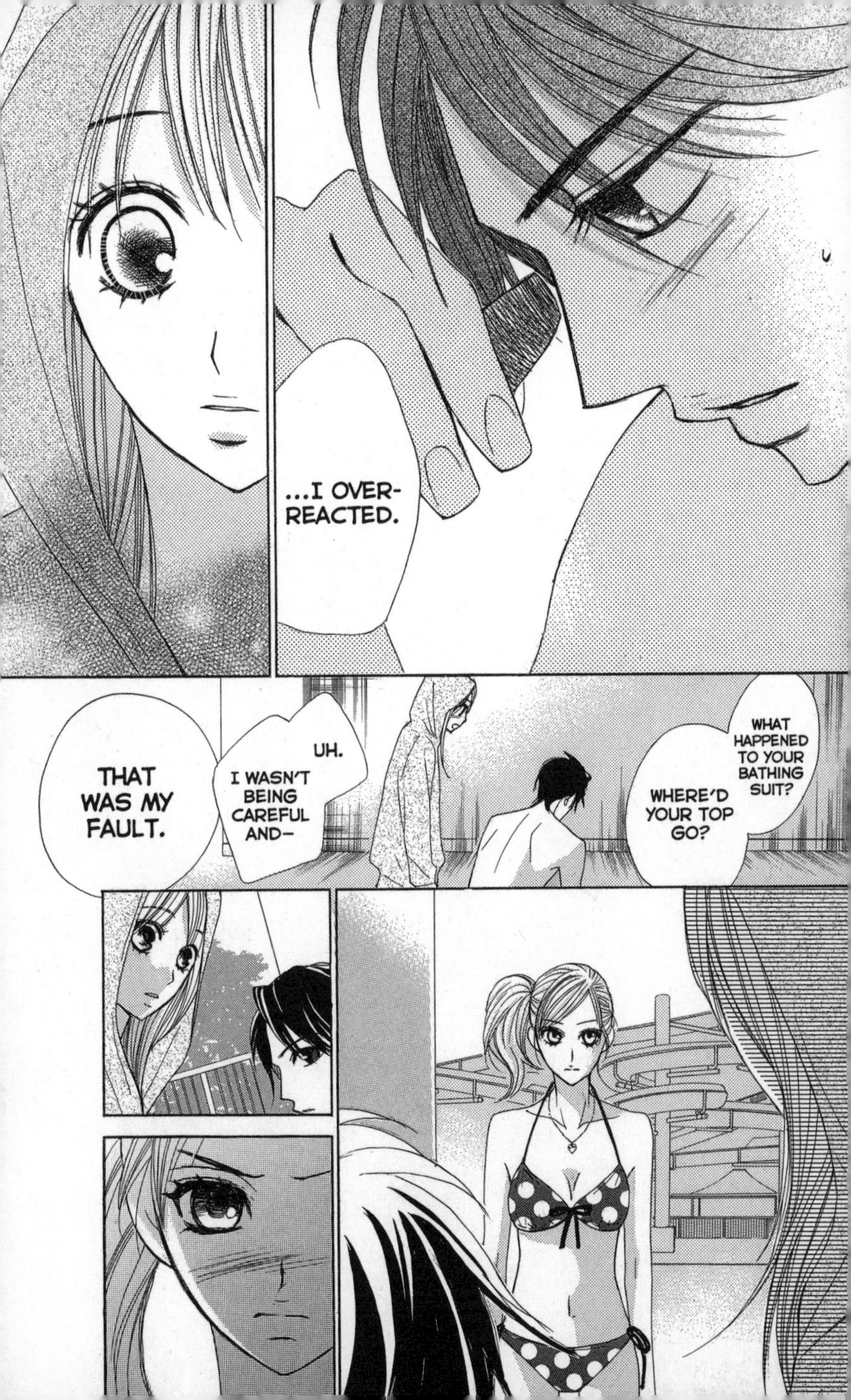
...I OVER-REACTED.
WHAT HAPPENED TO YOUR BATHING SUIT?
WHERE'D YOUR TOP GO?
UH.
I WASN'T BEING CAREFUL AND—
THAT WAS MY FAULT.

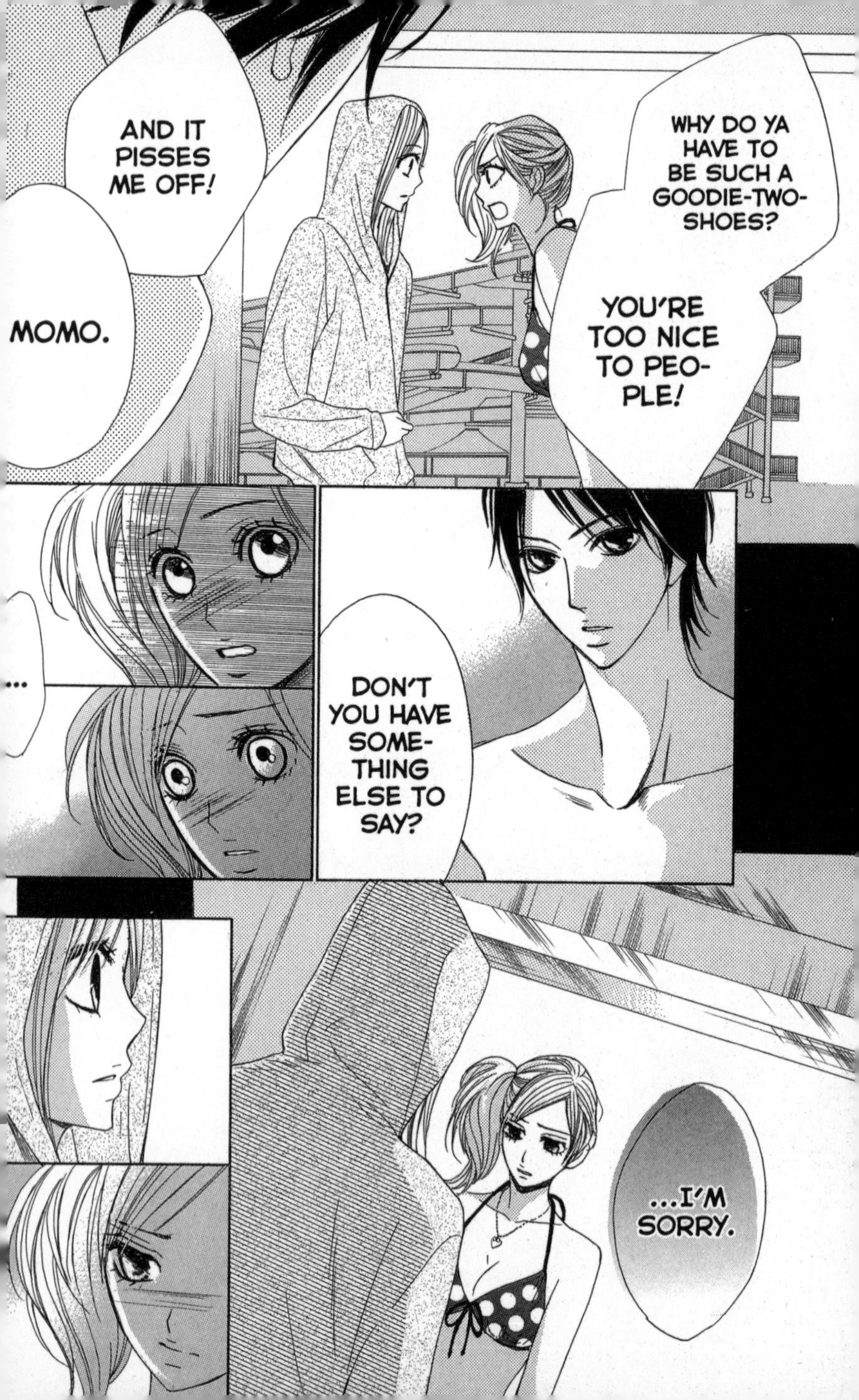
WHY DO YA HAVE TO BE SUCH A GOODIE-TWO-SHOES?
YOU'RE TOO NICE TO PEO-PLE!
AND IT PISSES ME OFF!
MOMO.
DON'T YOU HAVE SOME-THING ELSE TO SAY?
...
...I'M SORRY.

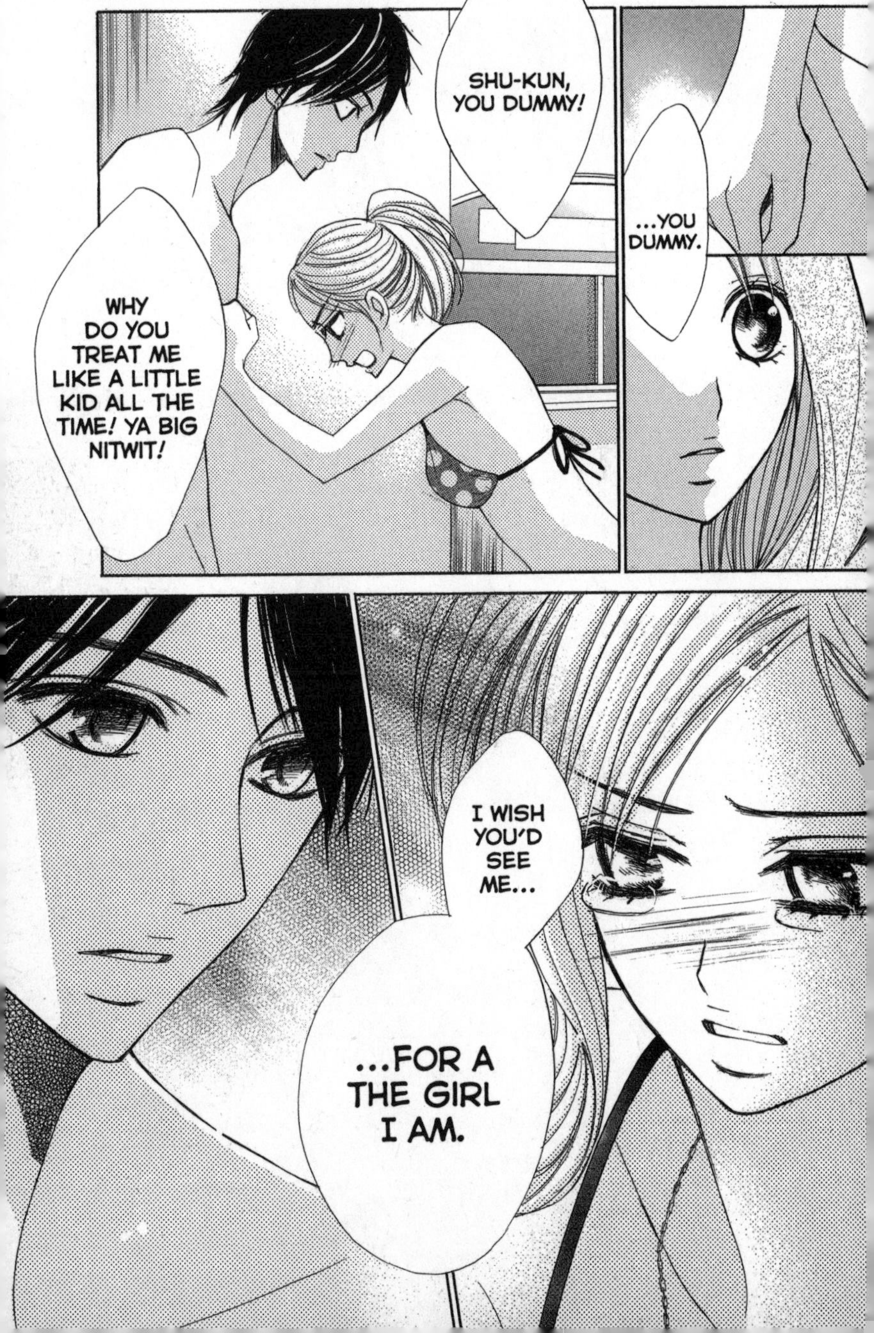
...YOU DUMMY.
SHU-KUN, YOU DUMMY!
WHY DO YOU TREAT ME LIKE A LITTLE KID ALL THE TIME! YA BIG NITWIT!
I WISH YOU'D SEE ME...
...FOR A THE GIRL I AM.

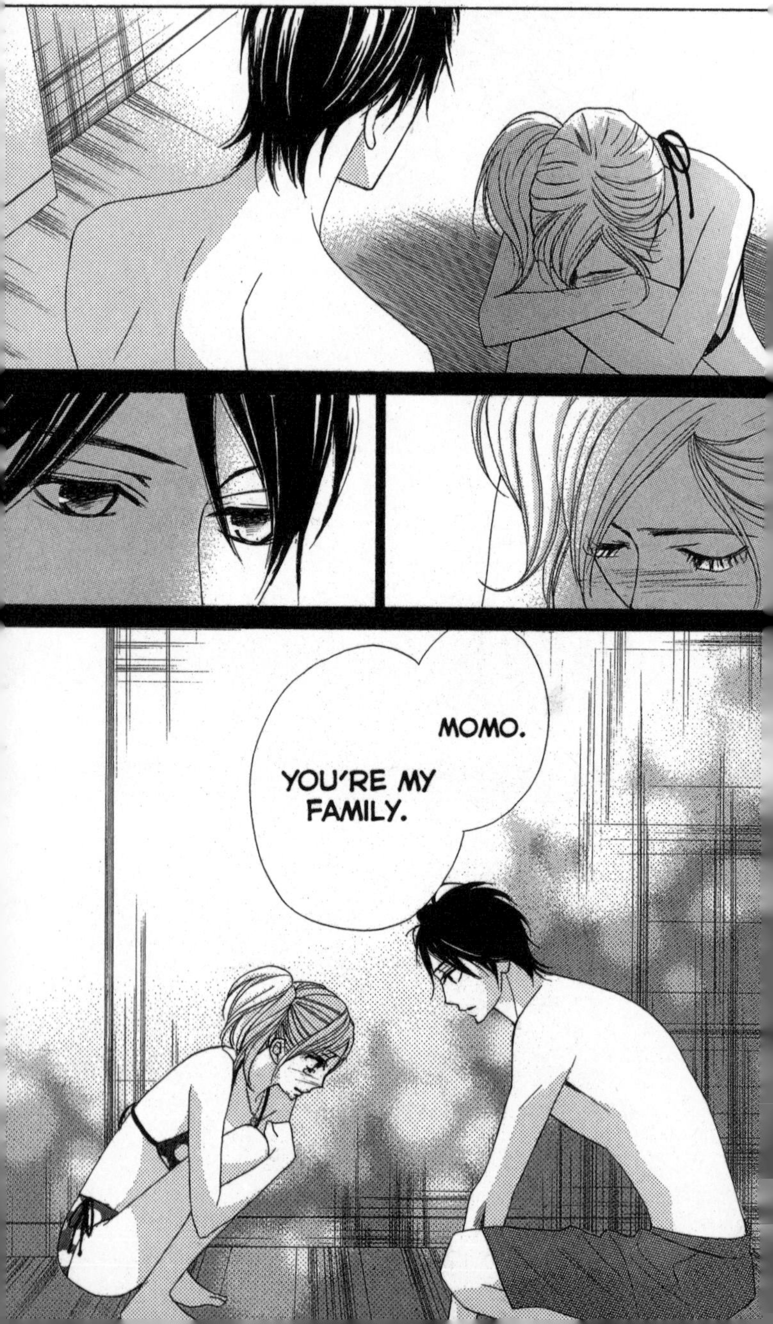
MOMO.
YOU'RE MY FAMILY.

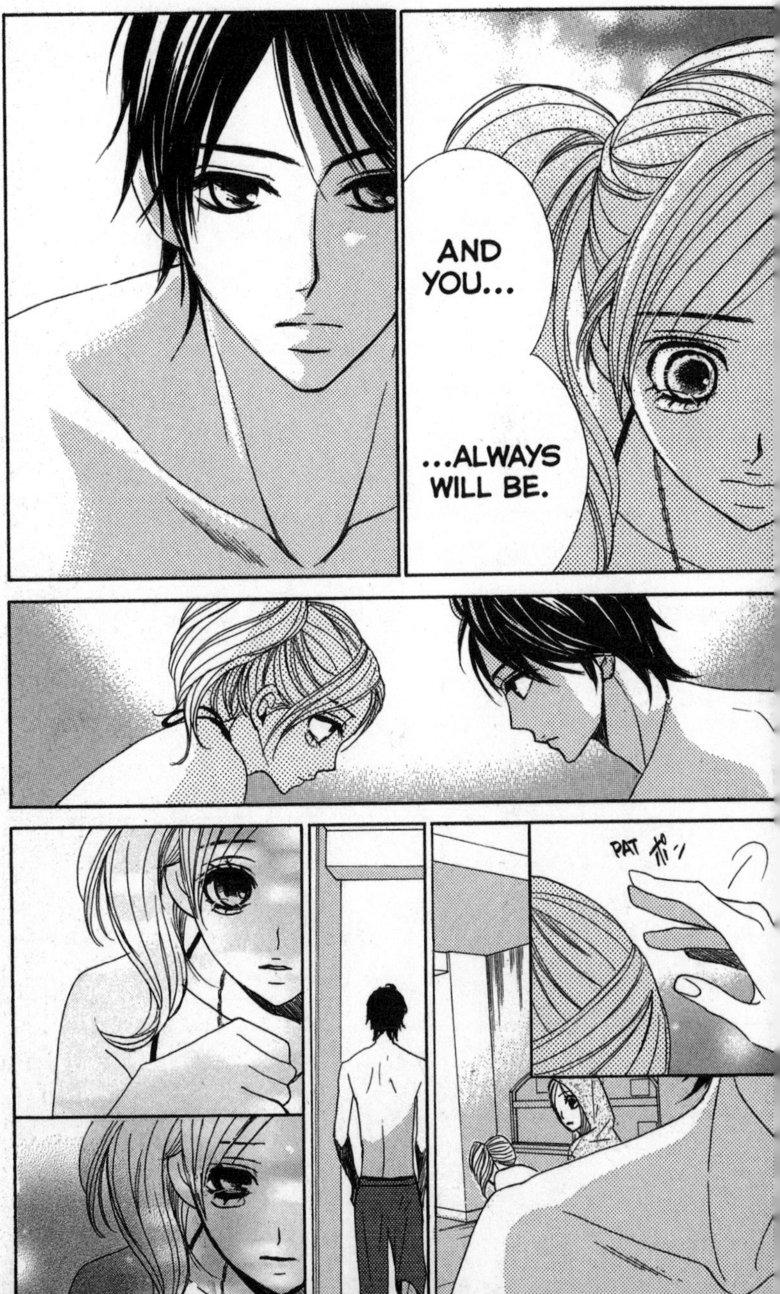
AND YOU...
...ALWAYS WILL BE.
PAT

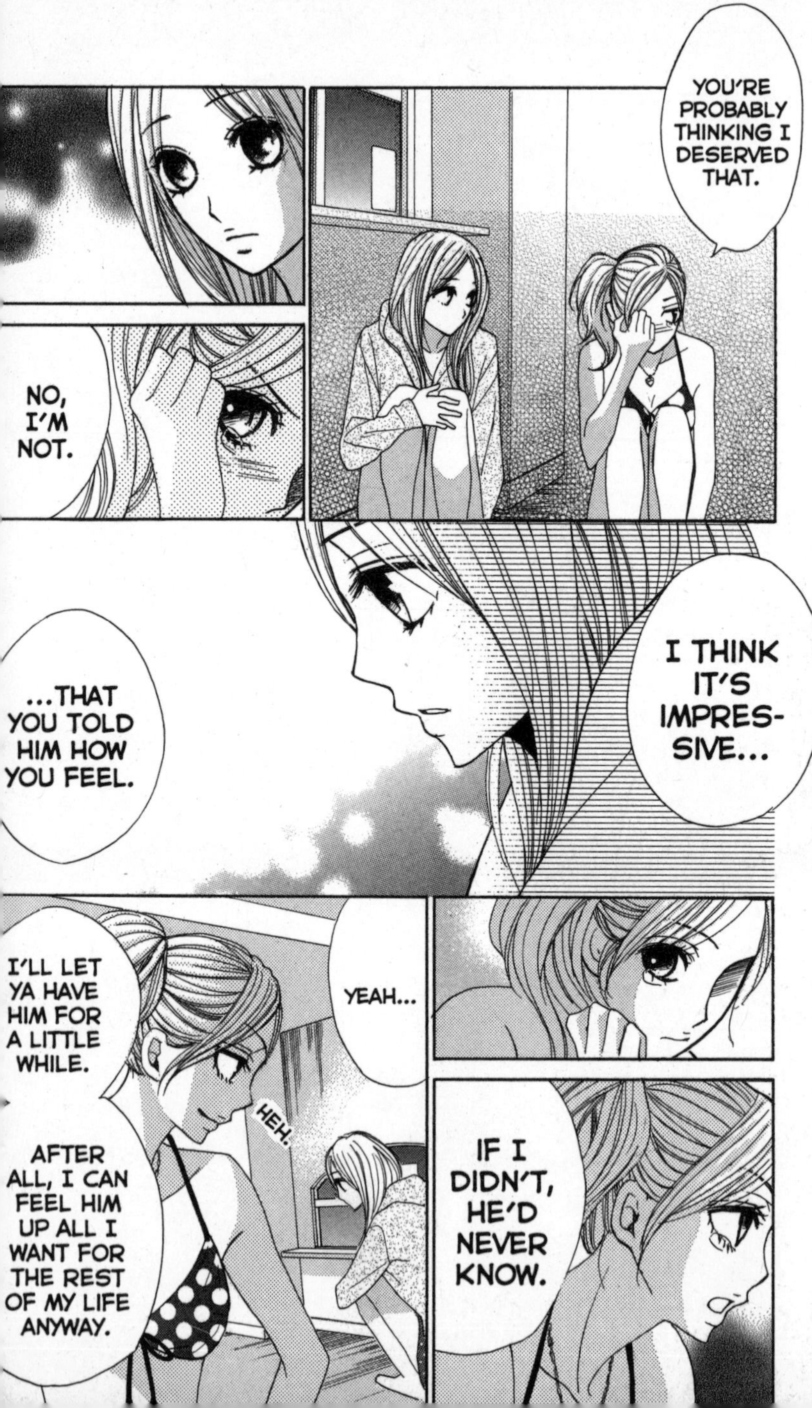
YOU'RE PROBABLY THINKING I DESERVED THAT.
NO, I'M NOT.
I THINK IT'S IMPRES-SIVE...
...THAT YOU TOLD HIM HOW YOU FEEL.
IF I DIDN'T, HE'D NEVER KNOW.
YEAH...
I'LL LET YA HAVE HIM FOR A LITTLE WHILE.
HEH.
AFTER ALL, I CAN FEEL HIM UP ALL I WANT FOR THE REST OF MY LIFE ANYWAY.

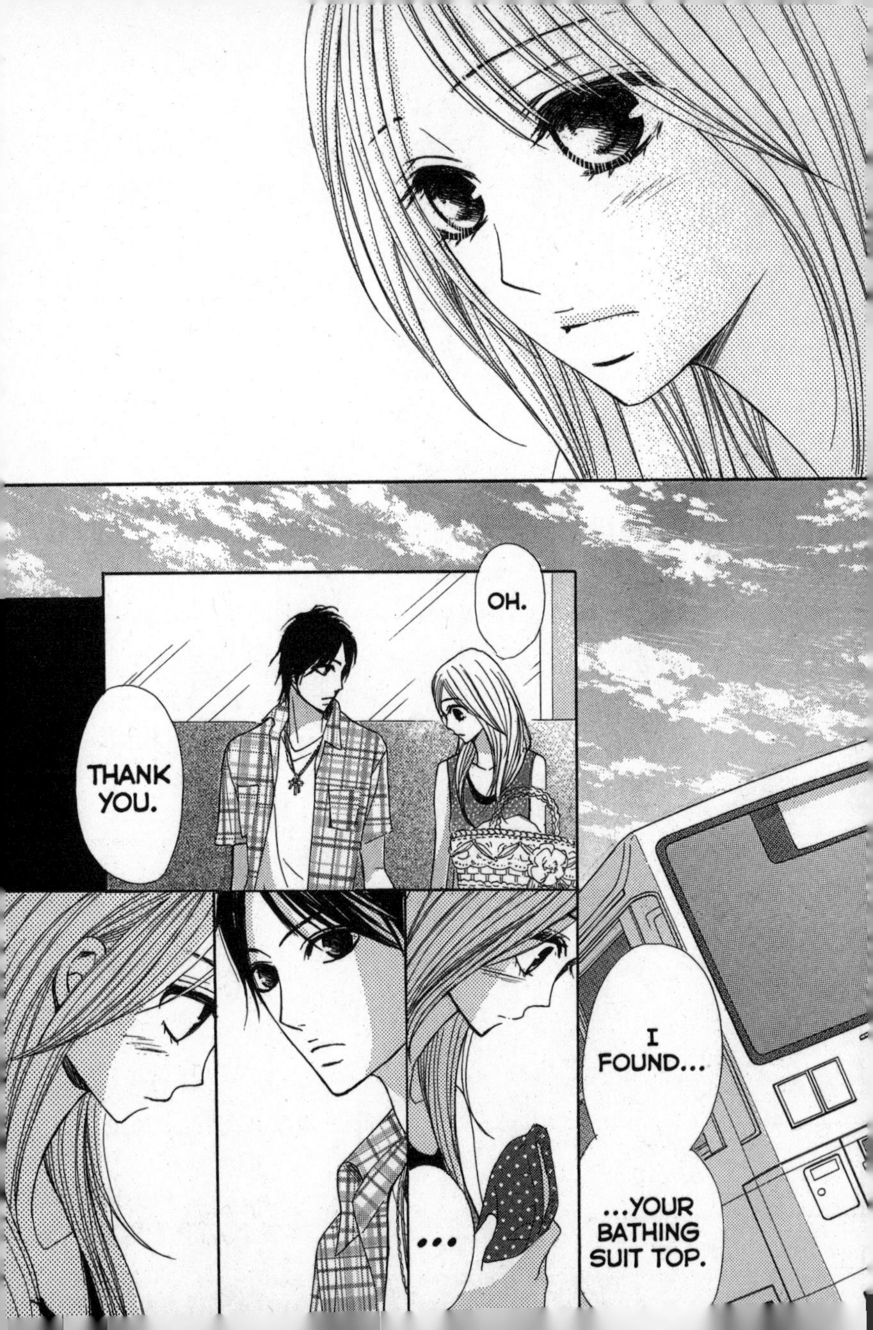
I FOUND...
...YOUR BATHING SUIT TOP.
OH.
THANK YOU.
...

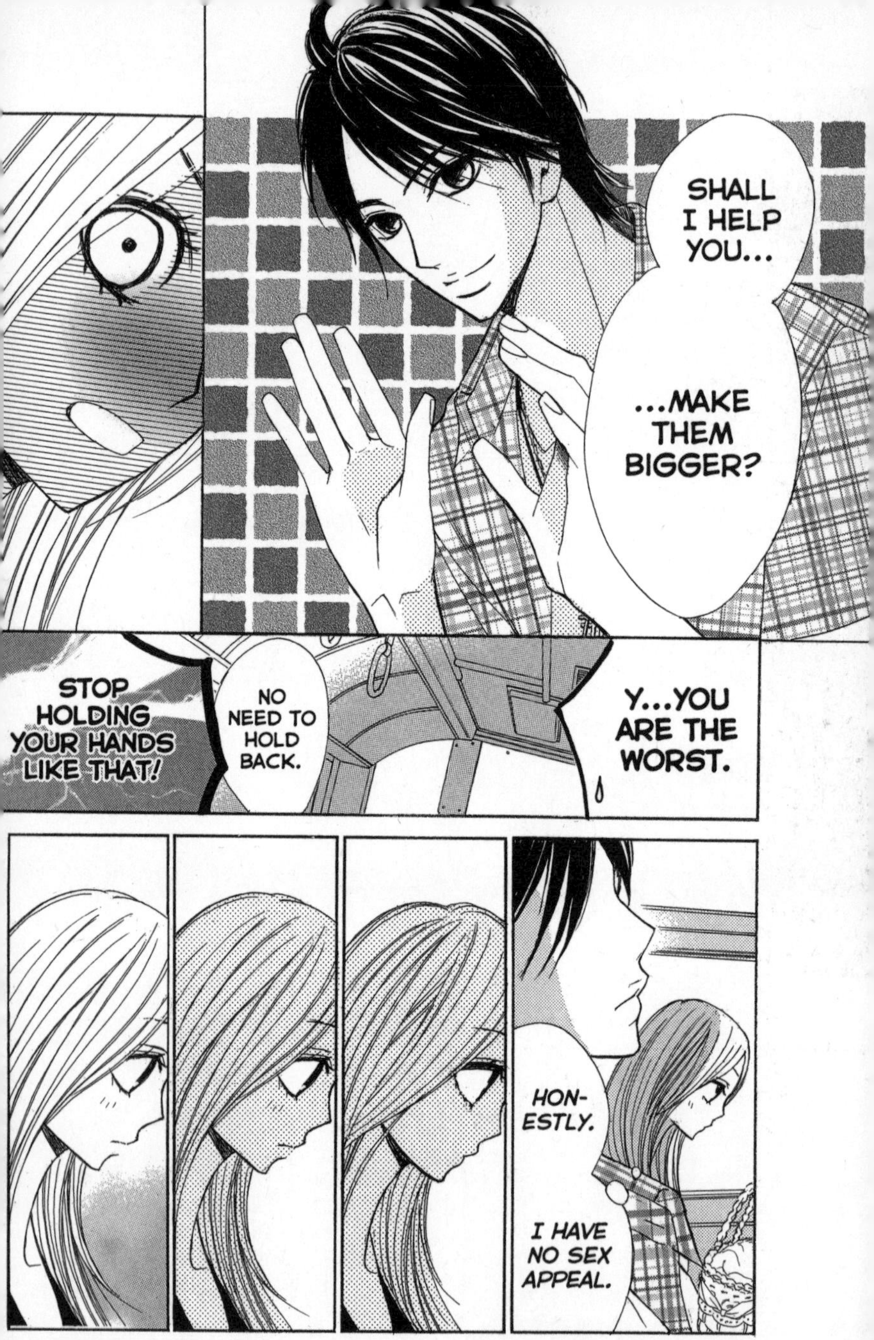
SHALL I HELP YOU...
...MAKE THEM BIGGER?
Y...YOU ARE THE WORST.
NO NEED TO HOLD BACK.
STOP HOLDING YOUR HANDS LIKE THAT!
HON-ESTLY.
I HAVE NO SEX APPEAL.

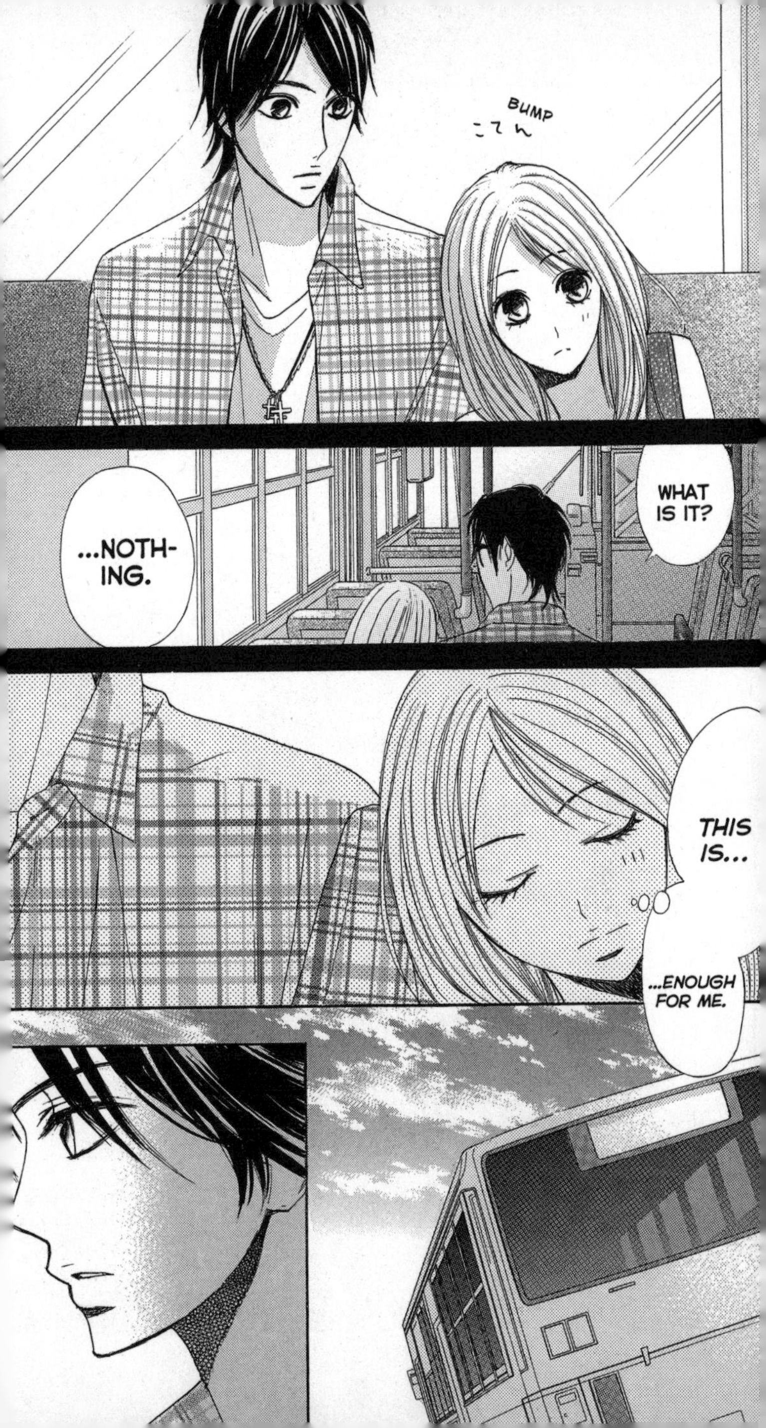
BUMP
こてん
WHAT IS IT?
...NOTH-ING.
THIS IS...
...ENOUGH FOR ME.

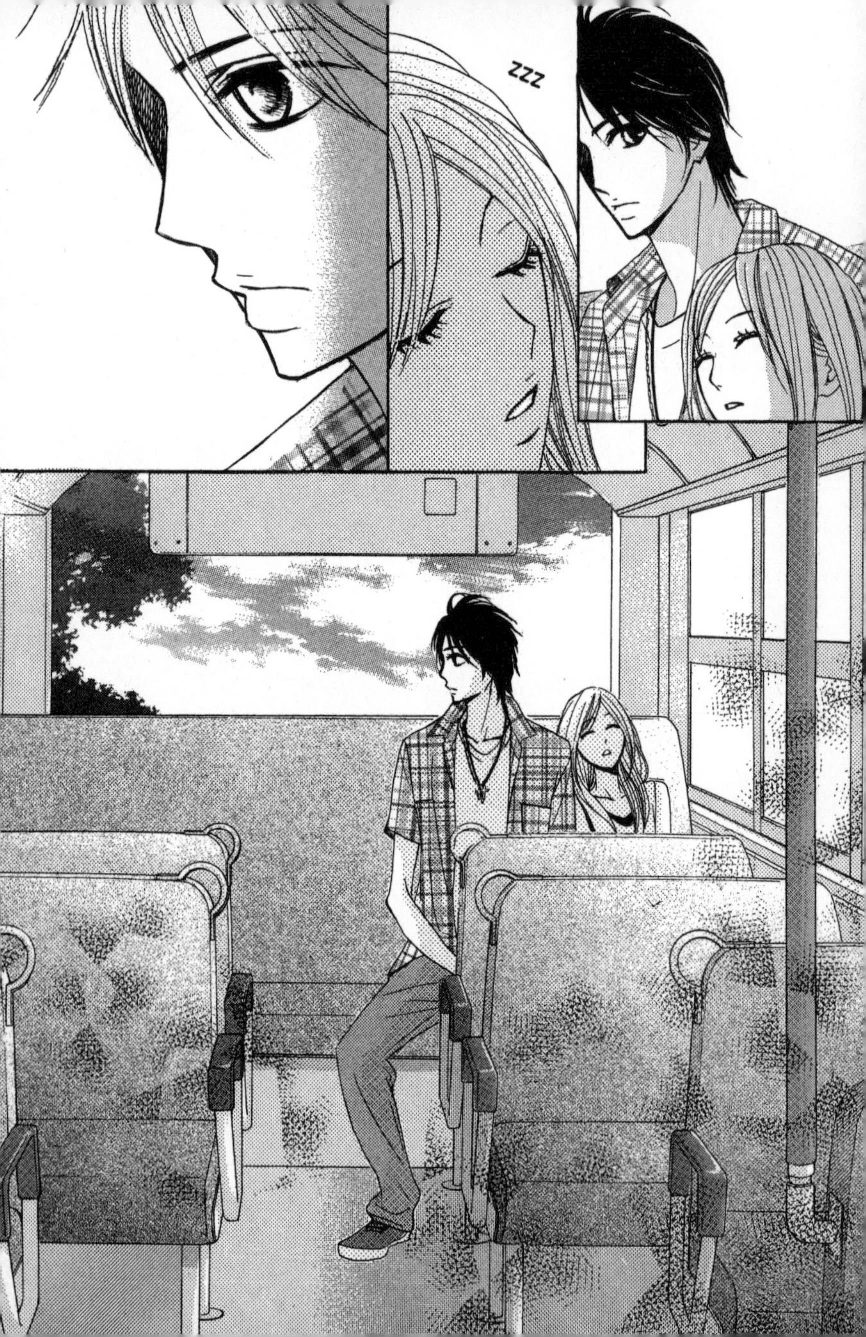
ZZZ

L♥DK

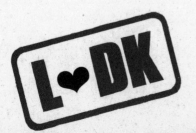

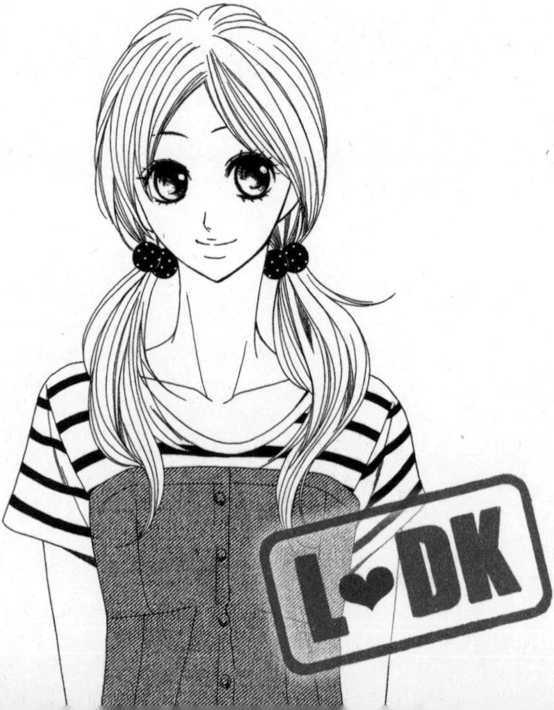
L♥DK

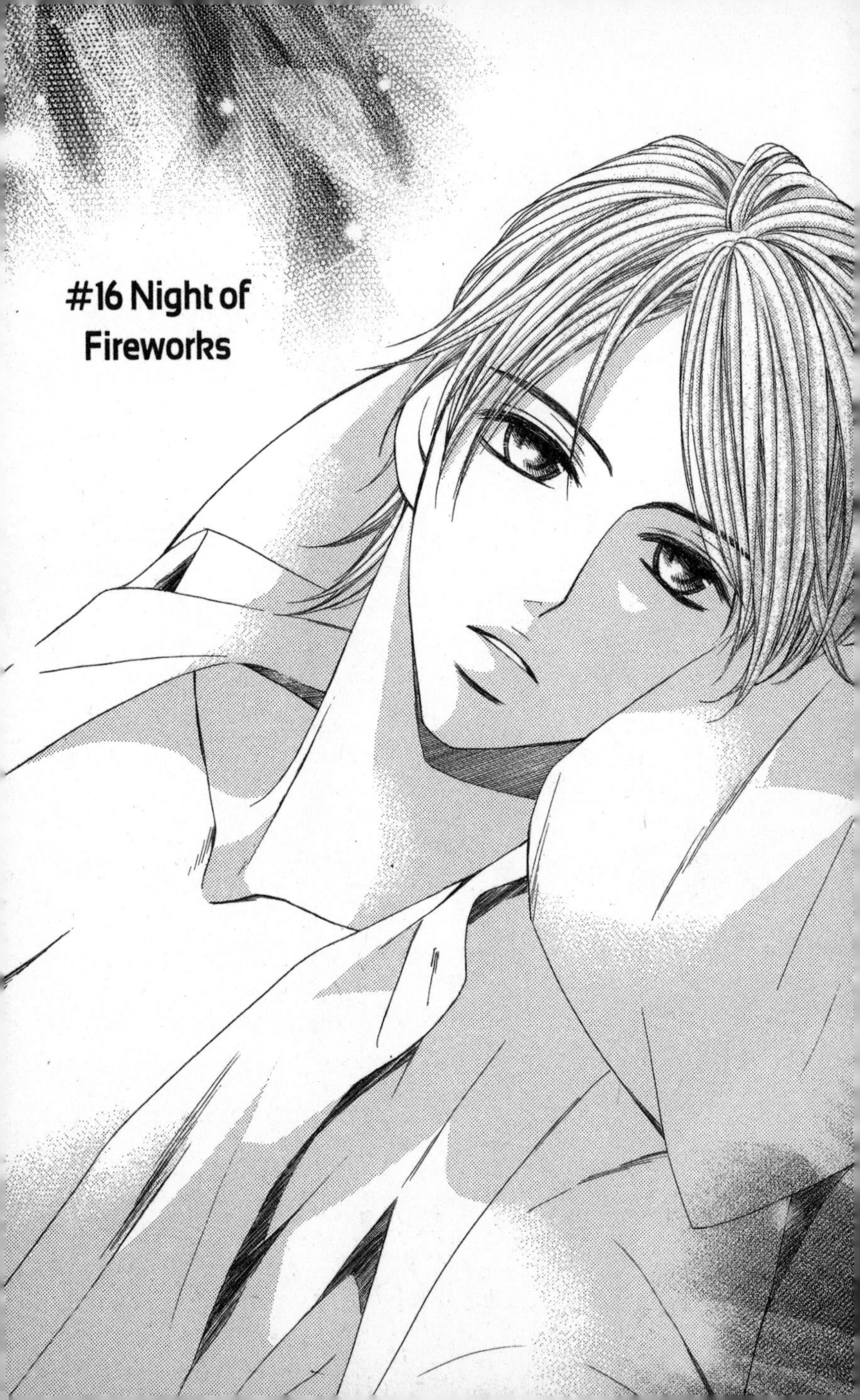
#16 Night of Fireworks

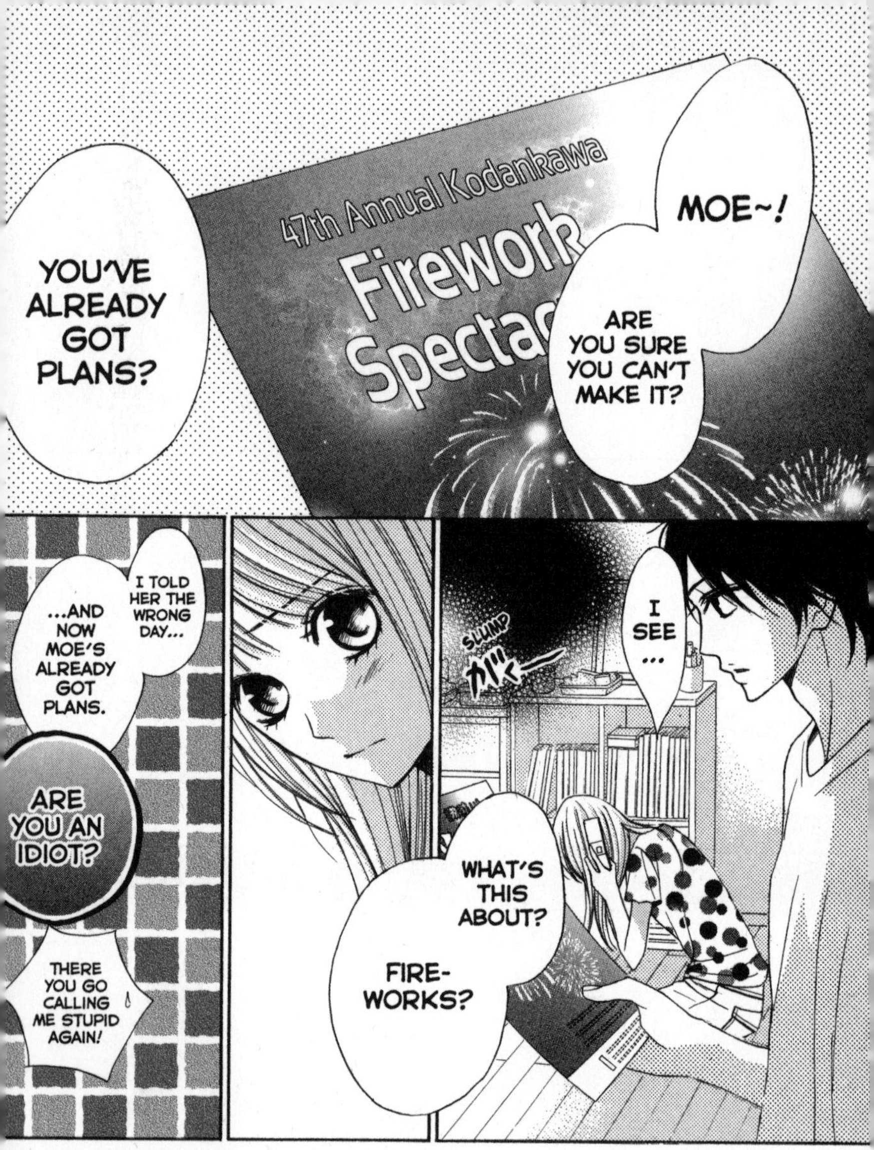
47th Annual Kodankawa
MOE~!
ARE YOU SURE YOU CAN'T MAKE IT?
YOU'VE ALREADY GOT PLANS?
I SEE...
SLUMP
WHAT'S THIS ABOUT?
FIRE-WORKS?
I TOLD HER THE WRONG DAY...
...AND NOW MOE'S ALREADY GOT PLANS.
ARE YOU AN IDIOT?
THERE YOU GO CALLING ME STUPID AGAIN!

L♥DK

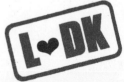

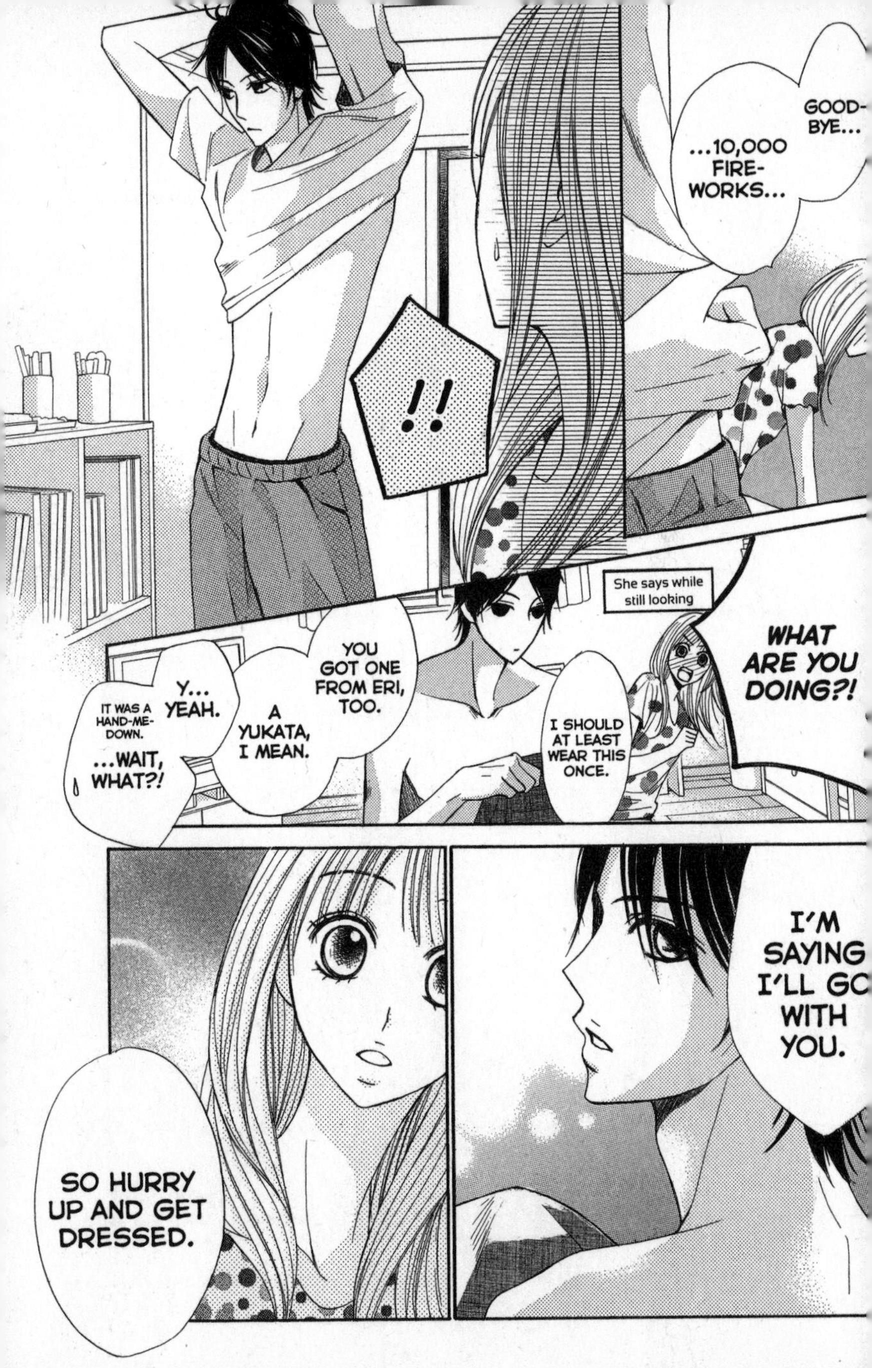
GOOD-BYE...
...10,000 FIRE-WORKS...
!!
WHAT ARE YOU DOING?!
She says while still looking
I SHOULD AT LEAST WEAR THIS ONCE.
YOU GOT ONE FROM ERI, TOO.
A YUKATA, I MEAN.
Y... YEAH.
IT WAS A HAND-ME-DOWN.
...WAIT, WHAT?!
I'M SAYING I'LL GO WITH YOU.
SO HURRY UP AND GET DRESSED.

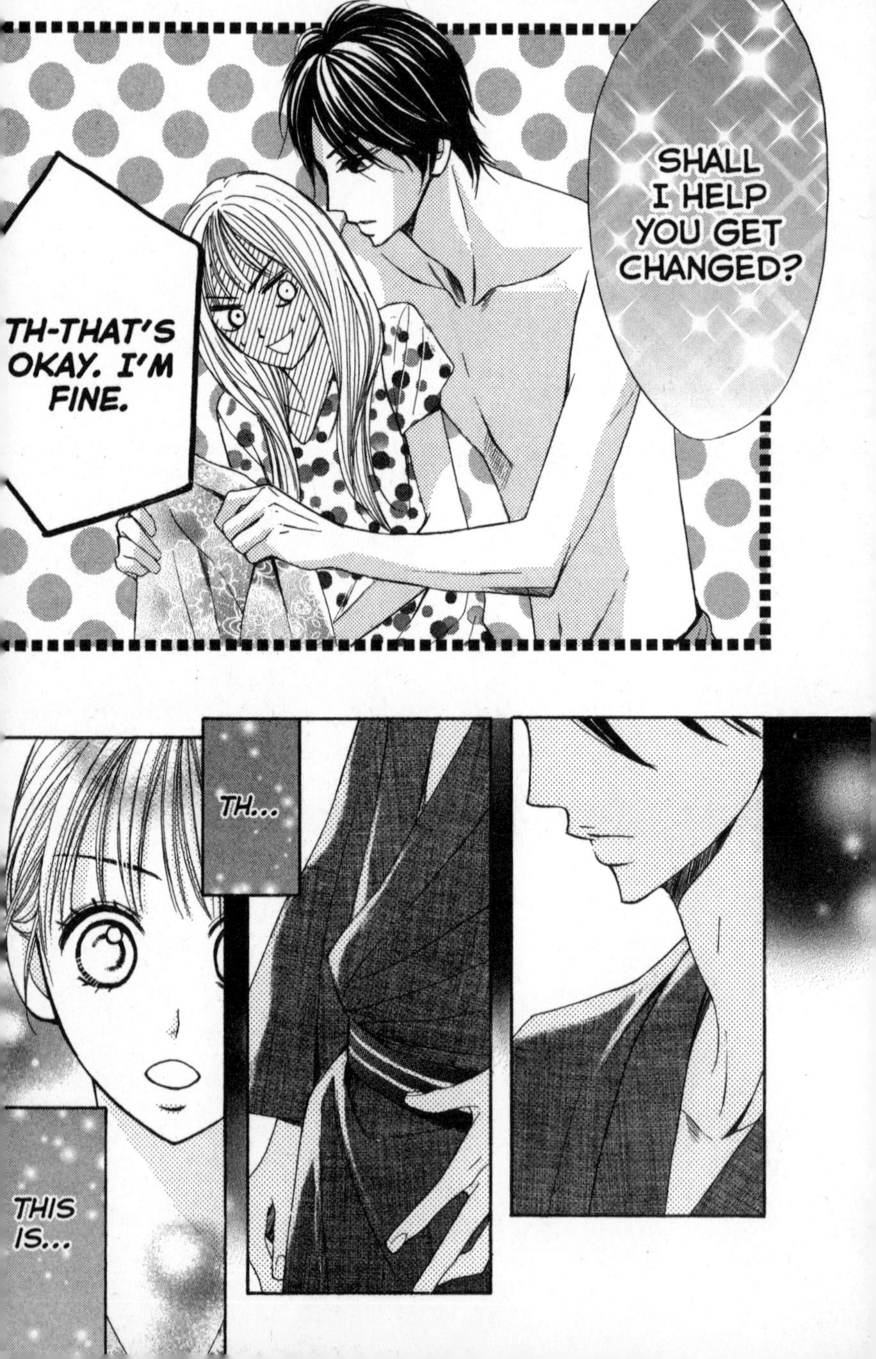
SHALL I HELP YOU GET CHANGED?
TH-THAT'S OKAY. I'M FINE.
TH...
THIS IS...

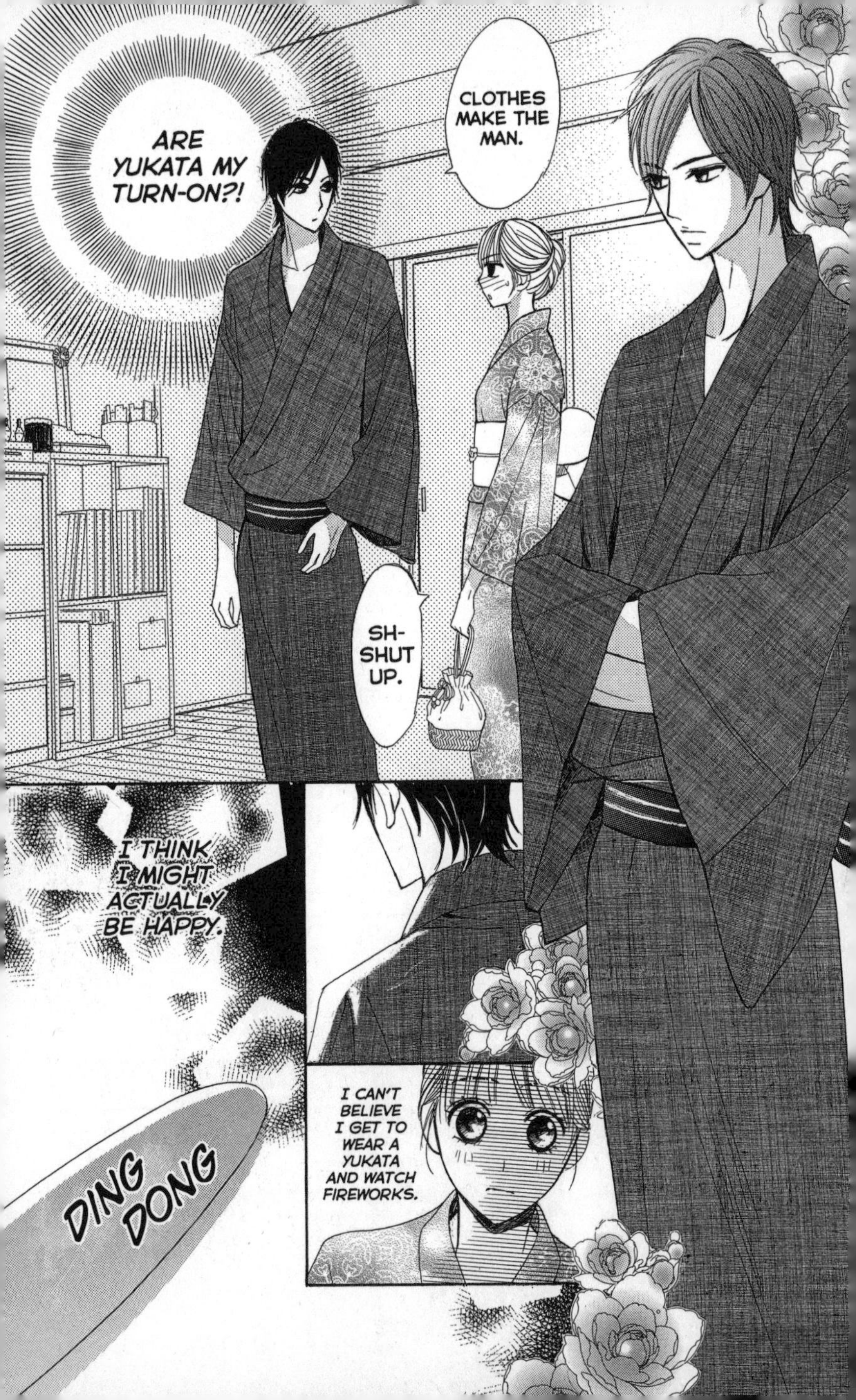
CLOTHES MAKE THE MAN.
ARE YUKATA MY TURN-ON?!
SH-SHUT UP.
I CAN'T BELIEVE I GET TO WEAR A YUKATA AND WATCH FIREWORKS.
I THINK I MIGHT ACTUALLY BE HAPPY.
DING DONG

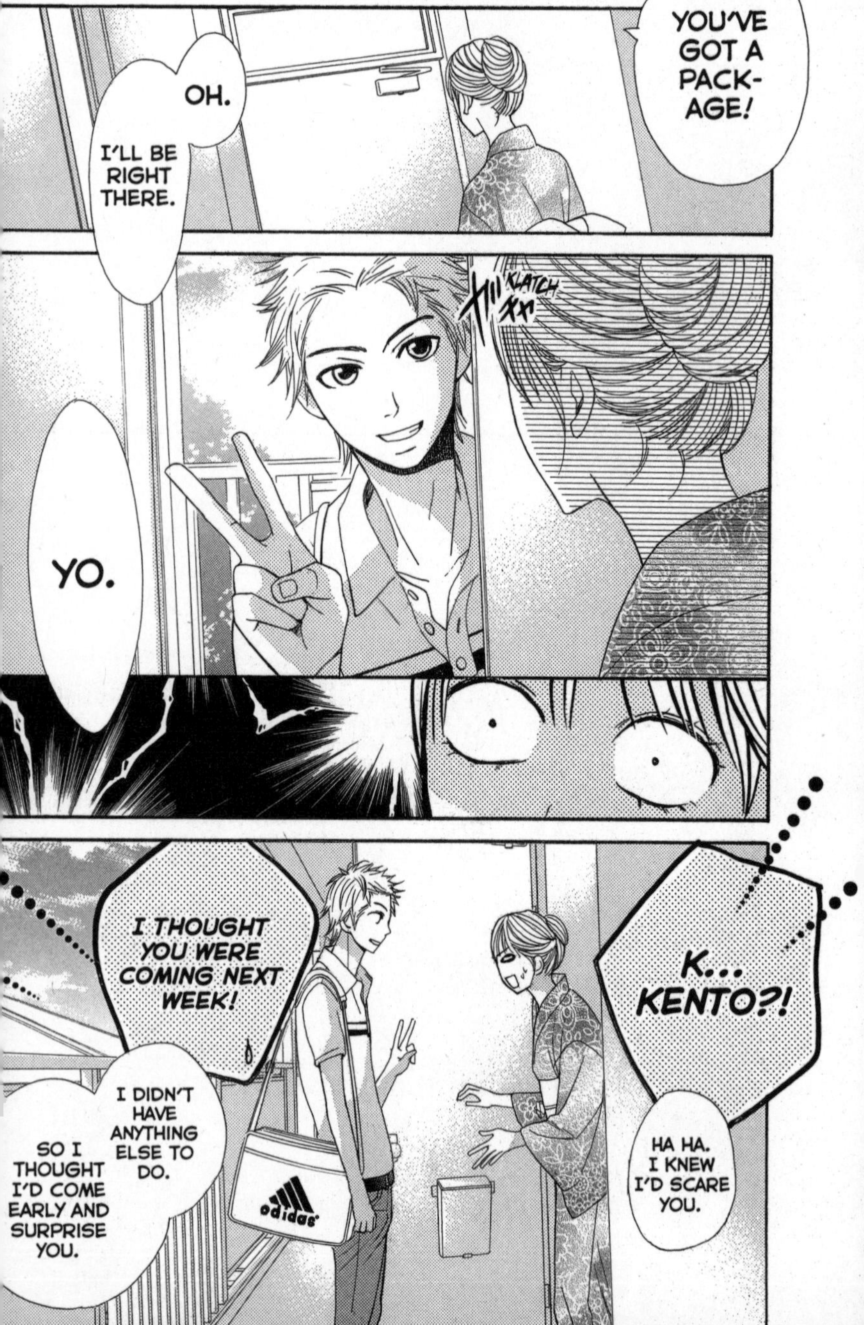
YOU'VE GOT A PACKAGE!
OH.
I'LL BE RIGHT THERE.
KLATCH
YO.
K... KENTO?!
I THOUGHT YOU WERE COMING NEXT WEEK!
HA HA. I KNEW I'D SCARE YOU.
I DIDN'T HAVE ANYTHING ELSE TO DO.
SO I THOUGHT I'D COME EARLY AND SURPRISE YOU.
adidas

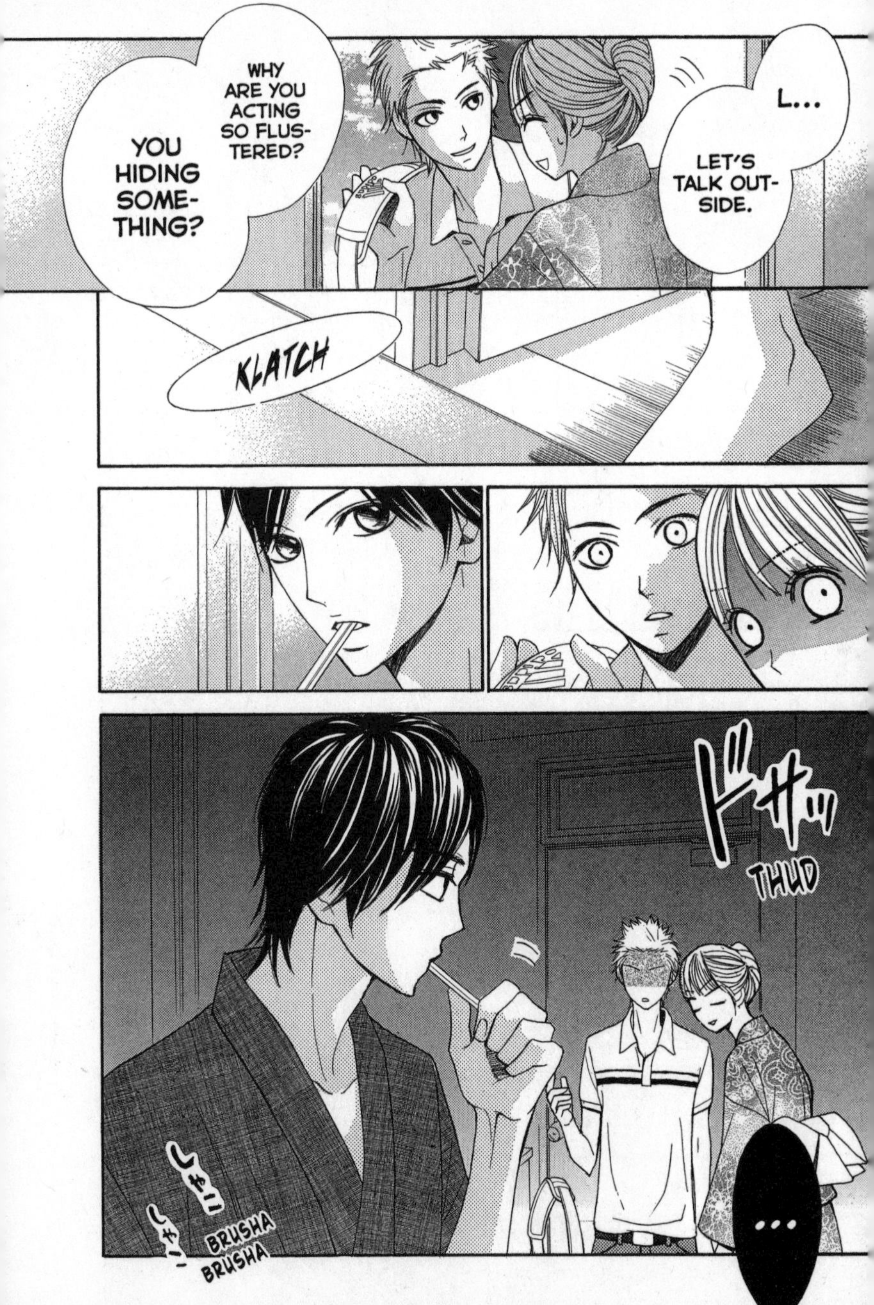
L...
LET'S TALK OUT-SIDE.
WHY ARE YOU ACTING SO FLUS-TERED?
YOU HIDING SOME-THING?
KLATCH
ドサッ
THUD
...
しゃこ しゃこ
BRUSHA BRUSHA

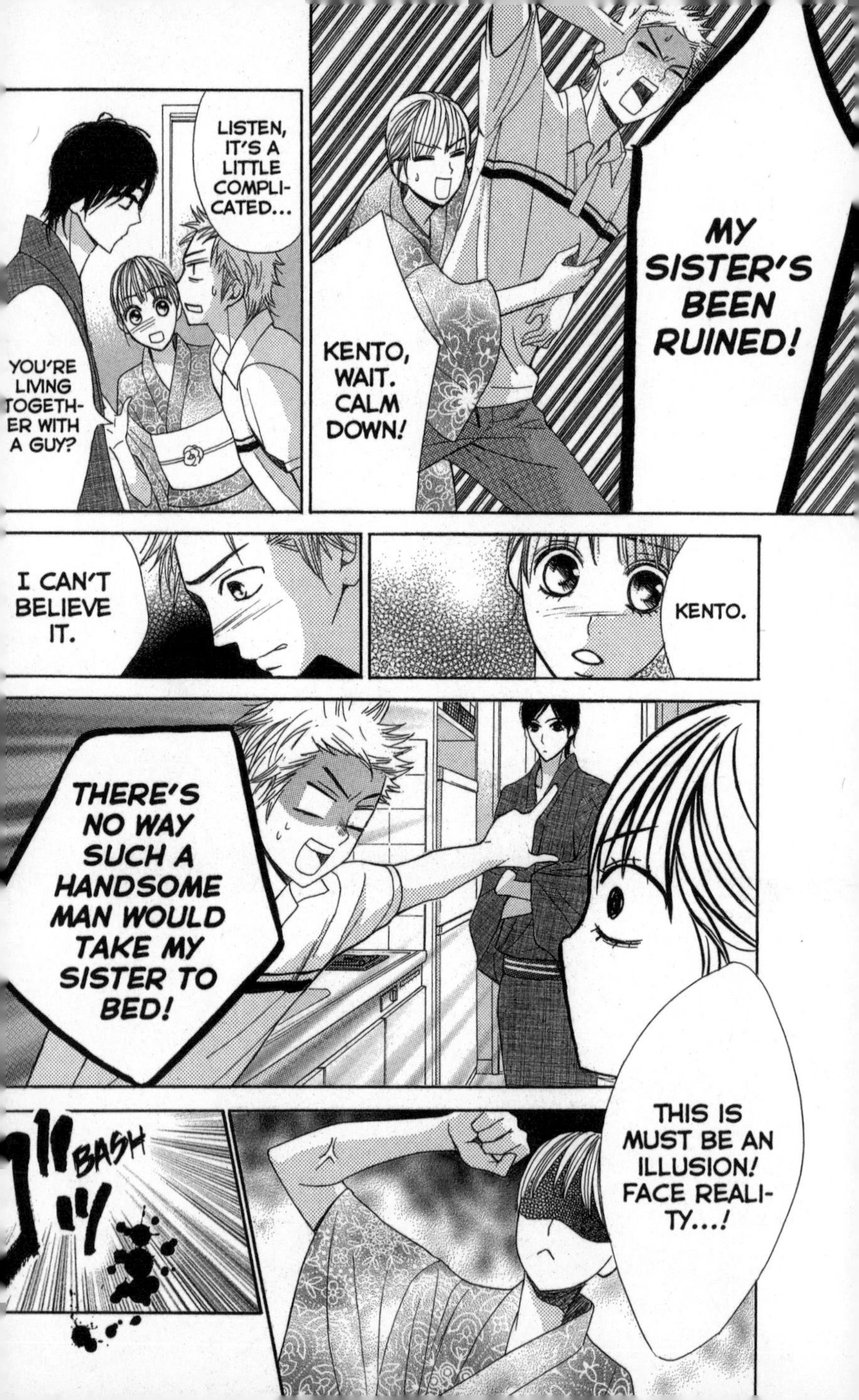
MY SISTER'S BEEN RUINED!
KENTO, WAIT. CALM DOWN!
LISTEN, IT'S A LITTLE COMPLICATED...
YOU'RE LIVING TOGETHER WITH A GUY?
KENTO.
I CAN'T BELIEVE IT.
THERE'S NO WAY SUCH A HANDSOME MAN WOULD TAKE MY SISTER TO BED!
THIS IS MUST BE AN ILLUSION! FACE REALITY...!
BASH

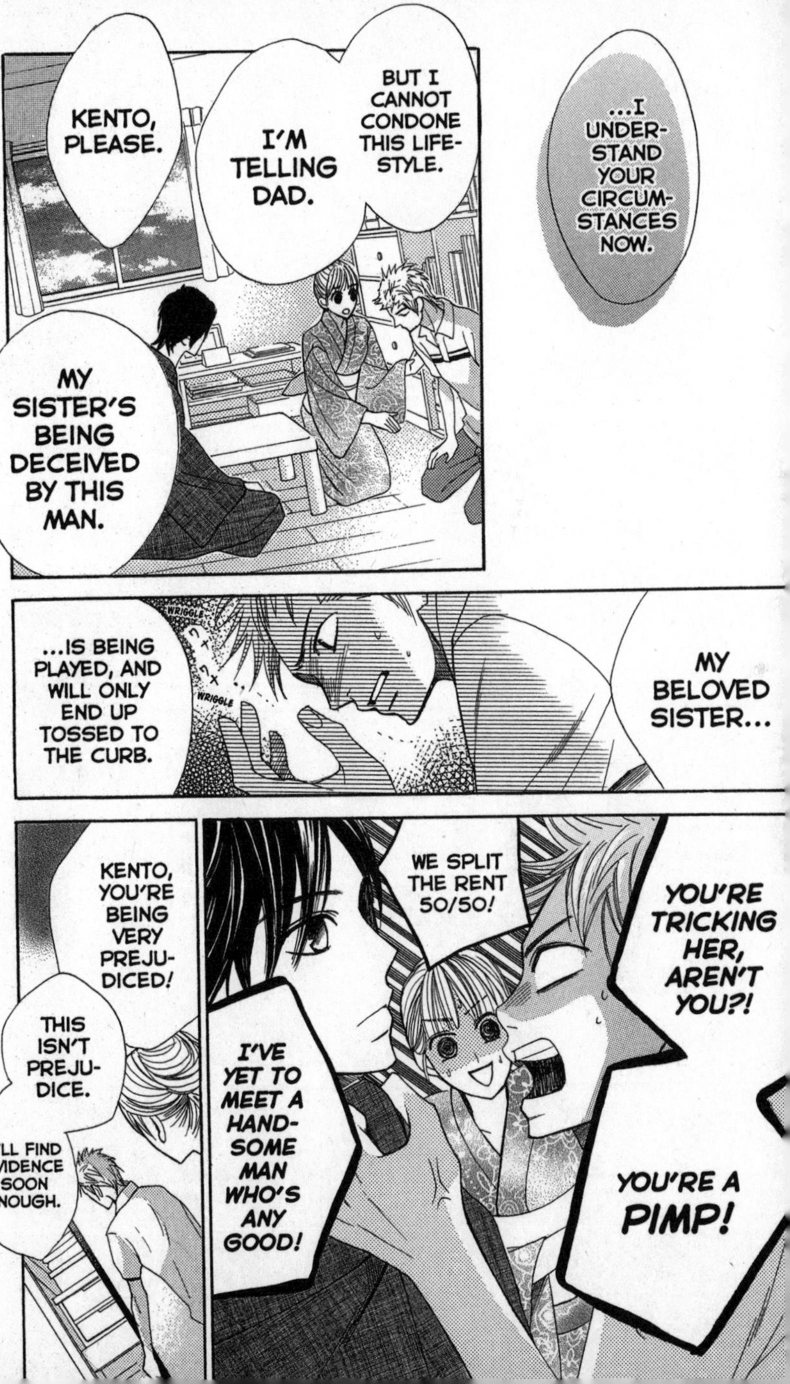
...I UNDERSTAND YOUR CIRCUMSTANCES NOW.
BUT I CANNOT CONDONE THIS LIFE-STYLE.
I'M TELLING DAD.
KENTO, PLEASE.
MY SISTER'S BEING DECEIVED BY THIS MAN.
MY BELOVED SISTER...
...IS BEING PLAYED, AND WILL ONLY END UP TOSSED TO THE CURB.
WRIGGLE
WRIGGLE
YOU'RE TRICKING HER, AREN'T YOU?!
WE SPLIT THE RENT 50/50!
YOU'RE A PIMP!
I'VE YET TO MEET A HANDSOME MAN WHO'S ANY GOOD!
KENTO, YOU'RE BEING VERY PREJUDICED!
THIS ISN'T PREJUDICE.
I'LL FIND EVIDENCE SOON ENOUGH.

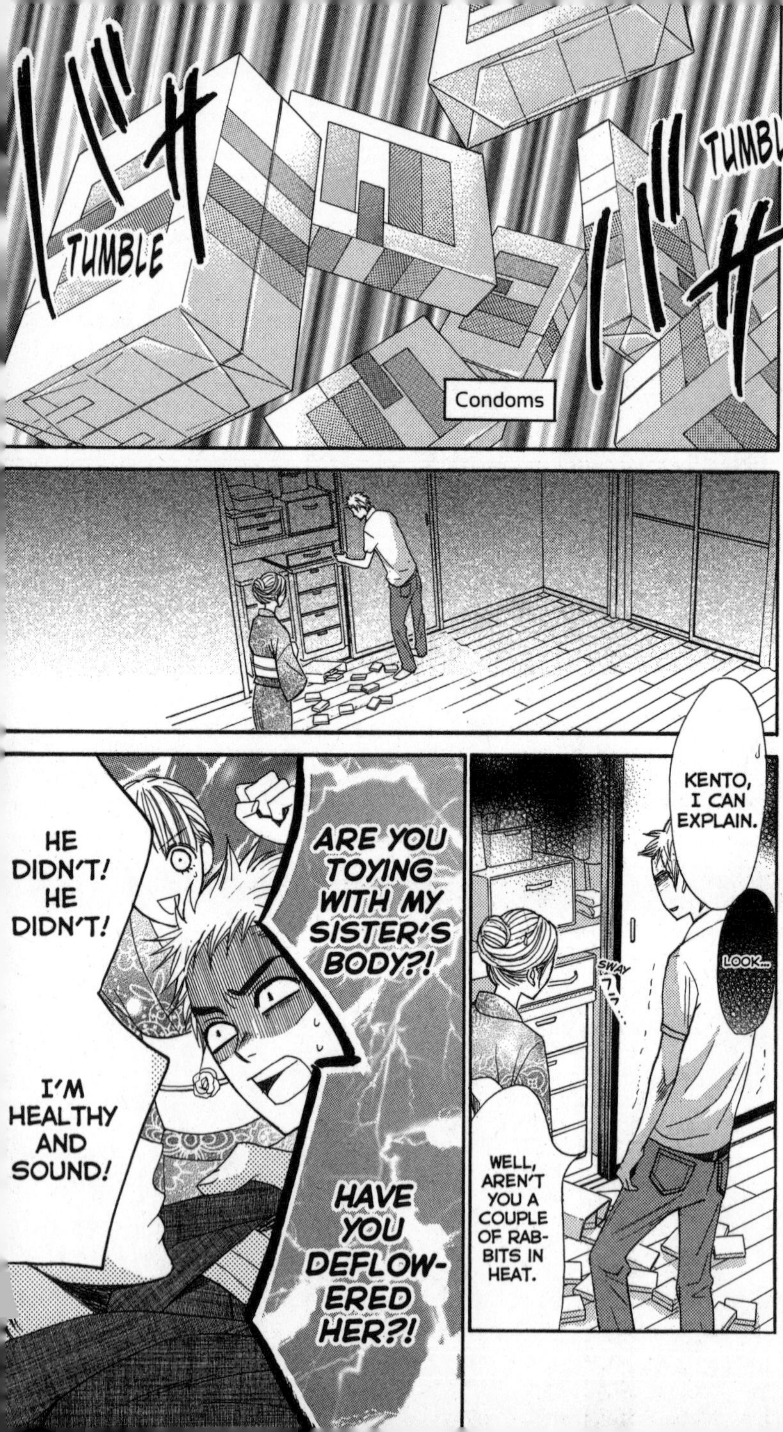
TUMBLE
TUMBLE
Condoms
KENTO, I CAN EXPLAIN.
LOOK...
SWAY
WELL, AREN'T YOU A COUPLE OF RAB-BITS IN HEAT.
ARE YOU TOYING WITH MY SISTER'S BODY?!
HAVE YOU DEFLOW-ERED HER?!
HE DIDN'T! HE DIDN'T!
I'M HEALTHY AND SOUND!

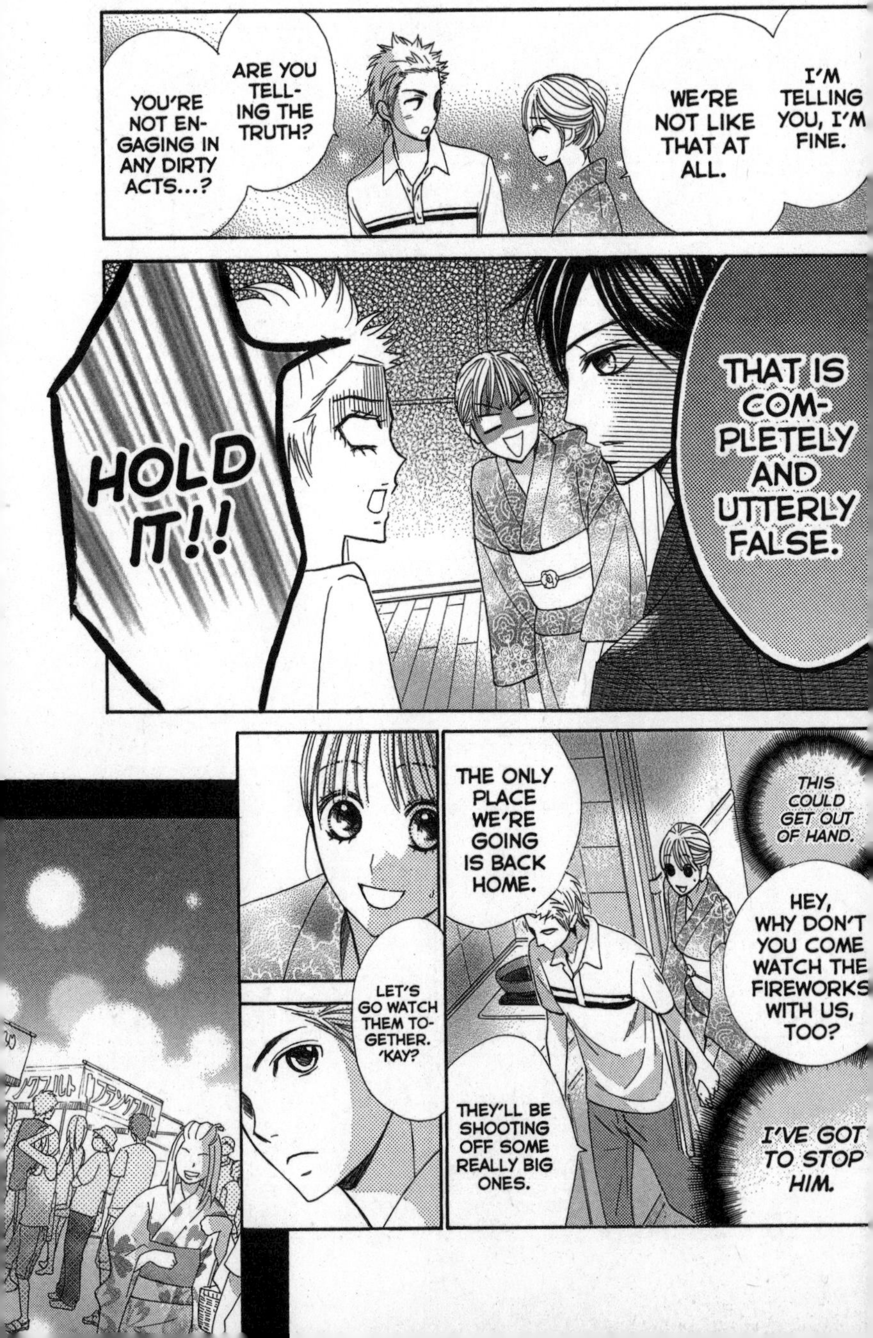
I'M TELLING YOU, I'M FINE.
WE'RE NOT LIKE THAT AT ALL.
ARE YOU TELLING THE TRUTH?
YOU'RE NOT ENGAGING IN ANY DIRTY ACTS...?
THAT IS COMPLETELY AND UTTERLY FALSE.
HOLD IT!!
THIS COULD GET OUT OF HAND.
HEY, WHY DON'T YOU COME WATCH THE FIREWORKS WITH US, TOO?
I'VE GOT TO STOP HIM.
THE ONLY PLACE WE'RE GOING IS BACK HOME.
THEY'LL BE SHOOTING OFF SOME REALLY BIG ONES.
LET'S GO WATCH THEM TOGETHER. 'KAY?

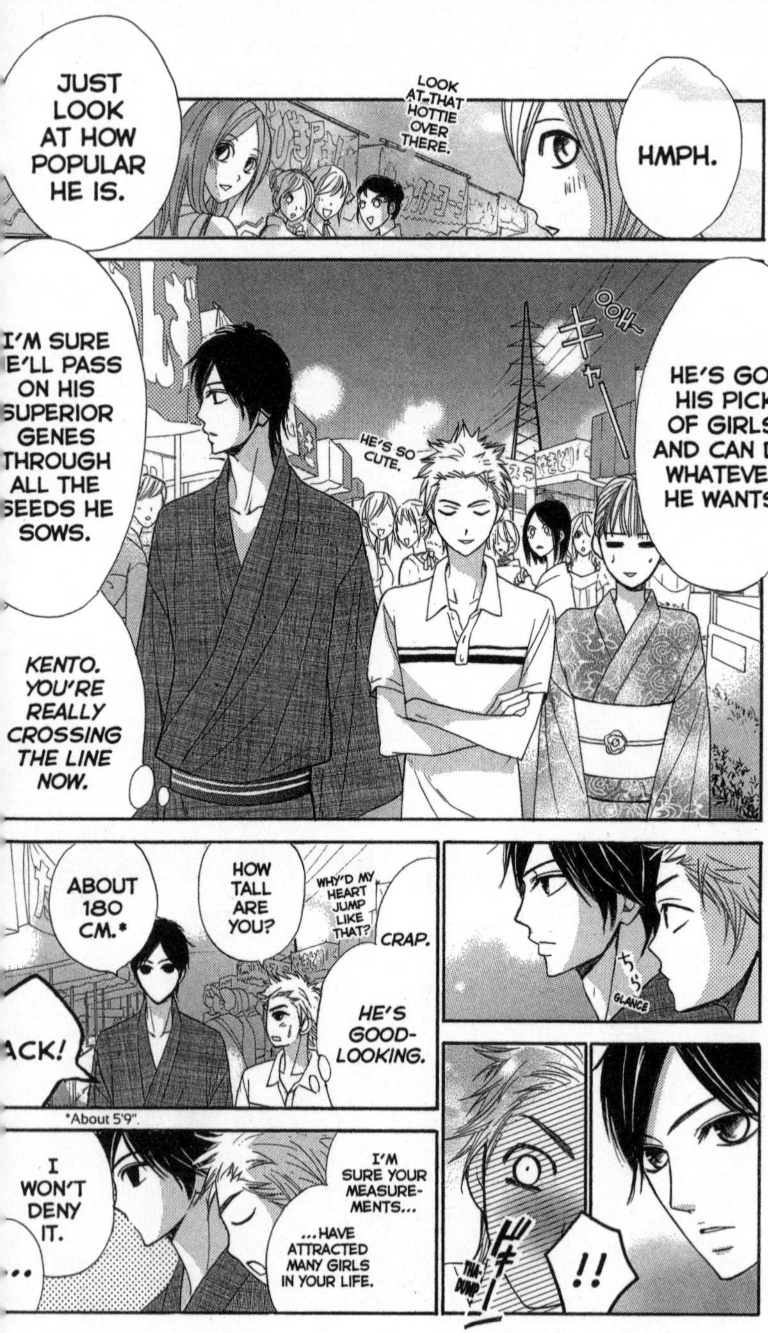
HMPH.
LOOK AT THAT HOTTIE OVER THERE.
JUST LOOK AT HOW POPULAR HE IS.
HE'S GOT HIS PICK OF GIRLS, AND CAN DO WHATEVER HE WANTS.
OOOH~
キャー
HE'S SO CUTE.
I'M SURE E'LL PASS ON HIS SUPERIOR GENES THROUGH ALL THE SEEDS HE SOWS.
KENTO. YOU'RE REALLY CROSSING THE LINE NOW.
ちら
GLANCE
WHY'D MY HEART JUMP LIKE THAT?
CRAP.
HOW TALL ARE YOU?
ABOUT 180 CM.*
HE'S GOOD-LOOKING.
ACK!
!!
ドキ
THA-DUMP
I'M SURE YOUR MEASUREMENTS...
...HAVE ATTRACTED MANY GIRLS IN YOUR LIFE.
I WON'T DENY IT.
...

*About 5'9".

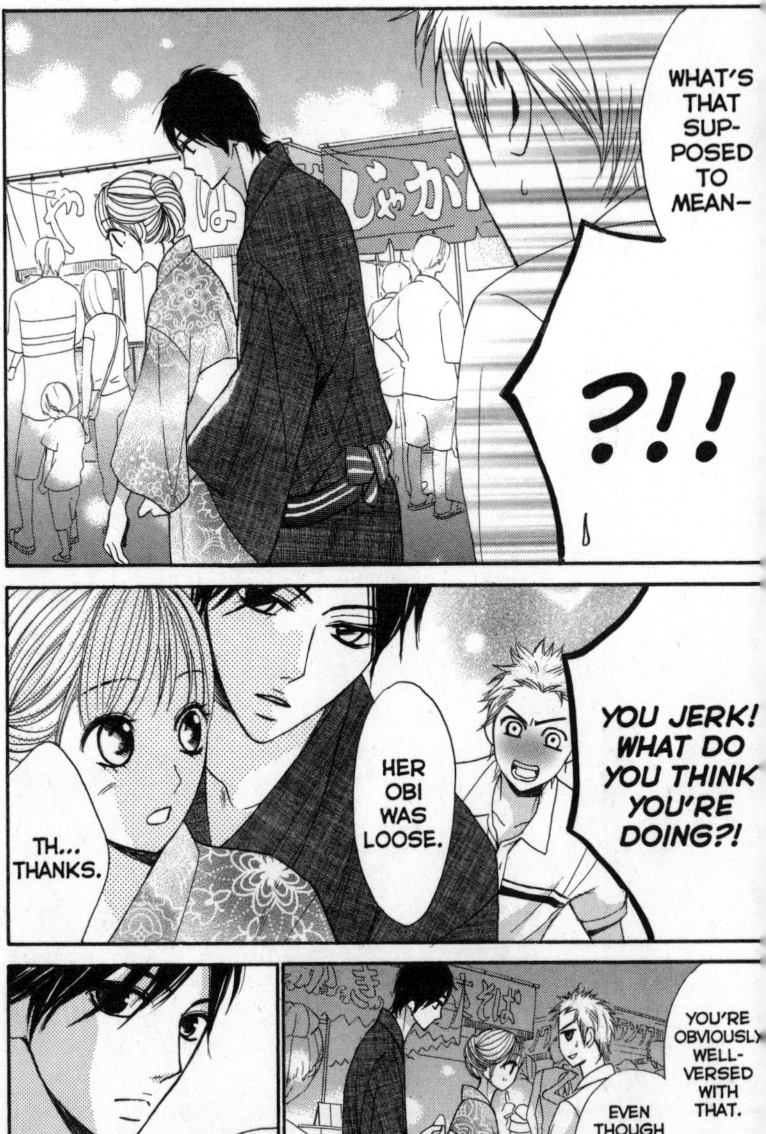
WHAT'S THAT SUPPOSED TO MEAN—
?!!
じゃが
YOU JERK! WHAT DO YOU THINK YOU'RE DOING?!
HER OBI WAS LOOSE.
TH... THANKS.
YOU'RE OBVIOUSLY WELL-VERSED WITH THAT.
EVEN THOUGH IT'S A GIRL'S YUKATA.

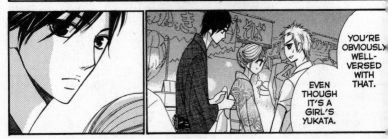

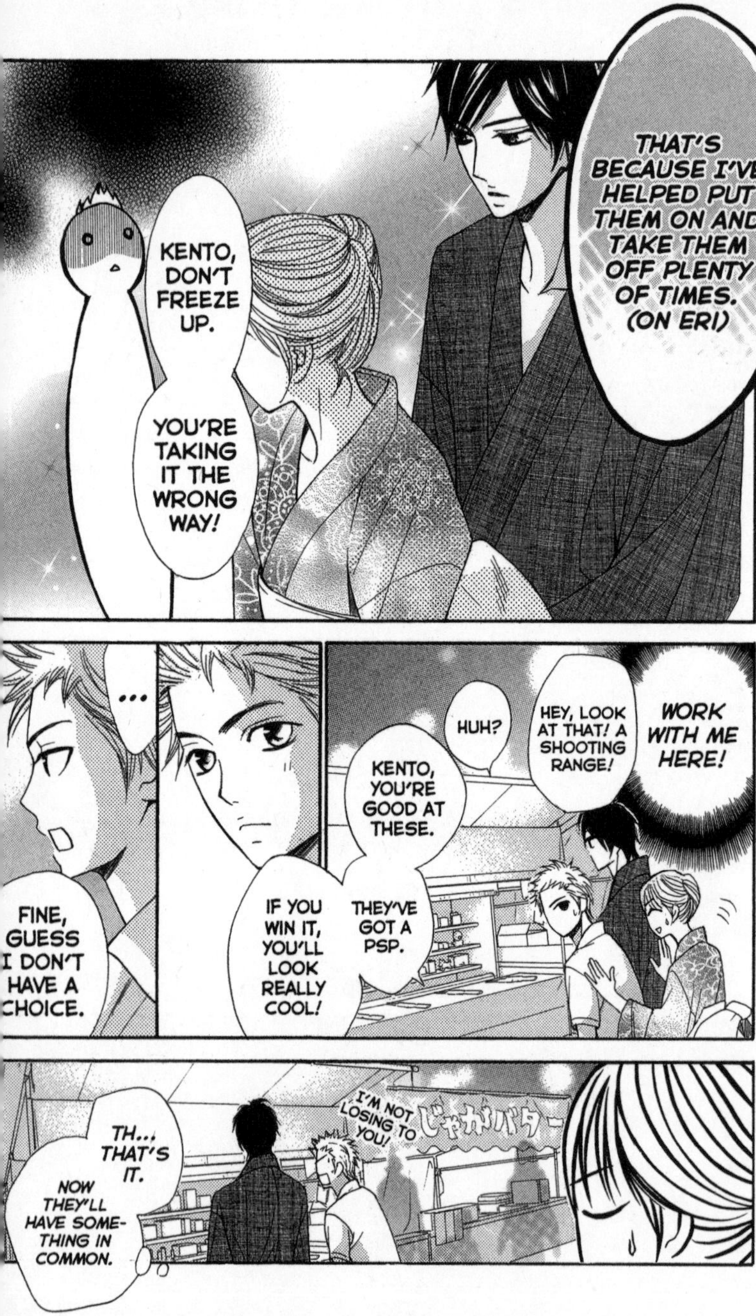
THAT'S BECAUSE I'VE HELPED PUT THEM ON AND TAKE THEM OFF PLENTY OF TIMES. (ON ERI)
KENTO, DON'T FREEZE UP.
YOU'RE TAKING IT THE WRONG WAY!
WORK WITH ME HERE!
HEY, LOOK AT THAT! A SHOOTING RANGE!
HUH?
KENTO, YOU'RE GOOD AT THESE.
THEY'VE GOT A PSP.
IF YOU WIN IT, YOU'LL LOOK REALLY COOL!
...
FINE, GUESS I DON'T HAVE A CHOICE.
じゃがバター
I'M NOT LOSING TO YOU!
TH... THAT'S IT.
NOW THEY'LL HAVE SOME-THING IN COMMON.

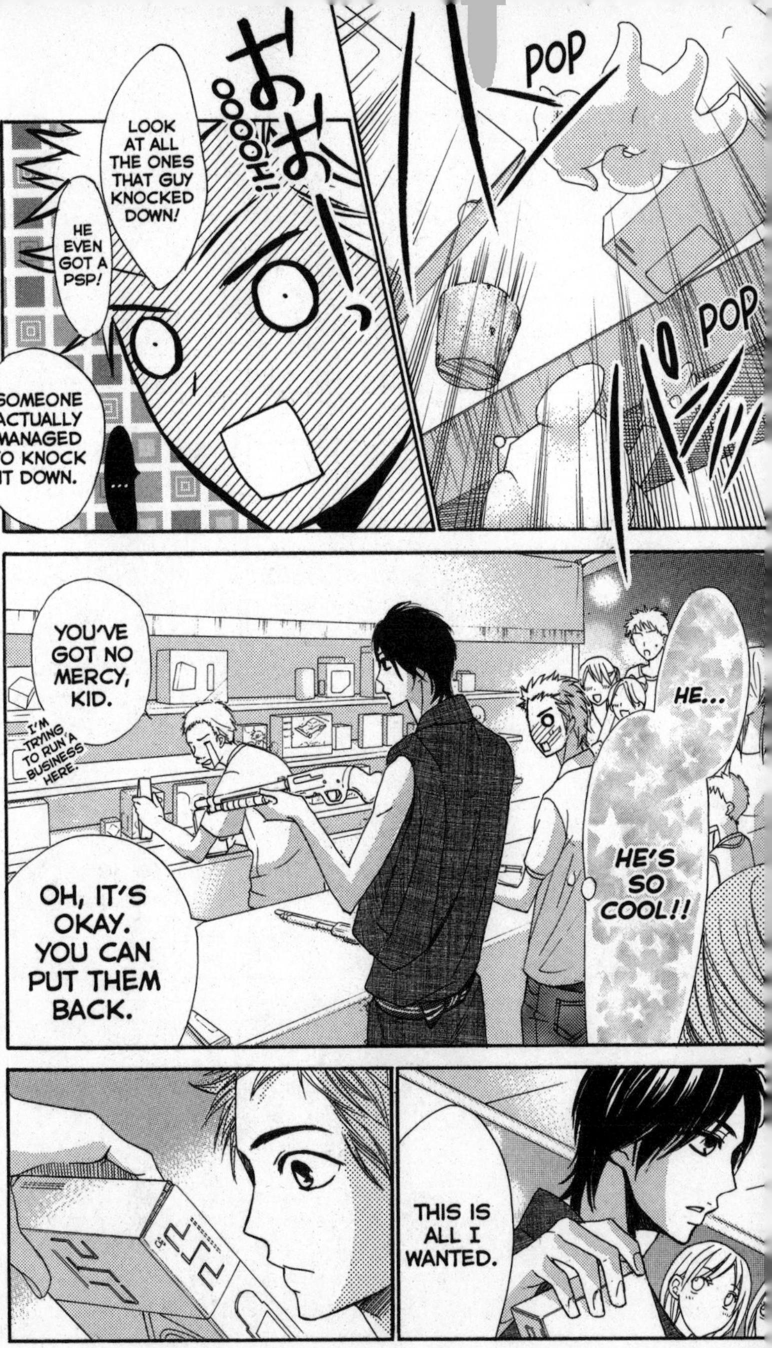
POP
POP
LOOK AT ALL THE ONES THAT GUY KNOCKED DOWN!
OOOOH!!
HE EVEN GOT A PSP!
SOMEONE ACTUALLY MANAGED TO KNOCK IT DOWN.
...
HE...
YOU'VE GOT NO MERCY, KID.
I'M TRYING TO RUN A BUSINESS HERE.
HE'S SO COOL!!
OH, IT'S OKAY. YOU CAN PUT THEM BACK.
THIS IS ALL I WANTED.

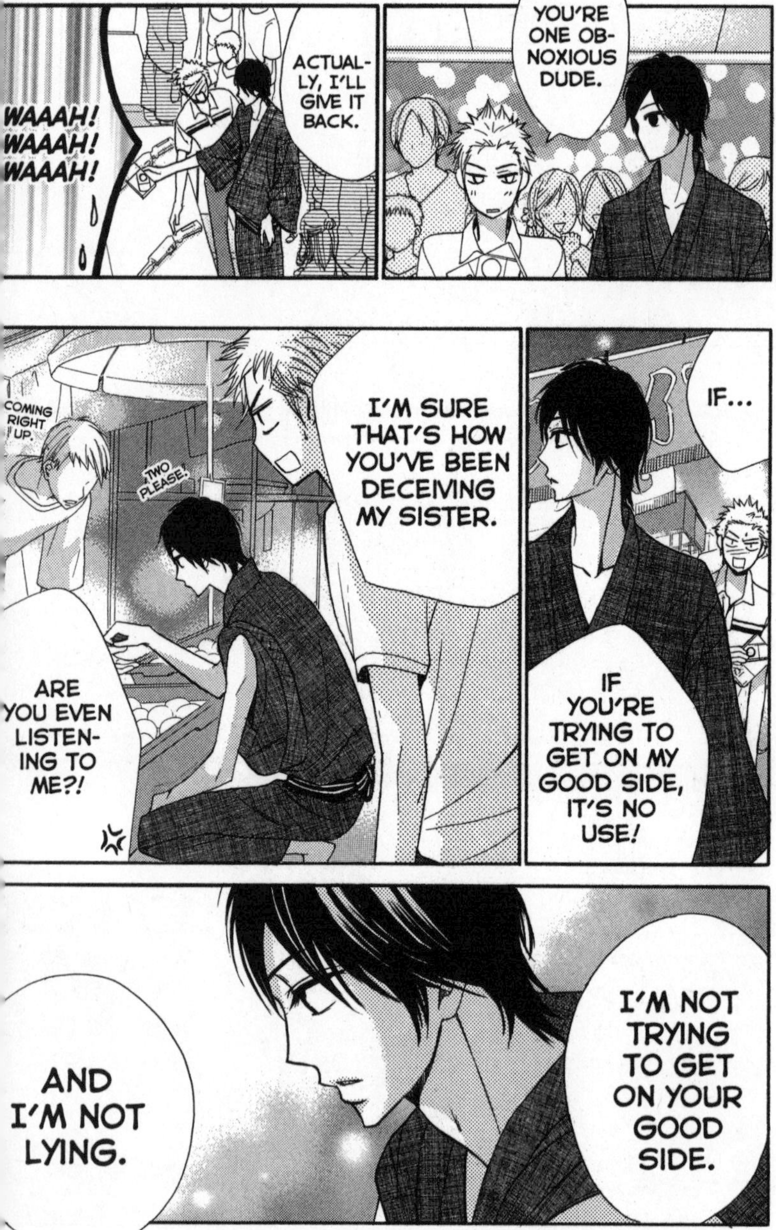

YOU'RE ONE OB-NOXIOUS DUDE.
ACTUAL-LY, I'LL GIVE IT BACK.
WAAAH! WAAAH! WAAAH!
IF...
IF YOU'RE TRYING TO GET ON MY GOOD SIDE, IT'S NO USE!
I'M SURE THAT'S HOW YOU'VE BEEN DECEIVING MY SISTER.
COMING RIGHT UP.
TWO PLEASE.
ARE YOU EVEN LISTEN-ING TO ME?!
I'M NOT TRYING TO GET ON YOUR GOOD SIDE.
AND I'M NOT LYING.

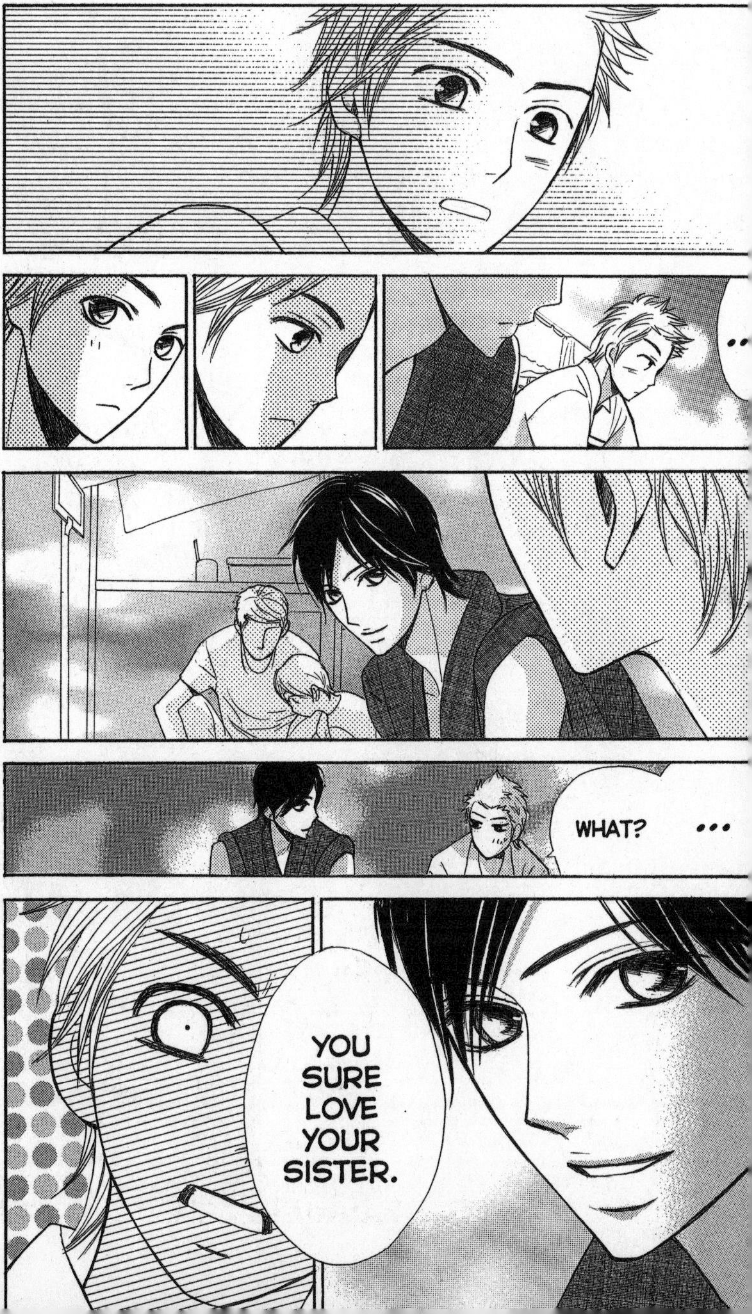
..
...
WHAT?
YOU SURE LOVE YOUR SISTER.

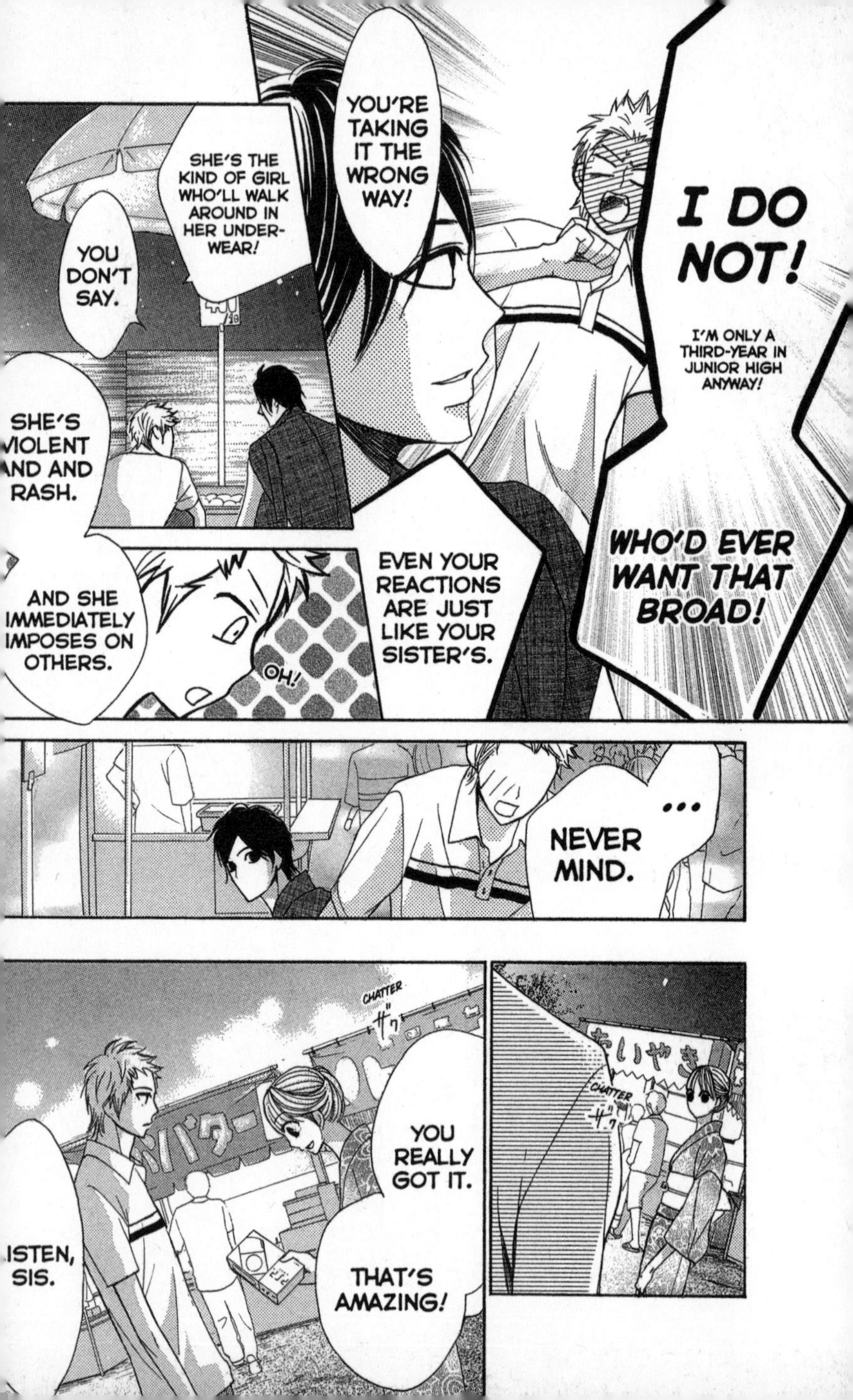
I DO NOT!
I'M ONLY A THIRD-YEAR IN JUNIOR HIGH ANYWAY!
WHO'D EVER WANT THAT BROAD!
YOU'RE TAKING IT THE WRONG WAY!
SHE'S THE KIND OF GIRL WHO'LL WALK AROUND IN HER UNDER-WEAR!
YOU DON'T SAY.
SHE'S VIOLENT AND AND RASH.
AND SHE IMMEDIATELY IMPOSES ON OTHERS.
EVEN YOUR REACTIONS ARE JUST LIKE YOUR SISTER'S.
OH!
... NEVER MIND.
CHATTER
CHATTER
YOU REALLY GOT IT.
THAT'S AMAZING!
LISTEN, SIS.

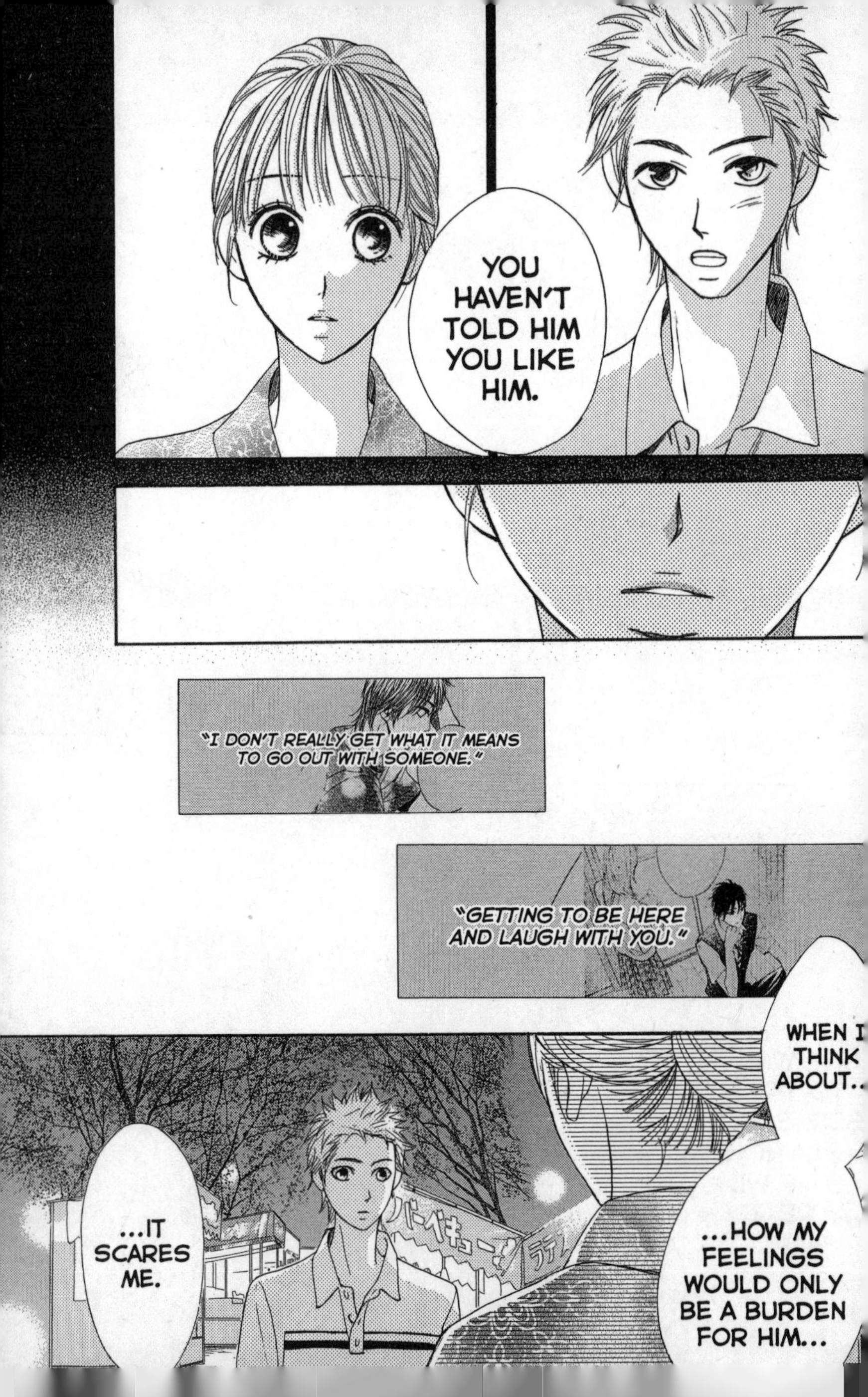
YOU HAVEN'T TOLD HIM YOU LIKE HIM.
"I DON'T REALLY GET WHAT IT MEANS TO GO OUT WITH SOMEONE."
"GETTING TO BE HERE AND LAUGH WITH YOU."
WHEN I THINK ABOUT...
...HOW MY FEELINGS WOULD ONLY BE A BURDEN FOR HIM...
...IT SCARES ME.

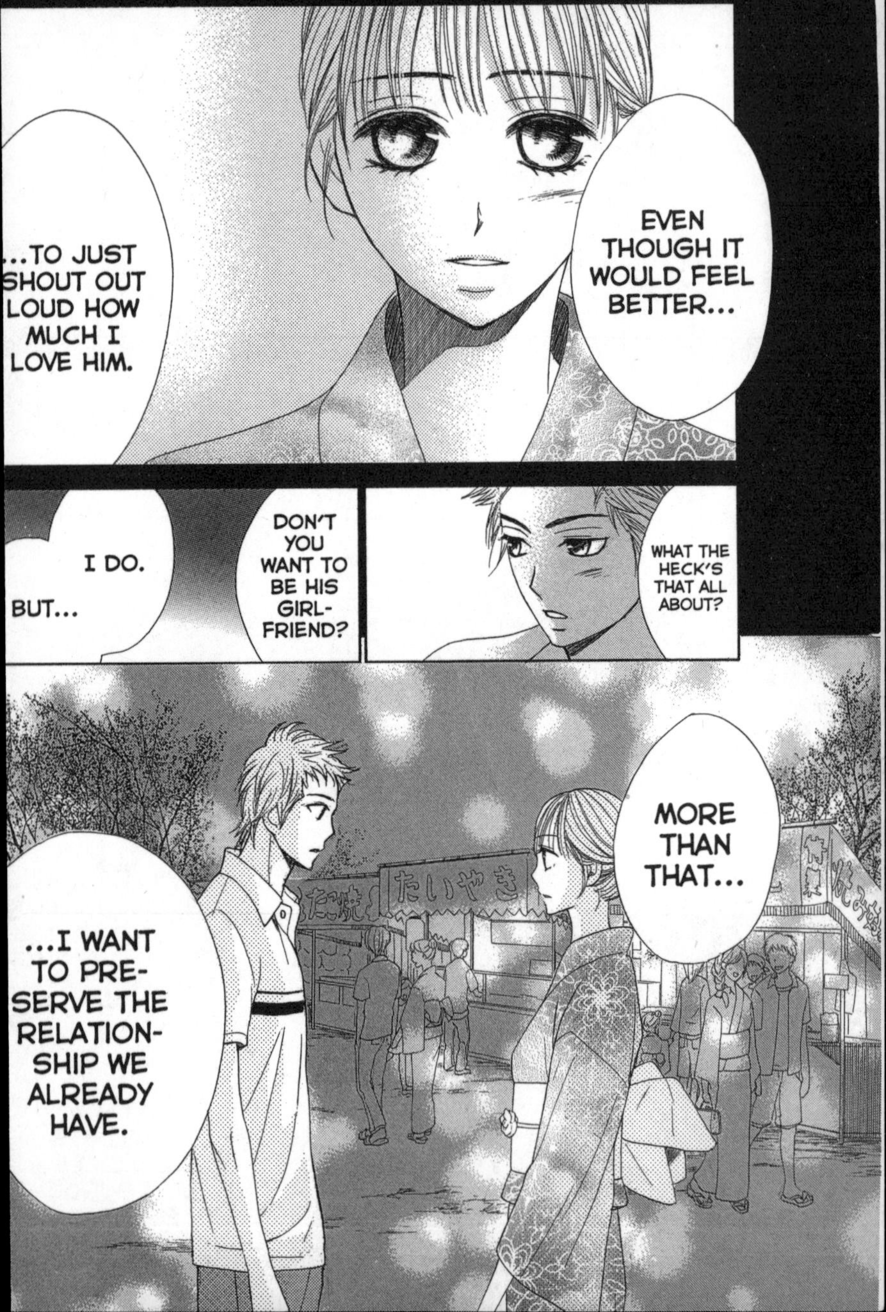
EVEN THOUGH IT WOULD FEEL BETTER...
...TO JUST SHOUT OUT LOUD HOW MUCH I LOVE HIM.
WHAT THE HECK'S THAT ALL ABOUT?
DON'T YOU WANT TO BE HIS GIRL-FRIEND?
I DO.
BUT...
MORE THAN THAT...
たいやき
...I WANT TO PRE-SERVE THE RELATION-SHIP WE ALREADY HAVE.

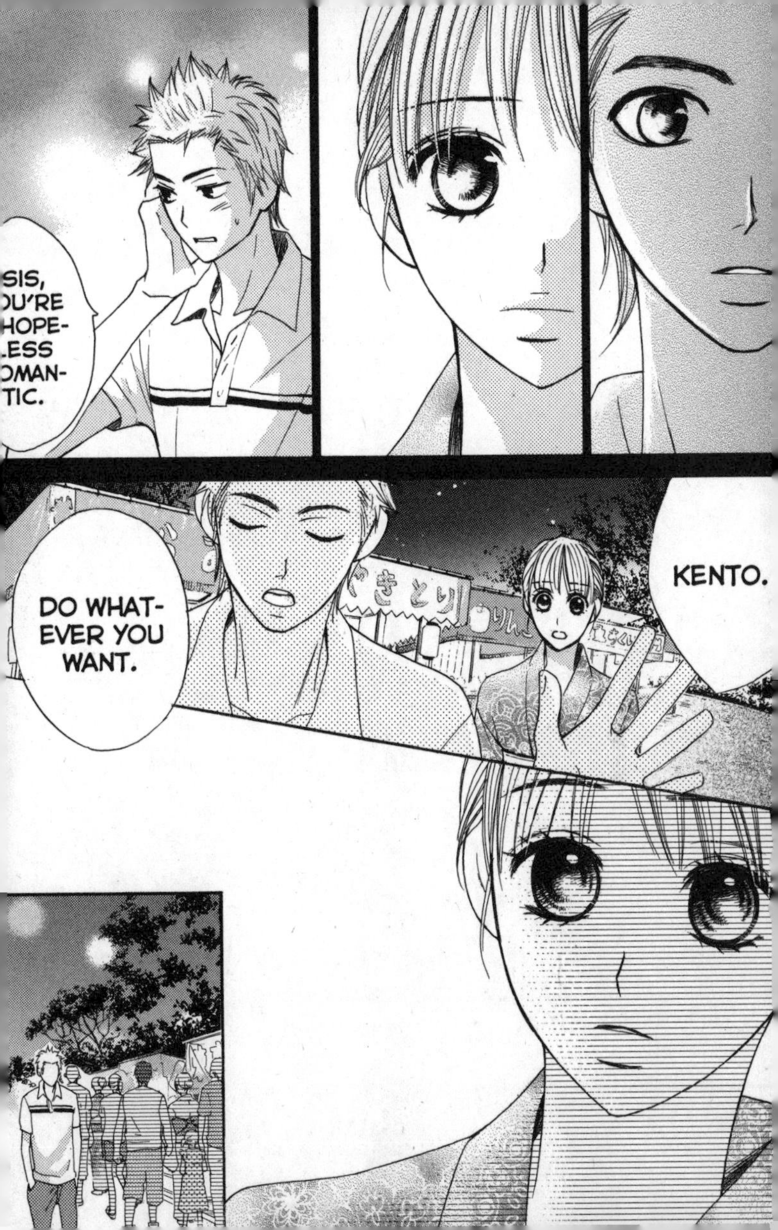
SIS, OU'RE HOPE-LESS OMAN-TIC.
KENTO.
DO WHAT-EVER YOU WANT.
やきとり

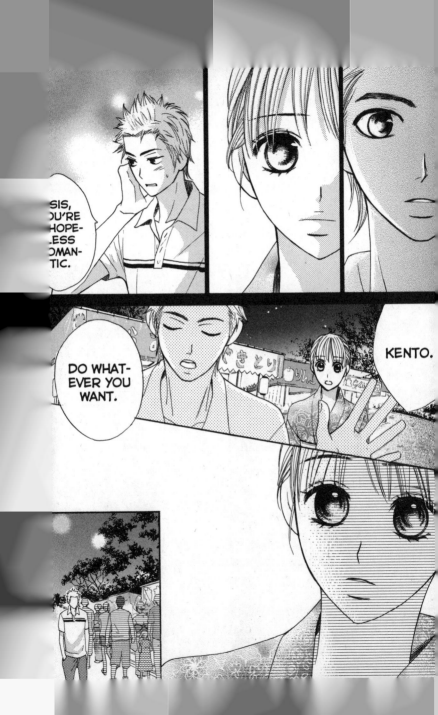

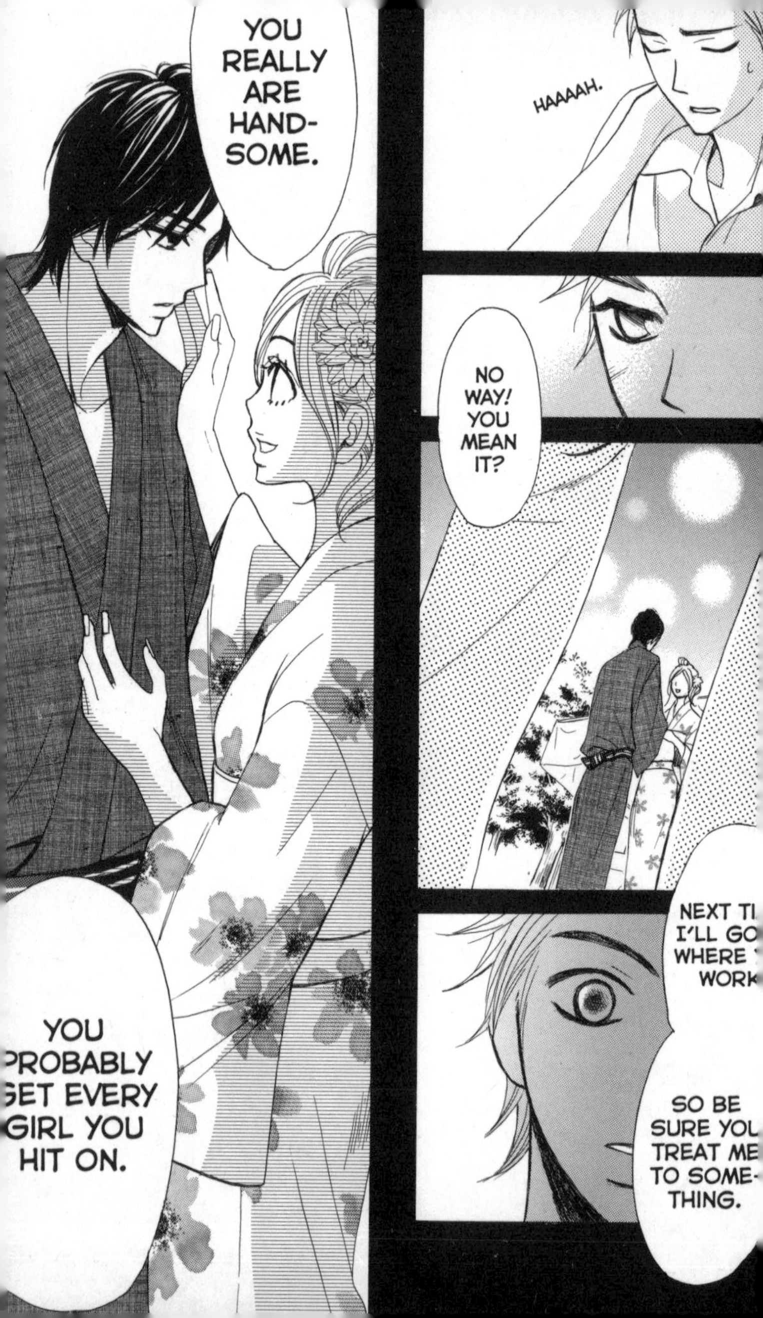
HAAAAH.
NO WAY! YOU MEAN IT?
NEXT TI I'LL GO WHERE WORK
SO BE SURE YOU TREAT ME TO SOME-THING.
YOU REALLY ARE HAND-SOME.
YOU PROBABLY GET EVERY GIRL YOU HIT ON.

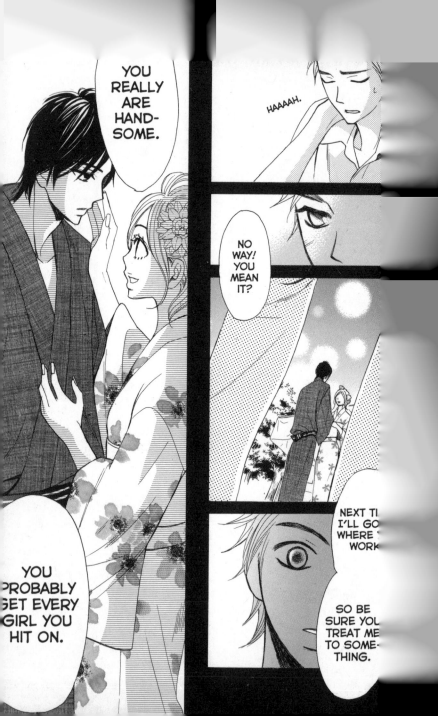

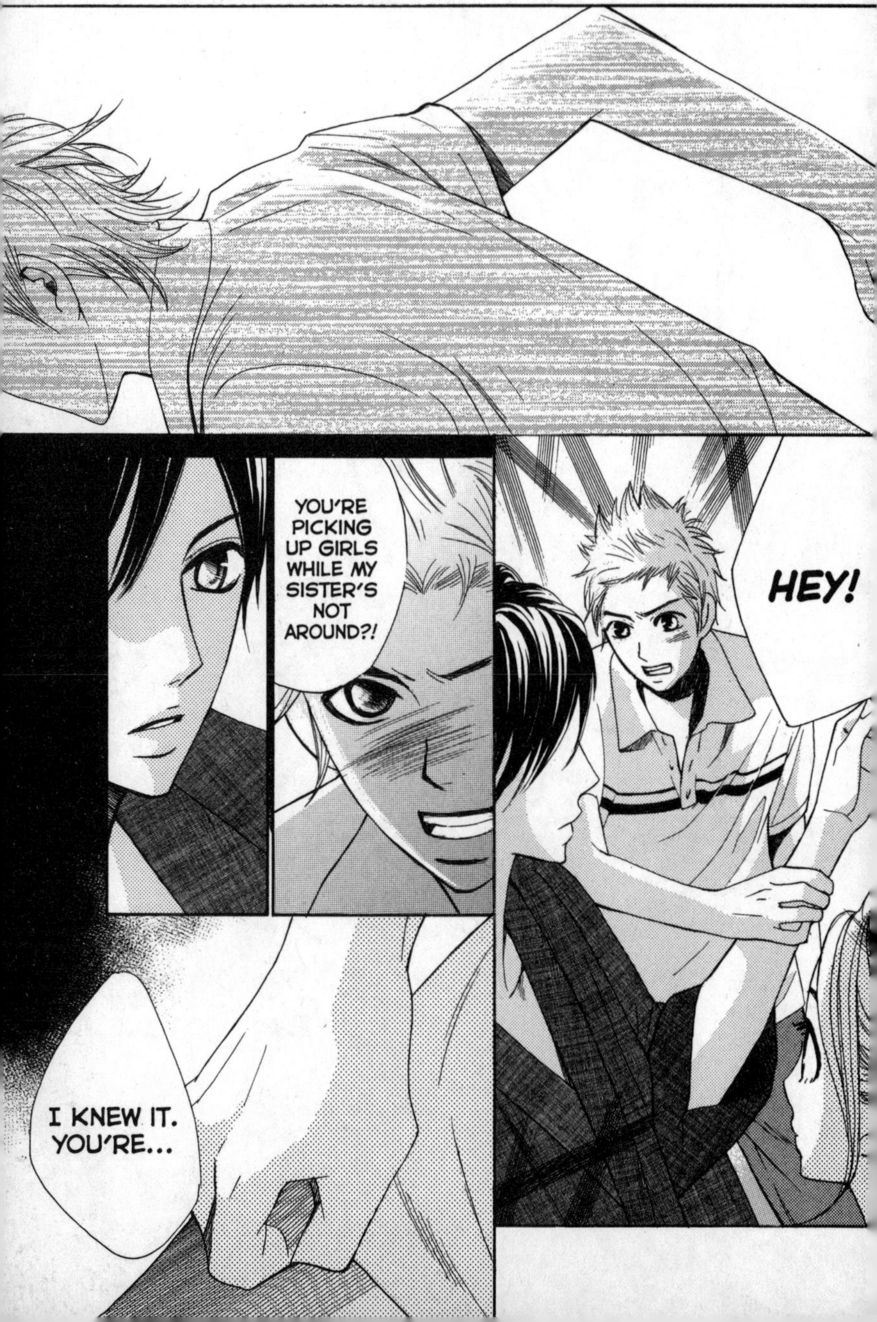
HEY!
YOU'RE PICKING UP GIRLS WHILE MY SISTER'S NOT AROUND?!
I KNEW IT. YOU'RE...

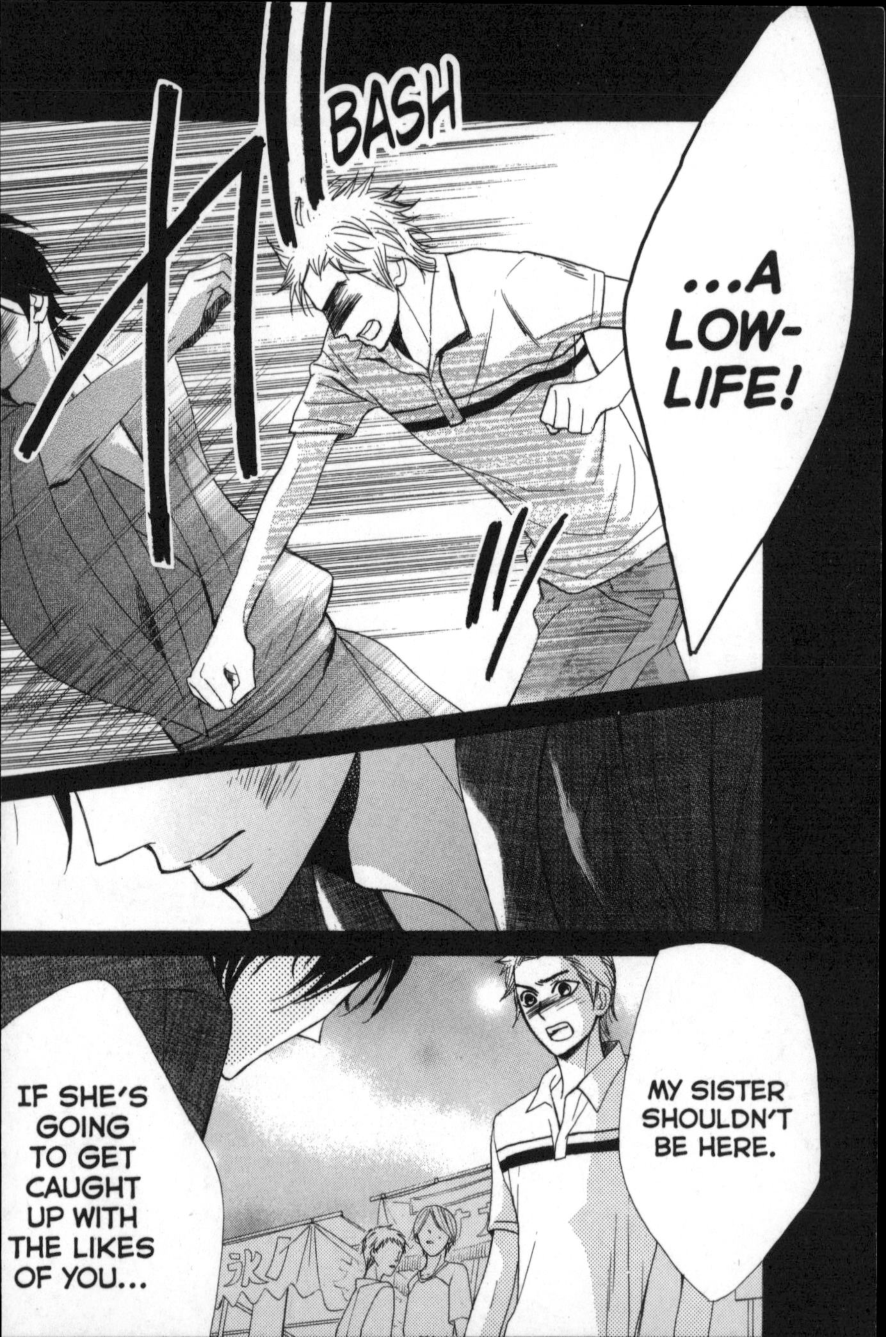
...A LOW-LIFE!
BASH
MY SISTER SHOULDN'T BE HERE.
IF SHE'S GOING TO GET CAUGHT UP WITH THE LIKES OF YOU...

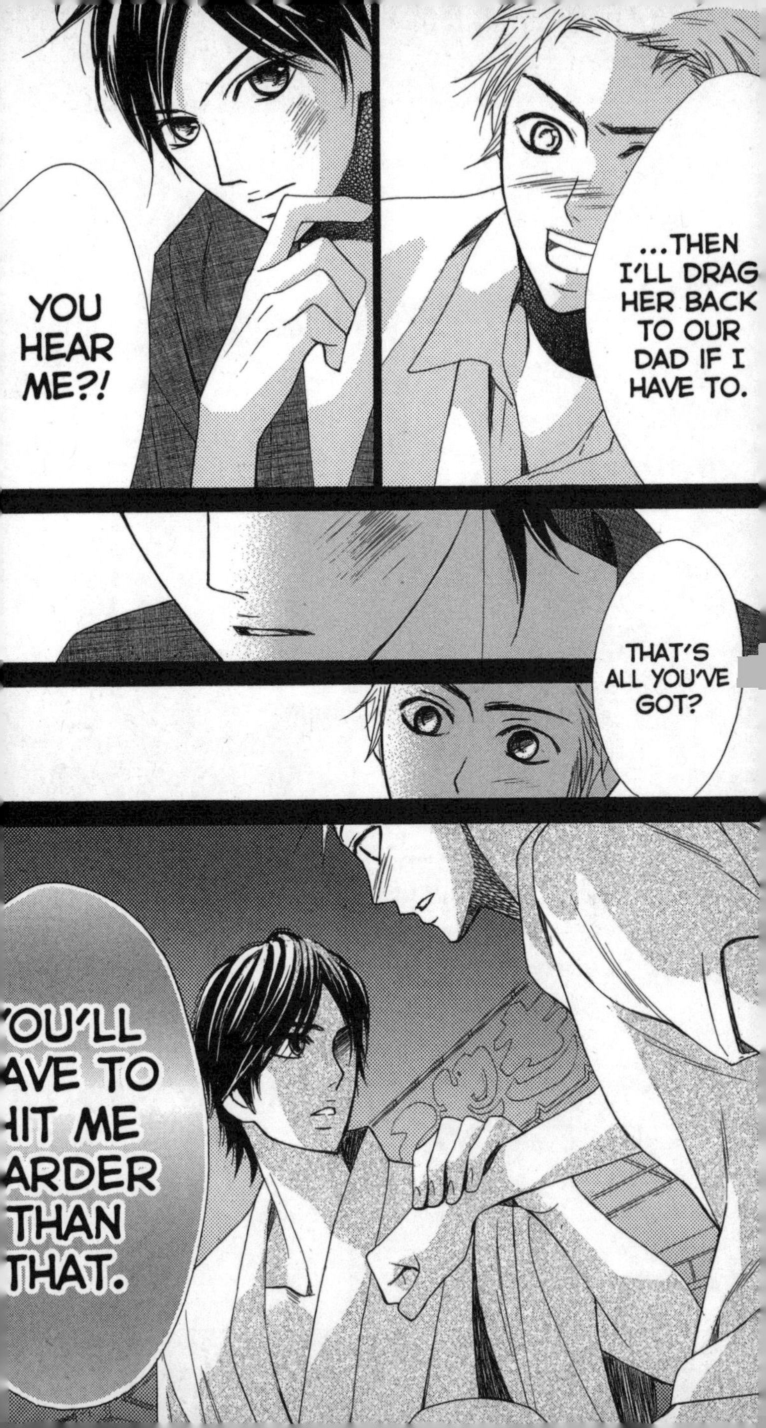
...THEN I'LL DRAG HER BACK TO OUR DAD IF I HAVE TO.
YOU HEAR ME?!
THAT'S ALL YOU'VE GOT?
OU'LL AVE TO IT ME ARDER THAN THAT.

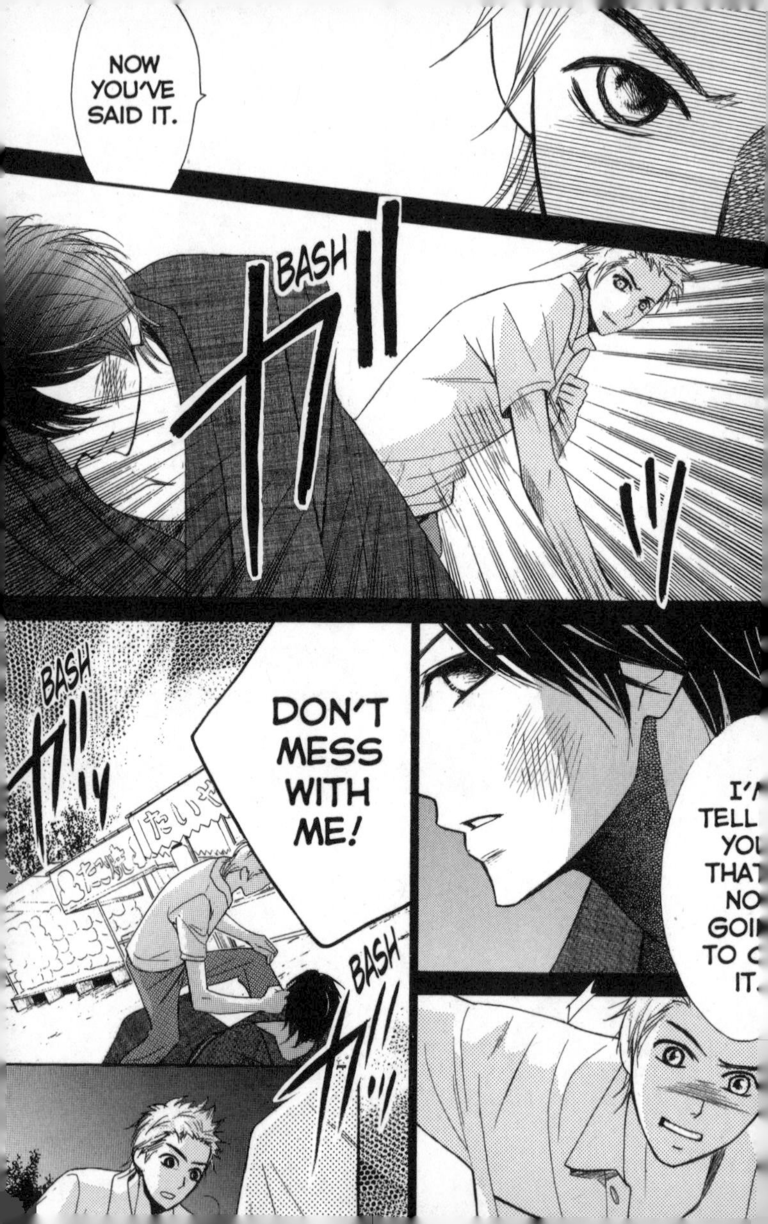
NOW YOU'VE SAID IT.
BASH
BASH
DON'T MESS WITH ME!
BASH

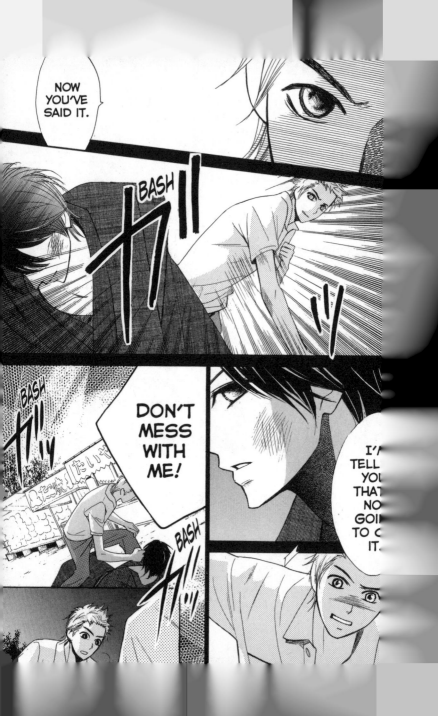

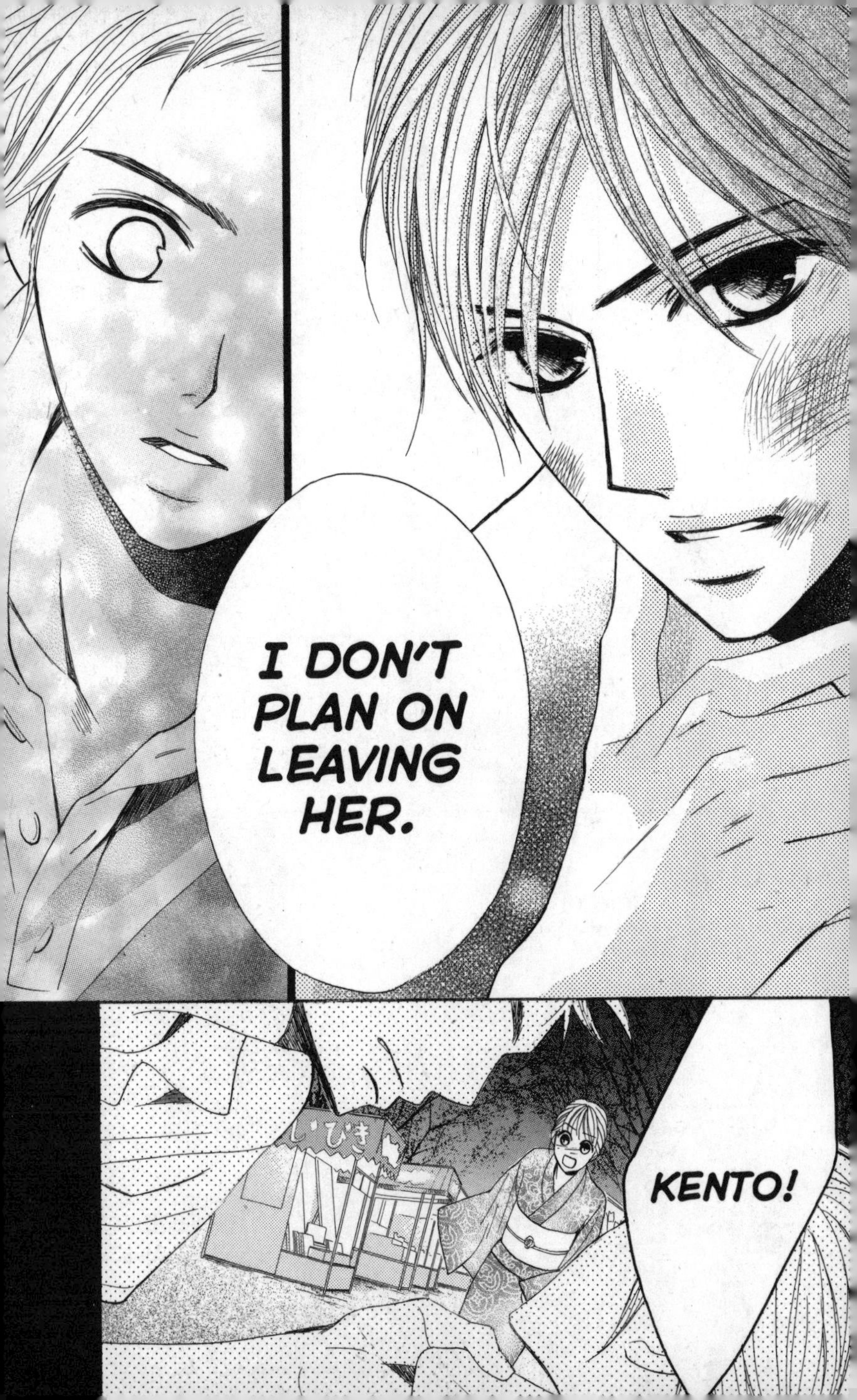
I DON'T PLAN ON LEAVING HER.
KENTO!

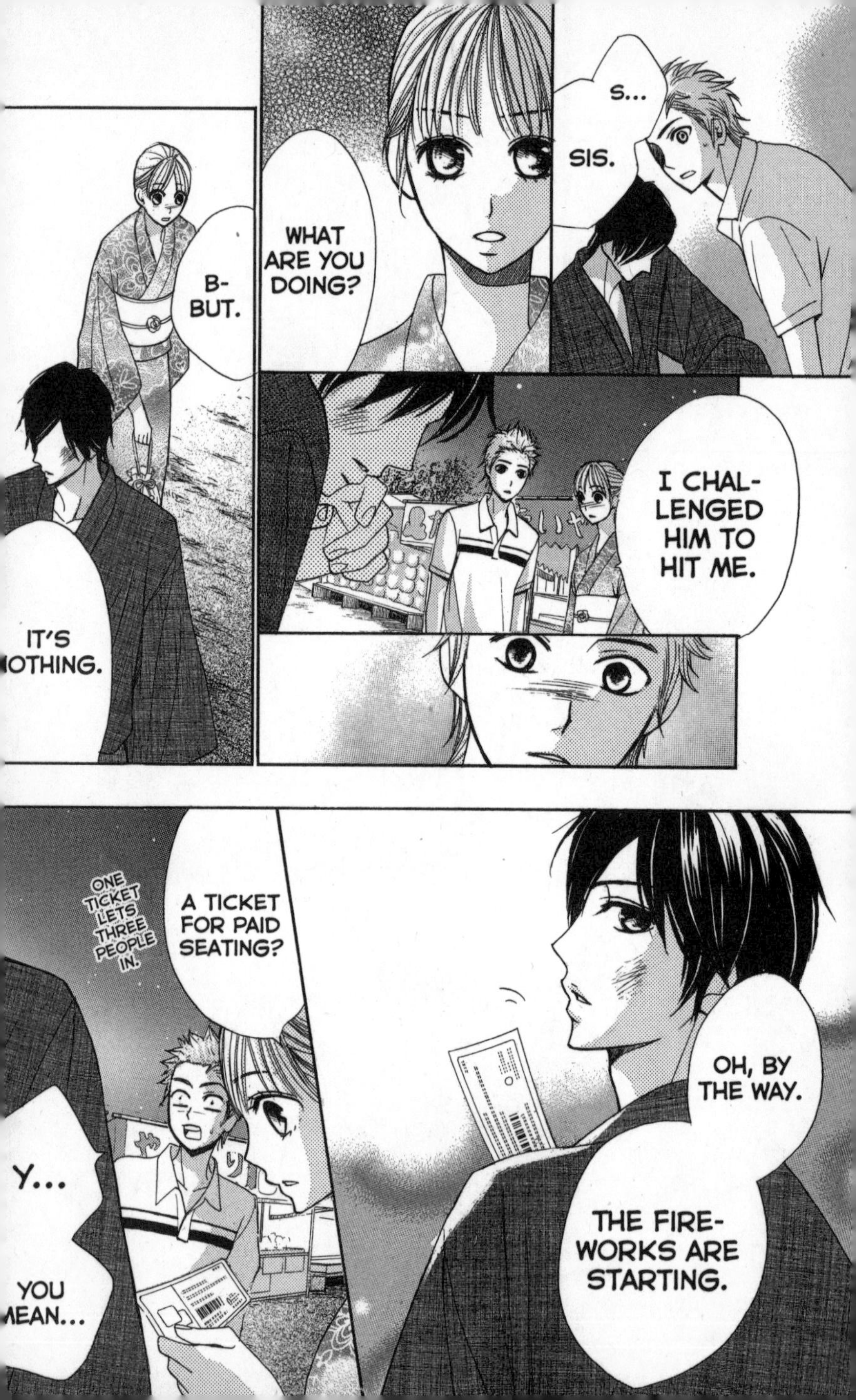
S...
SIS.
WHAT ARE YOU DOING?
I CHALLENGED HIM TO HIT ME.
B-BUT.
IT'S OTHING.
OH, BY THE WAY.
THE FIREWORKS ARE STARTING.
A TICKET FOR PAID SEATING?
ONE TICKET LETS THREE PEOPLE IN.
Y...
YOU EAN...

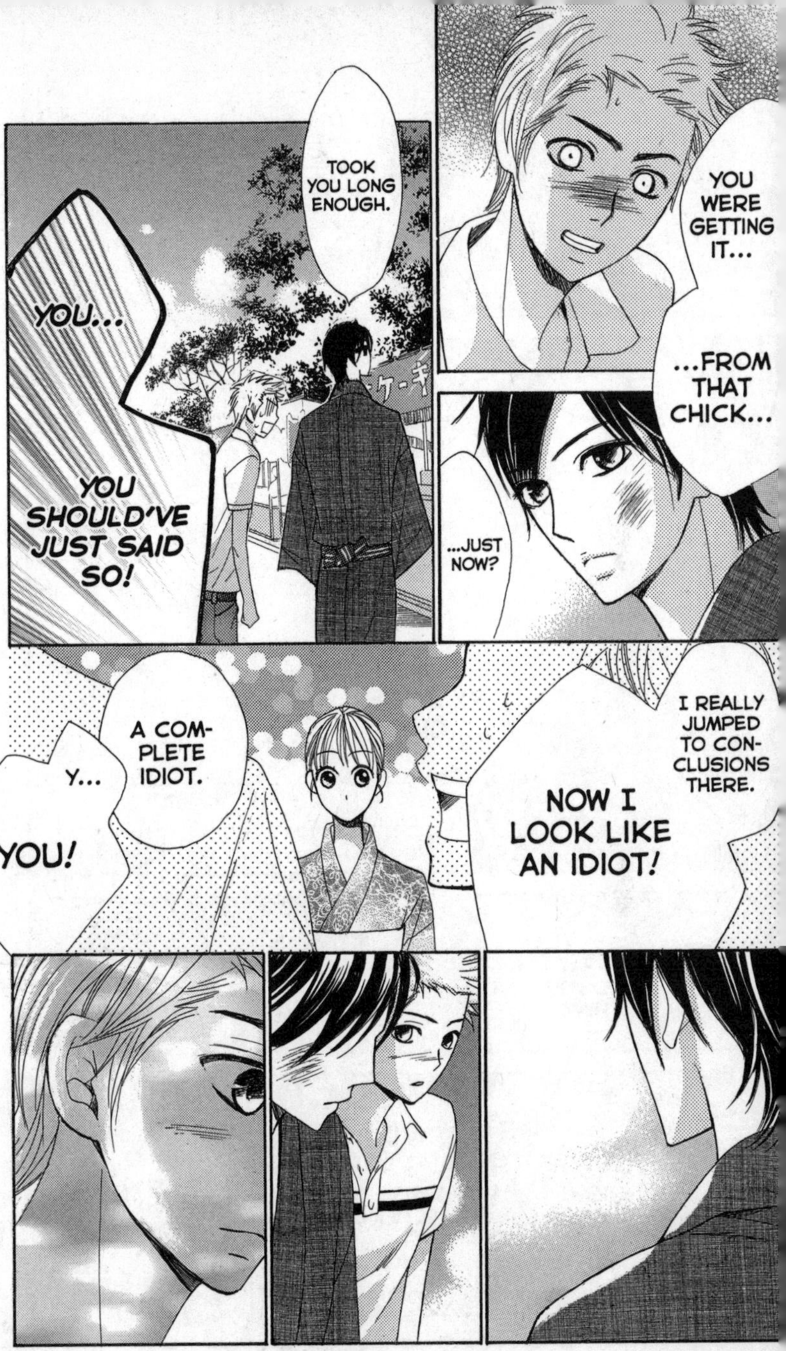
YOU WERE GETTING IT...
...FROM THAT CHICK...
...JUST NOW?
TOOK YOU LONG ENOUGH.
YOU...
YOU SHOULD'VE JUST SAID SO!
I REALLY JUMPED TO CON-CLUSIONS THERE.
NOW I LOOK LIKE AN IDIOT!
A COM-PLETE IDIOT.
Y...
YOU!

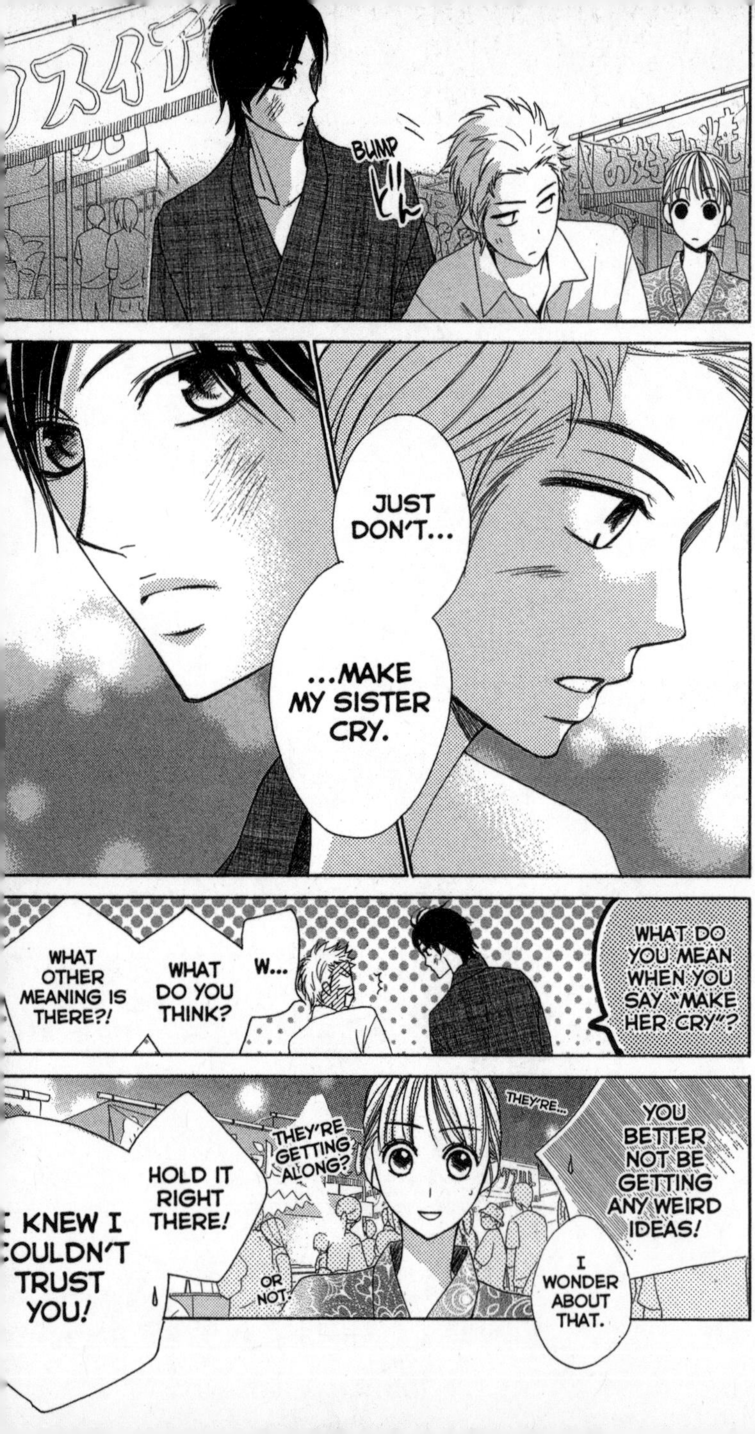
BUMP
JUST DON'T...
...MAKE MY SISTER CRY.
WHAT DO YOU MEAN WHEN YOU SAY "MAKE HER CRY"?
W...
WHAT DO YOU THINK?
WHAT OTHER MEANING IS THERE?!
YOU BETTER NOT BE GETTING ANY WEIRD IDEAS!
THEY'RE...
I WONDER ABOUT THAT.
THEY'RE GETTING ALONG?
OR NOT.
HOLD IT RIGHT THERE!
I KNEW I COULDN'T TRUST YOU!

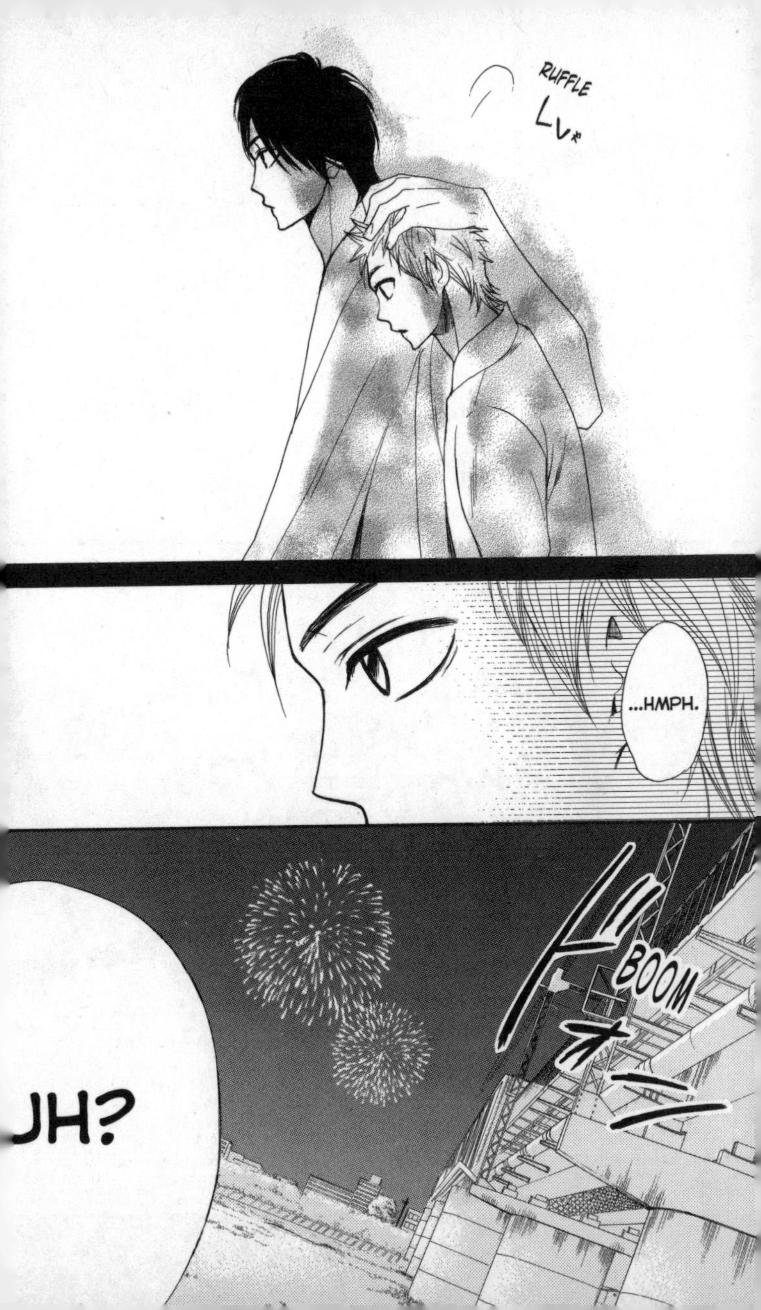
RUFFLE
しゃ
...HMPH.
BOOM
ドォーン
JH?

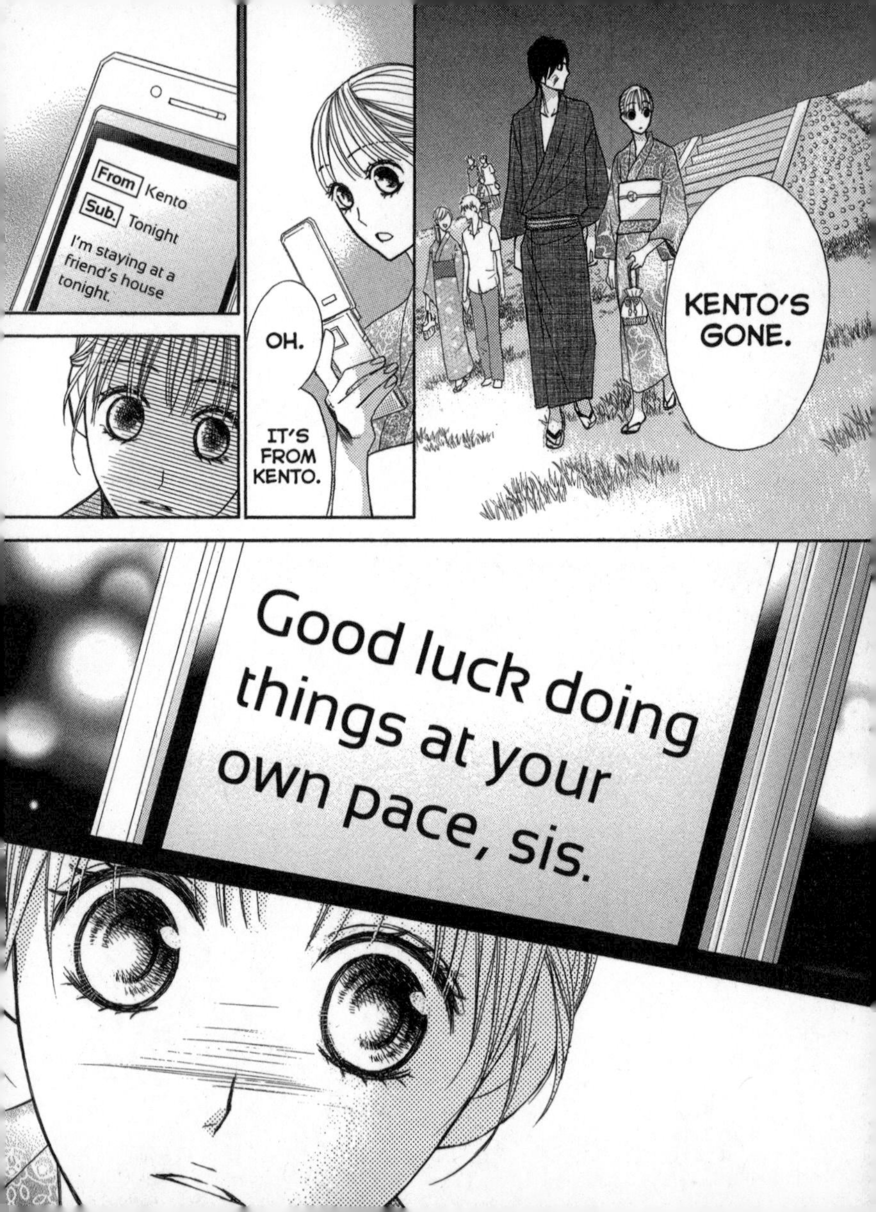
KENTO'S GONE.
OH.
IT'S FROM KENTO.
From Kento
Sub. Tonight
I'm staying at a friend's house tonight.
Good luck doing things at your own pace, sis.

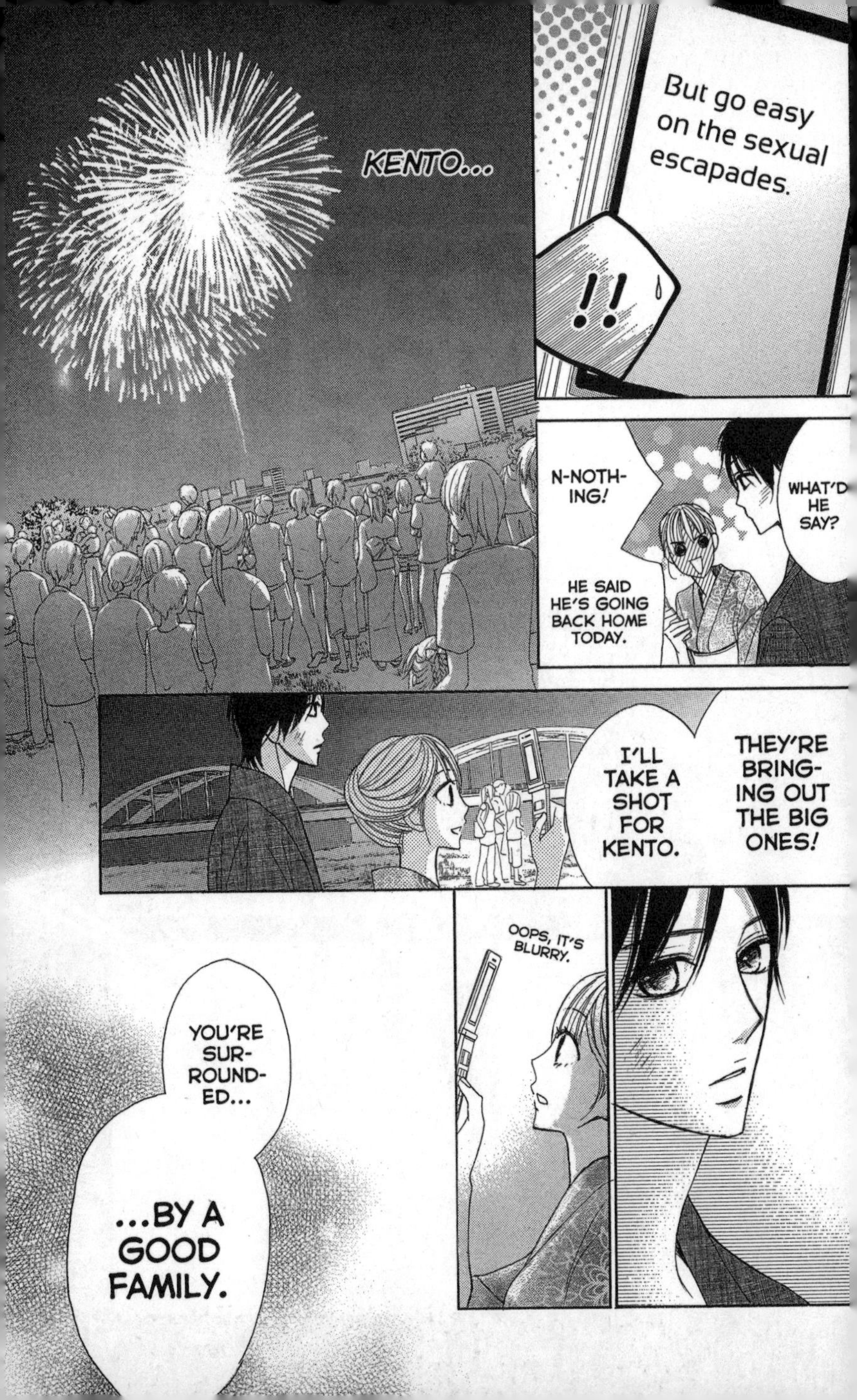

But go easy on the sexual escapades.
!!
WHAT'D HE SAY?
N-NOTHING!
HE SAID HE'S GOING BACK HOME TODAY.
KENTO...
THEY'RE BRINGING OUT THE BIG ONES!
I'LL TAKE A SHOT FOR KENTO.
OOPS, IT'S BLURRY.
YOU'RE SURROUNDED...
...BY A GOOD FAMILY.

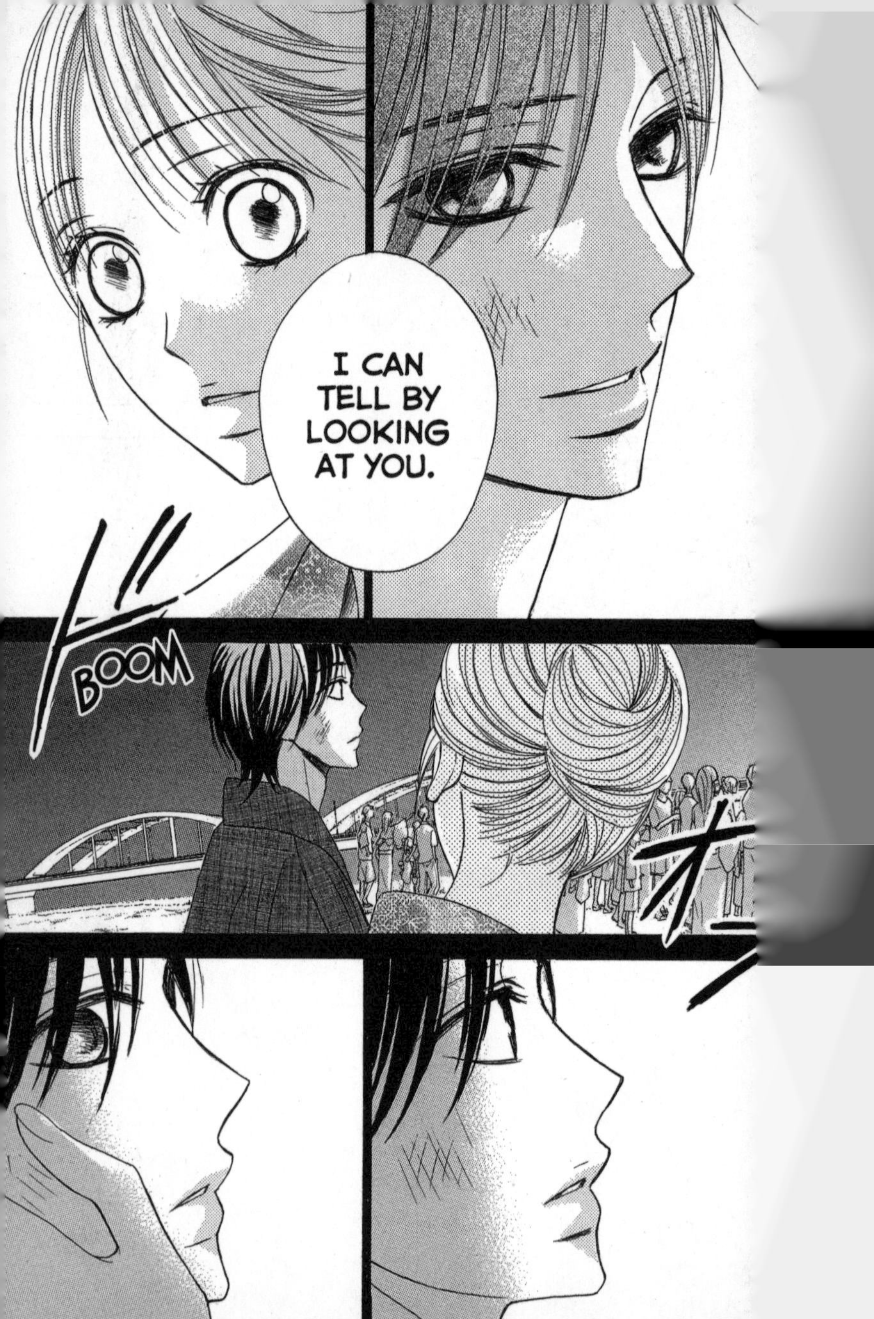
I CAN TELL BY LOOKING AT YOU.
BOOM

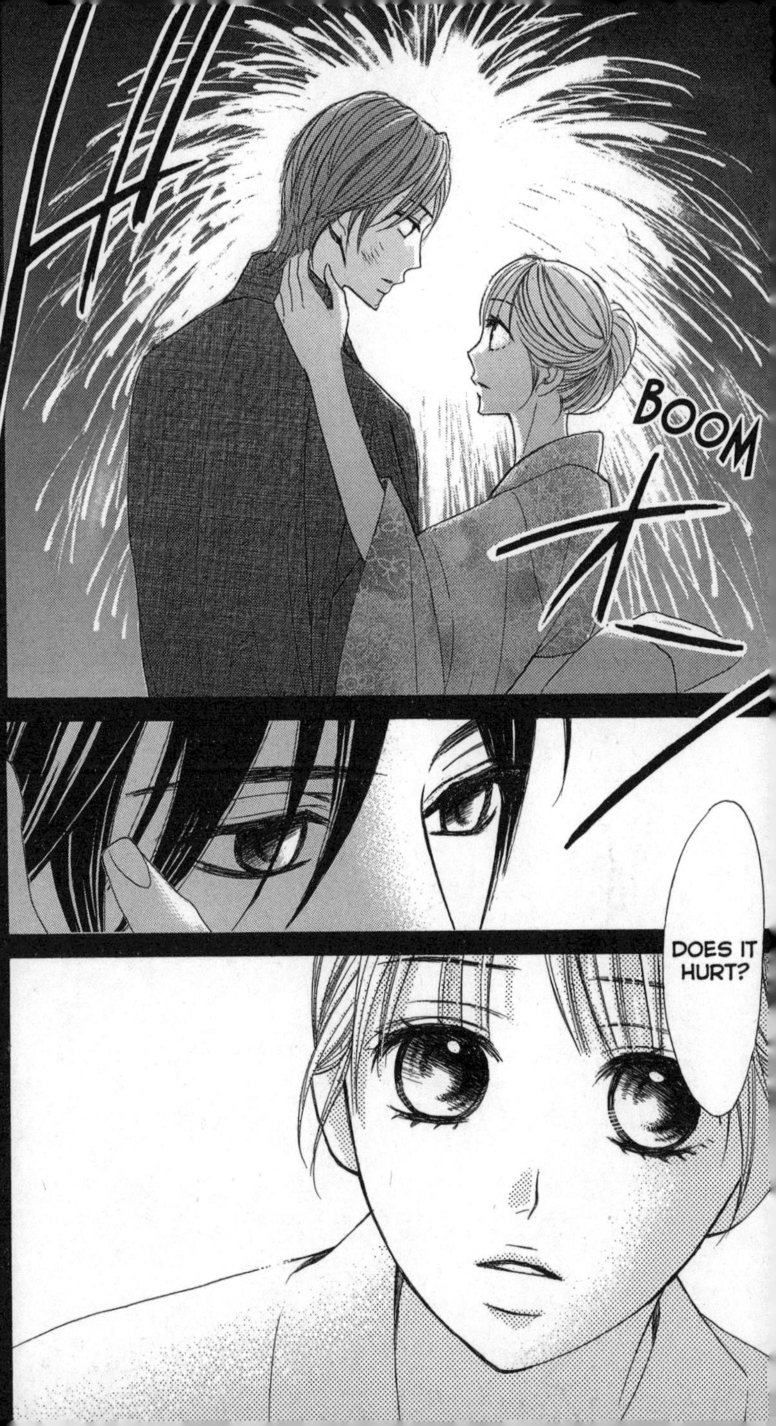
BOOM
DOES IT HURT?

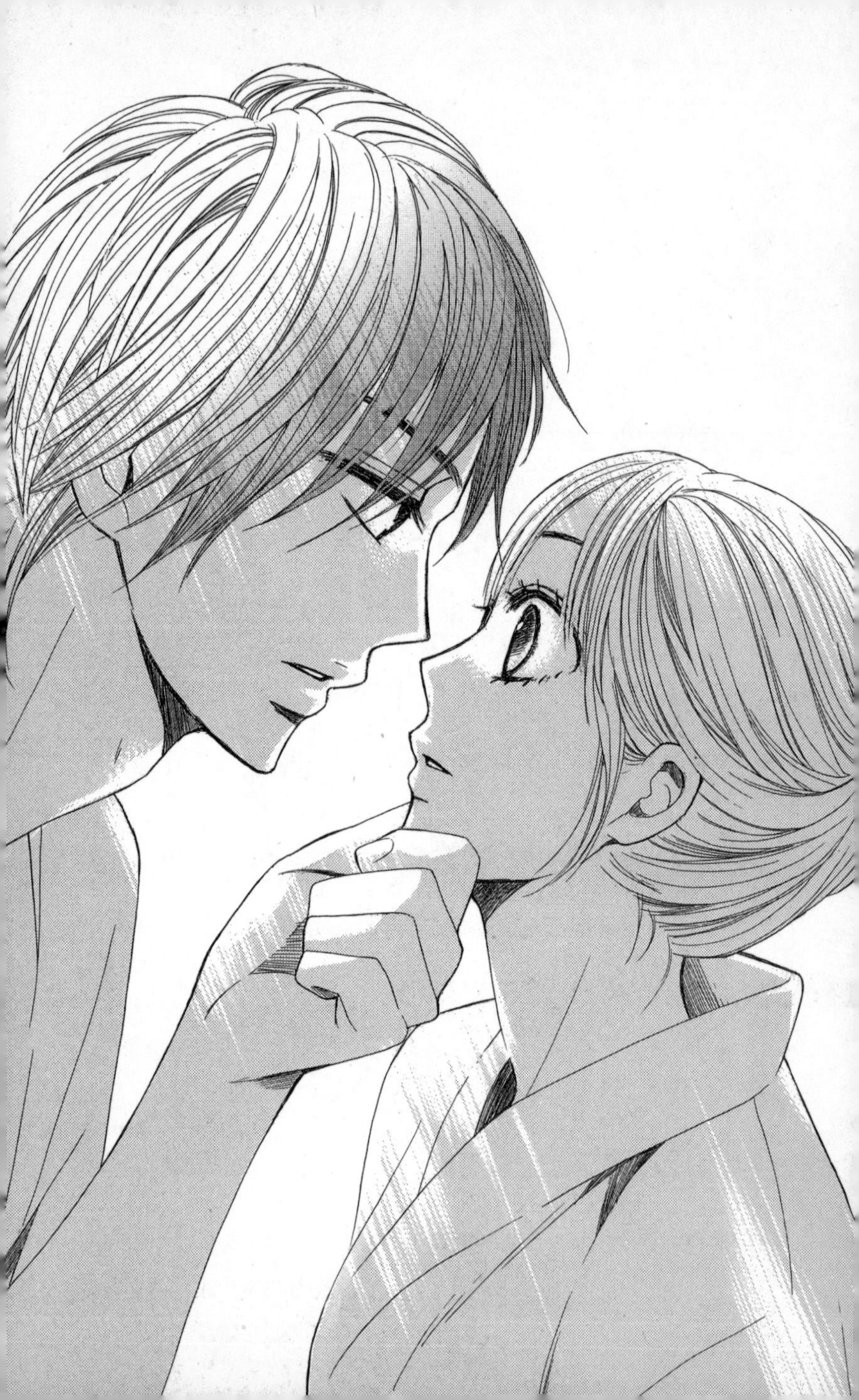

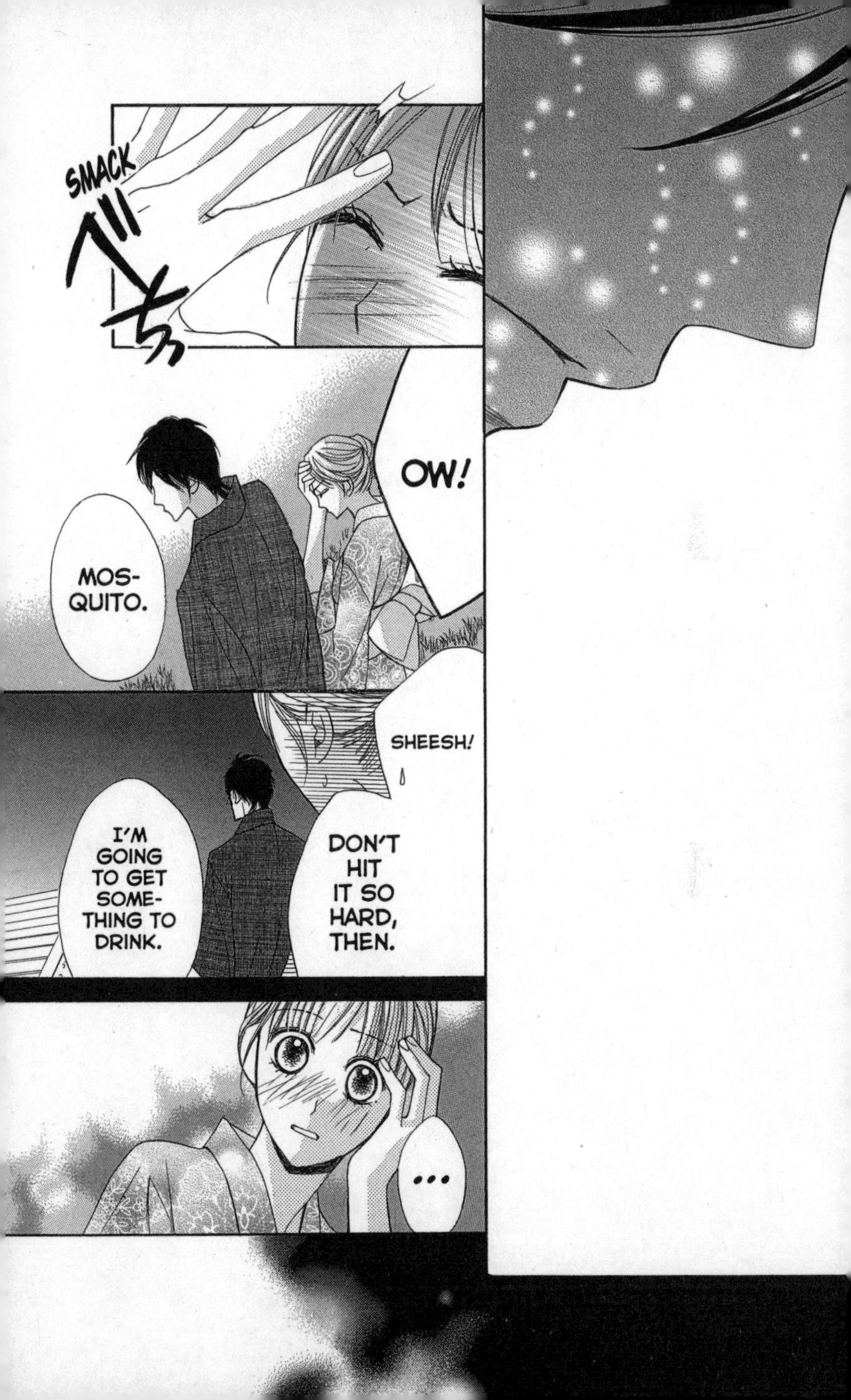
SMACK
OW!
MOS-QUITO.
SHEESH!
DON'T HIT IT SO HARD, THEN.
I'M GOING TO GET SOME-THING TO DRINK.
...

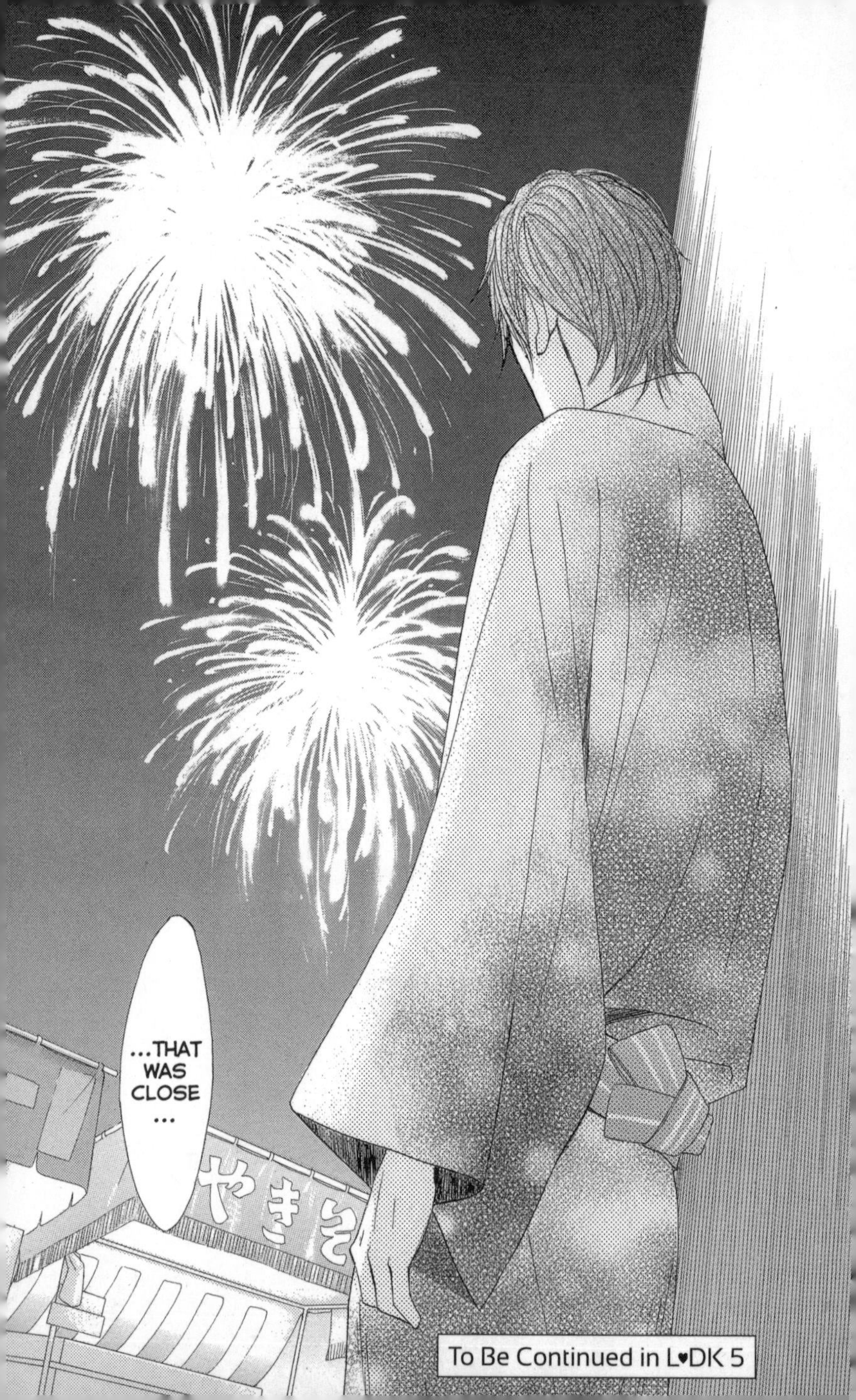
...THAT WAS CLOSE ...
やきそ
To Be Continued in L♥DK 5

L♥DK

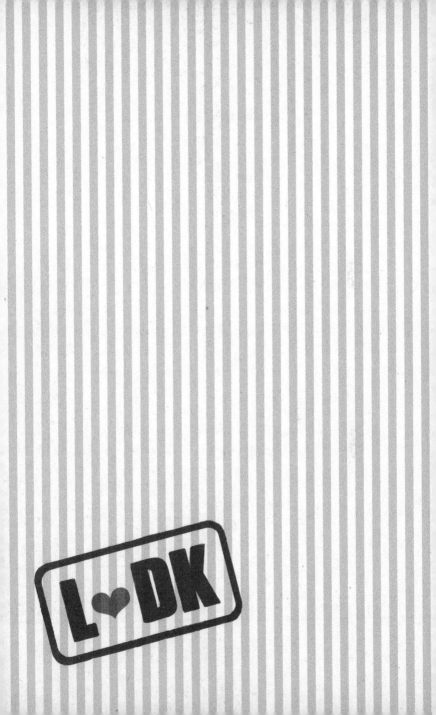

special thanks

K.Hamano
N.Imai
S.Sato

my family
my friends

M.Morita
M.Horiuchi
Y.Ikumi
A.Ichikawa

AND YOU

Ayu Watanabe
Jun.2010

**Everyday Essentials, Item 4
Eye Pillow**

This is an item for sleeping soundly
that helps comfort my tired eyes.
Since I tend to sleep after it's already
gotten light out, it completely darkens
my field of vision, making it incredibly
handy. Even though remedying my
late-night lifestyle would be the
quickest route to healthier living...

Translation Notes

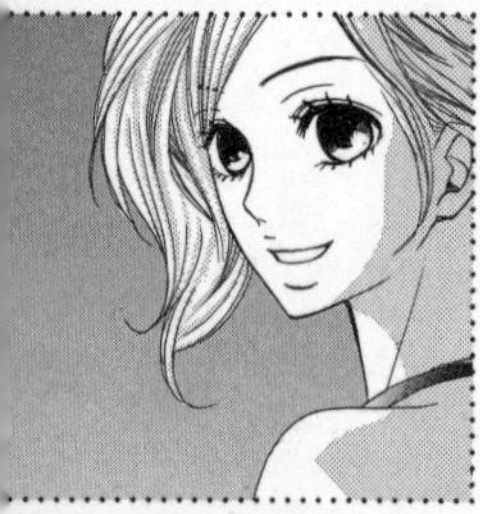

***Momo*-colored crush, page 87**
"Momo" is both Shusei's cousin's name and the Japanese word for "peach." In Japan, "peach-colored" refers to both the pink of peach blossoms, but also invokes images of young women, and may connote budding sexuality.

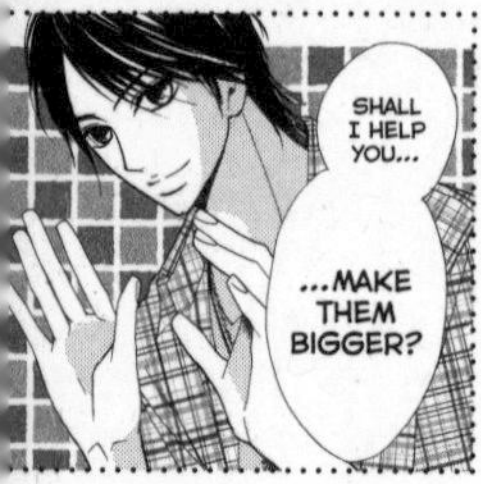
SHALL I HELP YOU...
...MAKE THEM BIGGER?

Touching breasts to make them bigger, page 122
Referring to the common teenage Japanese belief that touching breasts makes them grow in size.

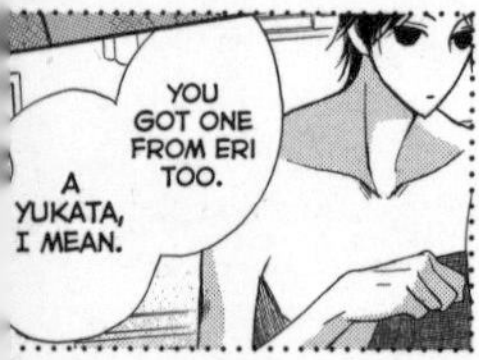
YOU GOT ONE FROM ERI TOO.
A YUKATA, I MEAN.

***Yukata*, page 129**
A *yukata* is a lighter, *kimono*-like garment worn primarily in the summer for summer events like festivals and firework displays.

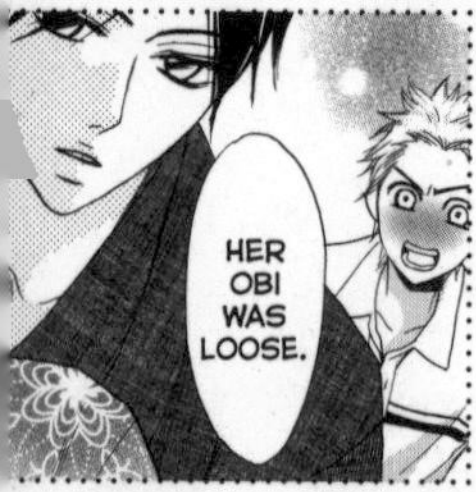
HER OBI WAS LOOSE.

***Obi*, page 139**
The *obi* is the belt part of the *yukata* outfit.

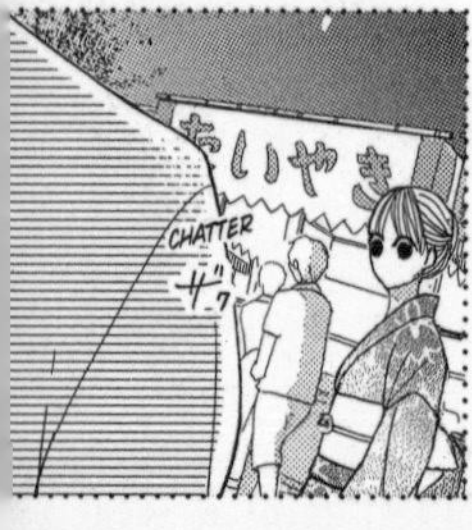
CHATTER

***Festival Food*, page 144**
Festivals in Japan have food stalls with a plethora of delicious food for snacking! This festival has stalls for: buttered potatoes, *yakisoba*, *taiyaki* (sweet, often fish-shaped filled pancake), barbeque, *takoyaki* (fried dough with octopus inside), *yakitori*, candied apples, shaved ice, and *okonomiyaki* (savory pancake with various toppings).

SWAPPED WITH A KISS?!

Class troublemaker Ryu Yamada is already having a bad day when he stumbles down a staircase along with star student Urara Shiraishi. When he wakes up, he realizes they have switched bodies—and that Ryu has the power to trade places with anyone just by kissing them! Ryu and Urara take full advantage of the situation to improve their lives, but with such an oddly amazing power, just how long will they be able to keep their secret under wraps?

Available now in print and digitally!

Praise for the anime:

"The show provides a pleasant window on the highs and lows of young love with two young people who are first-timers at the real thing."

–The Fandom Post

"Always it is smarter, more poetic, more touching, just plain better than you think it is going to be."

–Anime News Network

Say I Love You.

Mei Tachibana has no friends — and says she doesn't need them!

But everything changes when she accidentally roundhouse kicks the most popular boy in school! However, Yamato Kurosawa isn't angry in the slightest— in fact, he thinks his ordinary life could use an unusual girl like Mei. But winning Mei's trust will be a tough task. How long will she refuse to say, "I love you"?

My Little Monster

OPPOSITES ATTRACT...MAYBE?

Haru Yoshida is feared as an unstable and violent "monster." Mizutani Shizuku is a grade-obsessed student with no friends. Fate brings these two together to form the most unlikely pair. Haru firmly believes he's in love with Mizutani and she firmly believes he's insane.

KC

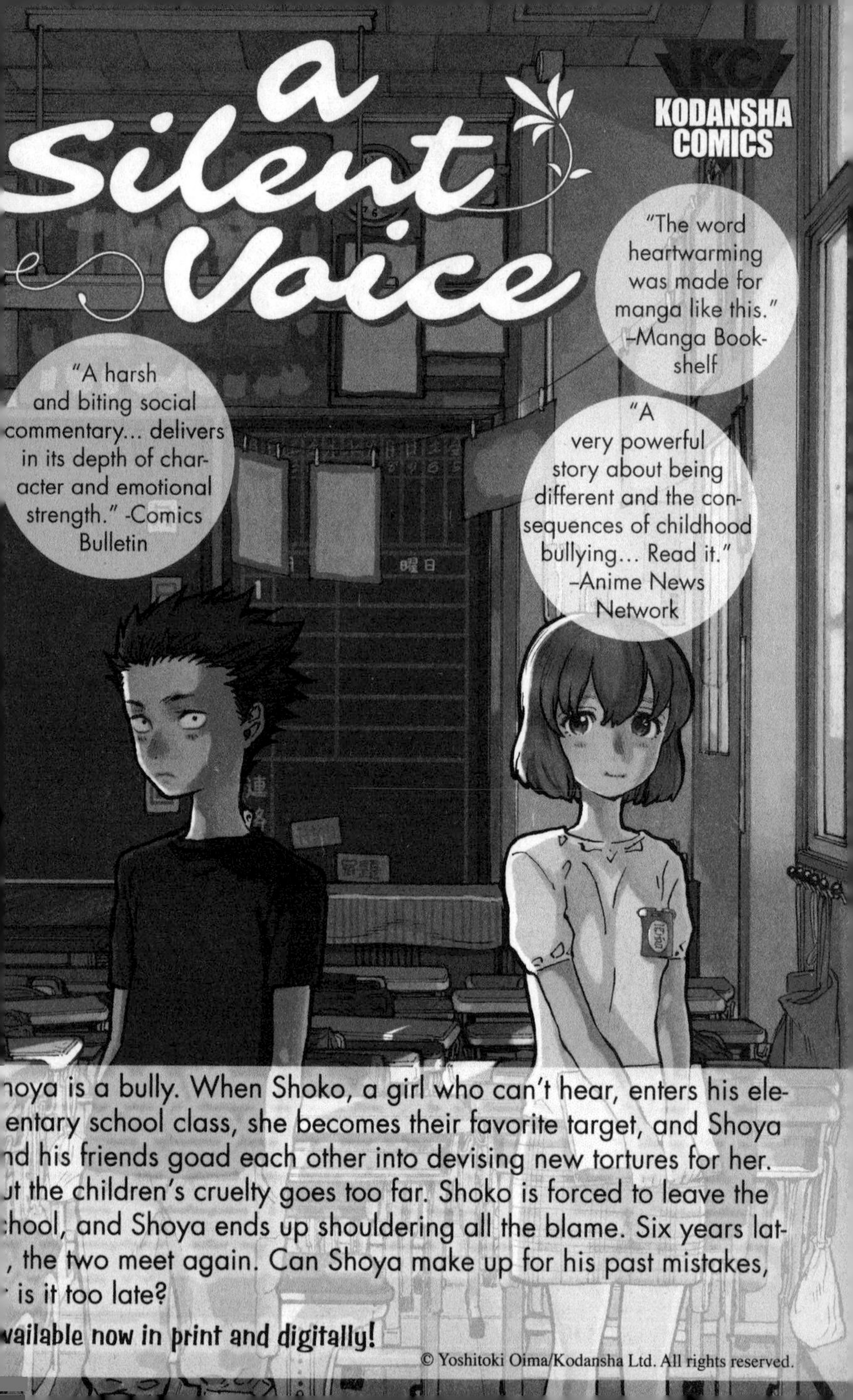
a Silent Voice
KODANSHA COMICS
"The word heartwarming was made for manga like this." –Manga Bookshelf
"A harsh and biting social commentary... delivers in its depth of character and emotional strength." -Comics Bulletin
"A very powerful story about being different and the consequences of childhood bullying... Read it." –Anime News Network
ioya is a bully. When Shoko, a girl who can't hear, enters his ele-
entary school class, she becomes their favorite target, and Shoya
nd his friends goad each other into devising new tortures for her.
ut the children's cruelty goes too far. Shoko is forced to leave the
hool, and Shoya ends up shouldering all the blame. Six years lat-
, the two meet again. Can Shoya make up for his past mistakes,
is it too late?
vailable now in print and digitally!
© Yoshitoki Oima/Kodansha Ltd. All rights reserved.

NORAGAMI
STRAY GOD

> "A FUN
> ADVENTURE WITH
> A COLORFUL AND
> MEMORABLE
> CAST OF
> CHARACTERS IN
> AN ENGROSSING
> MODERN-
> DAY FANTASY
> SETTING."
> -KOTAKU

READ THE SERIES THAT BECAME THE HIT ANIME!

YATO IS A HOMELESS GOD WITHOUT A SHRINE OR ANY WORSHIPPERS! SO TO ACHIEVE HIS AMBITIOUS GOAL OF A LAVISH TEMPLE, HE'S SET UP A SERVICE TO HELP THOSE IN NEED... FOR A SMALL FEE. SINCE HE CAN'T AFFORD TO BE PICKY, YATO ACCEPTS ANY JOB FROM FINDING LOST KITTENS TO HELPING BULLIED STUDENTS. MEANWHILE, HIYORI IKI, AN ORDINARY PRO-WRESTLING-LOVING MIDDLE SCHOOL GIRL, HAS TURNED INTO AN EXISTENCE THAT IS NEITHER HUMAN NOR AYAKASHI! IT'S UP TO YATO'S "DIVINE INTERVENTION" TO TURN HIYORI BACK TO NORMAL, BUT CAN SHE RELY ON THE SPONTANEOUS AND WAYWARD GOD?

AVAILABLE NOW IN PRINT AND DIGITALLY!

BY TOMOKO HAYAKAWA

It's a beautiful, expansive mansion, and four handsome, fifteen-year-old friends are allowed to live in it for free! But there is one condition—within three years the young men must take the owner's niece and transform her into a proper lady befitting the palace in which they all live! How hard can it be?

Enter Sunako Nakahara, the horror-movie-loving, pock-faced, frizzy-haired, fashion-illiterate hermit who has a tendency to break into explosive nosebleeds whenever she sees anyone attractive. This project is going to take far more than our four heroes ever expected; it needs a miracle!

Ages: 16 +

Special extras in each volume! Read them all!

SAVE THE DATE!

Celebrating **15** Years

FREE COMIC BOOK •DAY•

1st SATURDAY IN MAY!

May 7, 2016

www.freecomicbookday.com

FREE COMICS FOR EVERYONE!

Details @ www.freecomicbookday.com

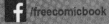 /freecomicbook @freecomicbook 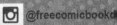 @freecomicbookd

A Kodansha Comics Trade Paperback Original.

Published in the United States by Kodansha Comics, an imprint of Kodansha USA Publishing, LLC, New York.

Publication rights for this English edition arranged through Kodansha Ltd., Tokyo.

First published in Japan in 2010 by Kodansha Ltd., Tokyo, as *L♡DK*, volume 4.

ISBN 978-1-63236-157-8

Printed in the United States of America.

www.kodanshacomics.com

9 8 7 6 5 4 3 2 1

Translation: Christine Dashiell
Lettering: Sara Linsley
Editing: Lauren Scanlan
Kodansha Comics Edition Cover Design: Phil Balsman